"This is an exceptional resource for anyone interested in mindfulness and college student mental health. It provides summaries of a variety of mindfulness approaches as well as practical applications to clinical situations and empirical research. I plan on sharing the book with our counseling service and finding ways to implement many aspects of it into my daily clinical work with students. It is an important addition to the mindfulness-based literature."

> —**Gregory T. Eells, PhD**, director of counseling and
> psychological services at Cornell University and past
> president of the Association for University and College
> Counseling Center Directors (AUCCCD)

"Pistorello and her colleagues have created an incredible and timely resource for anyone treating the fully wired and constantly connected Generation Z college student. This easy-to-read book effortlessly guides the reader through practical, evidence-based applications of dialectical behavioral therapy (DBT), acceptance and commitment therapy (ACT), mindfulness-based stress reduction (MBSR), and mindfulness-based cognitive therapy (MBCT) designed specifically for college students receiving treatment at college counseling centers. Judicious use of case vignettes and transcripts brings concepts to life. Whether you are new to mindfulness and acceptance-based therapies or they are deep in your bones, this creative and well-written book will positively influence your clinical practice with this high-risk population."

> —**Linda A. Dimeff, PhD**, author of *Brief Alcohol Screening and
> Intervention for College Students* and *DBT in Clinical Practice*

"This book should quickly become a treasured resource on college campuses. It is a practical and accessible presentation of best practices based on mindfulness and acceptance. A timely and valuable contribution to improving the mental health and wellbeing of college students!"

> —**Daniel Eisenberg, PhD**, associate professor at the University
> of Michigan School of Public Health and principal
> investigator of the Healthy Minds Study, a national survey
> study of college student mental health

THE MINDFULNESS & ACCEPTANCE PRACTICA SERIES

As mindfulness and acceptance-based therapies gain momentum in the field of mental health, it is increasingly important for professionals to understand the full range of their applications. To keep up with the growing demand for authoritative resources on these treatments, *The Mindfulness and Acceptance Practica Series* was created. These edited books cover a range of evidence-based treatments, such as acceptance and commitment therapy (ACT), cognitive behavioral therapy (CBT), compassion-focused therapy (CFT), dialectical behavioral therapy (DBT), and mindfulness-based stress reduction (MBSR) therapy. Incorporating new research in the field of psychology, these books are powerful tools for mental health clinicians, researchers, advanced students, and anyone interested in the growth of mindfulness and acceptance strategies.

Visit www.newharbinger.com for
more books in this series.

MINDFULNESS & ACCEPTANCE FOR COUNSELING COLLEGE STUDENTS

Theory and Practical Applications for Intervention, Prevention & Outreach

Edited by
JACQUELINE PISTORELLO, PhD

CONTEXT PRESS
An Imprint of New Harbinger Publications, Inc.

Copyright © 2013 by Jacqueline Pistorello
New Harbinger Publications, Inc.
5674 Shattuck Avenue
Oakland, CA 94609
www.newharbinger.com

Distributed in Canada by Raincoast Books

Acquired by Catharine Meyers; Cover design by Amy Shoup; Edited by Melanie Bell; Text design by Tracy Carlson

---

Library of Congress Cataloging-in-Publication Data

Mindfulness and acceptance for counseling college students : theory and practical applications for intervention, prevention, and outreach / edited by Jacqueline Pistorello, PhD.
    pages cm. -- (The context press mindfulness and acceptance practica series)
    Summary: "In Mindfulness and Acceptance for Counseling College Students, clinical researcher Jacqueline Pistorello explores how mindfulness and acceptance-based approaches such as acceptance and commitment therapy (ACT), dialectical behavioral therapy (DBT), mindfulness-based cognitive therapy (MBCT), and mindfulness-based stress reduction (MBSR) are being utilized by college counseling centers around the world to treat student mental health problems like severe depression, substance abuse, and eating disorders. This book offers easy-to-use applications for college counselors and therapists, and includes a website link for downloadable worksheets for students, a sample podcast, and interactive web-based materials"-- Provided by publisher.
    Includes bibliographical references and index.
    ISBN 978-1-60882-222-5 (pbk.) -- ISBN 978-1-60882-223-2 (pdf e-book) -- ISBN 978-1-60882-224-9 (epub) 1. College students--Mental health services. 2. Psychotherapy. I. Pistorello, Jacqueline.
    RC451.4.S7M56 2013
    616.89'14--dc23
                                2013009845

Printed in the United States of America

15 14 13   10 9 8 7 6 5 4 3 2 1   First printing

Contents

Acknowledgments ix

How to Use This Book 1

Jacqueline Pistorello, Ph.D., *University of Nevada, Reno*

1   Mindfulness and Acceptance in
    College Students: Why it Matters. . . 9

Steven C. Hayes, Jacqueline Pistorello, and Michael E. Levin,
University of Nevada, Reno

2   Dialectical Behavior Therapy (DBT)
    Applied to Severely Distressed
    College Students 23

Jacqueline Pistorello, Chelsea MacLane, Alan Fruzzetti, and Karen
Erikson, *University of Nevada, Reno;* Carrie Guthrie, Holly Landsbaum,
and Abby Bjornsen, *University of California, Berkeley*

3   Acceptance and Commitment
      Therapy (ACT): Processes and
      Application 47

Matthew S. Boone, *Cornell University*

4   Acceptance and Commitment
      Therapy (ACT) in Groups 73

Matthew S. Boone, *Cornell University*;
and James Canicci, *University of Texas at Dallas*

5   Mindfulness-Based Cognitive
      Therapy (MBCT) and Acceptance
      and Commitment Therapy (ACT) at
      a College Counseling and
      Psychological Service 95

Philomena Renner and Elizabeth Foley, *University of Sydney,
Counseling and Psychological Services*

6   Mindfulness-Based Stress Reduction
      (MBSR) with College Students . . . 119

Michael C. Murphy, PhD, *University of Florida Counseling and Wellness
Center*

7   Using Acceptance and Commitment Therapy (ACT) to Treat Perfectionism in College Students 139

Jesse M. Crosby, *Utah State University, Department of Psychology, McLean Hospital/Harvard Medical School*; Andrew B. Armstrong, *Utah State University, Department of Psychology, University of Missouri-Columbia, Counseling Center*; Mark A. Nafziger, *Utah State University, Department of Psychology, Utah State University, Counseling and Psychological Services*; and Michael P. Twohig, *Utah State University, Department of Psychology*

8   Podcasts to Help Students Overcome Academic Barriers in Australia and Italy 159

Giovanni Miselli, Anna B. Prevedini, and Francesco Pozzi, *IULM University Milan, IESCUM Italy*; Julian McNally, M.Psych, *Counseling Psychologist, Melbourne, Australia*

9   Web-Based Values Training and Goal Setting 183

Todd A. Ward and Ramona Houmanfar, *University of Nevada-Reno, Department of Psychology*; and Jared Chase, *Chrysalis, Inc.*

10 Teaching Mindfulness and Acceptance within College Communities to Enhance Peer Support.................. 203

Charles Morse, *Worcester Polytechnic Institute (WPI)*

11 **Acceptance and Commitment Therapy (ACT) in Classroom Settings** 223

Jacqueline Pistorello, Steven C. Hayes, Jason Lillis, and Douglas M. Long, *University of Nevada, Reno*; Vasiliki Christodoulou, *City University, London, UK*; Jenna LeJeune, *Portland Psychotherapy*; Jennifer Villatte, *University of Nevada, Reno*; John Seeley, *Oregon Research Institute*; Matthieu Villatte, Tami Jeffcoat, Jennifer Plumb-Vilardaga, and Jamie Yadavaia, *University of Nevada, Reno*

12 **Mindfulness in Student Affairs Practice** 251

Eileen Hulme and Christy Tanious, *Azusa Pacific University*

Index 273

Acknowledgments

The editor would like to thank a number of individuals who have contributed to this book, starting with the chapter authors. For some of the authors, writing a chapter was a novel experience and required taking time out of a busy clinical schedule to write a paragraph at a time. For others, writing a "how-to" book, instead of an empirical piece, posed its own challenges. Editing a book was a new experience for me as well, and I thank all the authors for their psychological flexibility! One of the pleasant surprises in this journey was the incredible opportunity I had to interact with a thoughtful, perspicacious, and caring group of individuals whose interests overlap so much with my own.

There is another group of authors I'd like to acknowledge: those not included in this book. It is a testament to the relevance of these processes to college students that, since first organizing this book, I have learned of a number of additional initiatives underway to implement mindfulness and acceptance on college campuses. The present volume is not meant to be a comprehensive description of every effort under way, but rather a description of some key initiatives that hopefully will inspire readers to continue their work with students using new methods, or, conversely, continue their work with mindfulness and acceptance but now with college students.

I think I speak for all the authors when I say that we are extremely grateful to the college students we have known, have treated, taught, supervised, or otherwise interacted with, in our respective careers. This is an exciting population to work with, and their courage, strength, and wish to "give back" to other students continue to astound me. Their willingness to try out the different approaches discussed here made this book possible.

This book would not have happened without the support of New Harbinger visionaries, including Matt McKay and Catharine Meyers, and of a cadre of highly capable, thoughtful, and caring professionals who made sure this book was the best that it could be. Thanks also go to Spondita Goswami, my research assistant, for her tireless help double-checking references!

I am grateful to my husband, Steven Hayes, for his support, encouragement, and patience—it means a lot to me that you always act as if I can do anything, even when my passengers say otherwise. Thanks also to my son, Stevie Pistorello-Hayes, for reminding me every day of what matters most in life.

I would like to dedicate this book to my amazing nieces and nephews (Fernanda, Gisele, Marquinho, Alexsandro, Daiane, Vanessa, Melissa, Gesiane, Diane, Clarissa, e Amanda) for allowing me to bear witness to the wonders of growing up and for showing me how much vitality a sense of humor, strong community, and perseverance can bring to the young adult years (and beyond). Every single one of you has taught me something important and meaningful for my work with college students: obrigada.

—Jacqueline Pistorello

How to Use This Book

Jacqueline Pistorello, Ph.D.
University of Nevada, Reno

There has been a proliferation of a variety of mindfulness- and acceptance-based approaches throughout college campuses. The field has gone from finding mindfulness "exotic" to seeing it almost as mainstream. This book brings together several of these different innovative initiatives into one single volume, so that readers will be able to quickly get a glimpse of the type of mindfulness- and acceptance-based programs currently being applied in higher education settings.

The Chapters

The book has twelve chapters. Chapter 1 discusses the unique context in higher education and society in general that lends itself to mindfulness- and acceptance-based interventions. Chapter 2 presents the application of Dialectical Behavior Therapy (DBT; Linehan, 1993) to college students, both as a comprehensive approach, now empirically validated with this population, and as skills training only as an adjunctive form of treatment. Chapter 3 provides an overview of the theory and model behind Acceptance and Commitment Therapy (ACT; Hayes, Strosahl, & Wilson, 2011), which is a topic in many of the chapters in this book. Chapter 4 focuses specifically on the use of ACT groups with college students presenting with different types of concerns. Chapter 5 juxtaposes two different approaches: Mindfulness-Based Cognitive Therapy (MBCT; Segal, Williams, & Teasdale, 2002) and ACT as applied in a college counseling center; results from a controlled study are presented. Chapter 6 provides a detailed outline of an 8-week group utilized with college students based on Mindfulness-Based Stress Reduction (MBSR; Kabat-Zinn, 1990). Chapter 7 specifically addresses perfectionism in college students, utilizing ACT. Whereas chapters 2-7 outline approaches utilized within college counseling centers buildings, Chapters 8-9 focus on technological innovations such as downloadable podcasts (Chapter 8) and online values training (Chapter 9). Chapters 10-12 address other aspects of campus life: Chapter 10 illustrates the utility of mindfulness and acceptance in informing peer mentoring, Chapter 11 describes four adaptations of ACT into classroom settings, and Chapter 12 describes how Ellen Langer's concepts of mindful learning (1997) can be applied to programs in Student Affairs, such as leadership training.

This book describes mindfulness- and acceptance-based initiatives not only from across the U.S., but also across other parts of the world (See Chapters 5, 8, and 10).

Chapters' Structure

Each chapter follows a particular structure:

1. It will start out with clinical vignettes to illustrate which student presentations may benefit from the approach discussed in the chapter.

2. It includes a "how to" section, with a description of at least a couple of exercises or applications of the technology described in that chapter. This may include **fictional** therapy transcripts to give the reader a feel for the intervention.

3. It includes an *Empirical Considerations* section that will summarize the state of empirical knowledge on the technology described in the chapter (i.e., DBT), as well as any data collected by the authors on their specific program (i.e., DBT with college students). This section is meant to help the reader surmise the gist of the evidence in an easily digestible format.

4. It will include a *Final Words* section to highlight a few issues or challenges in using the chapter technology with college students and/or higher education settings.

Appendix Materials

Most chapters make reference to Appendix materials, all of which are available at www.newharbinger.com/22225. Appendix materials vary from one chapter to another and include PowerPoint presentations, therapy handouts, group instructions, scripts of exercises, and the like. These materials consist of three files:

- 22225_Bonus.pdf (16.7 MB): This navigable PDF contains all of the appended materials for the book, including reproductions of all the slides and worksheets.

- 22225_PowerPointSlides.zip (41.7 MB): This zip file contains playable Microsoft PowerPoint sideshows in .pptx format for some chapters.

- 22225_WordDocuments.zip (381 kb): This zip file contains editable Microsoft Word worksheets in .dox format for some chapters.

Note that you don't need to download the zip files in order to view all the appended material. All files are reproduced for viewing in 22225_Bonus.pdf. You will only need to download the zip files if you want the application files contained in each.

See the back of the book for more information.

Who Can Use This Book

This sub-section will outline for whom this book is intended and how it can be used.

Counselors at College Counseling Centers or Student Health Centers

This book is indeed primarily intended for mental health professionals (psychologists, counselors, social workers, psychiatrists) working at college counseling centers and/or student health centers, regardless of levels of expertise with these approaches:

- If you are already familiar with some of the methods described in the book (e.g., ACT, DBT, mindfulness), but not in the context of higher education, this book can guide you on how to use that approach with college students and/or college campuses specifically.

- If you are already applying these methods in your work with college students, some of the handouts/materials in the Appendix can provide you with options to further innovate with relatively little effort, as you may edit the handouts or presentations, for example, to your own needs/setting.

- If you are not yet familiar with these methods, this book will provide you an overview of mindfulness and acceptance methods applied to college students. The book will give you enough information on a particular approach to allow you to decide whether or not you want to learn more.

- If you are medical staff working with students in a student health center regularly, these approaches may also be of help, even when delivered via relatively brief interactions with students. Some of these approaches have been successfully used in primary care settings.

Instructors or Professors

If you are an instructor or professor, the following uses might apply:

- If you are someone who is familiar with mindfulness, for example, some of these chapters will give you ideas on how to infuse these concepts and technologies into educational contexts, including the classroom. Chapter 11 in particular will present four different ways to present ACT in a classroom setting. Other chapters may also be relevant, such as Chapter 12 that describes a version of mindfulness particularly geared towards learning.

- If you are routinely faced with students in your class who are distressed or distressing, or who write about psychological struggles, this book will help you become better informed. These chapters will describe some of the cutting-edge counseling approaches that are being utilized with college students. This may help you in understanding students in your class and possibly making more effective referrals.

Other Student Affairs Personnel

If you are a professional working in Student Affairs/Services, this book could be helpful in many ways:

- If you are someone who regularly teaches First Year Seminars (FYS), several chapters may help you generate useful ideas on how to make such seminars more experiential in nature and less didactic. In Chapter 11, for example, there is a description of an FYS based on mindfulness and acceptance.

- If you are someone doing trainings in peer mentoring or leadership training, and would like to incorporate concepts and/or techniques from mindfulness and acceptance-based approaches, this book can help you. Chapter 10 describes a peer mentoring system infused with ACT and related concepts that is being applied in dozens of campuses nationwide. Chapter 12 describes a mindfulness-based approach to leadership training.

- If you work in other Student Affairs offices, mindfulness-based approaches may still be of help. Student Affairs personnel are the front line in dealing directly with students about a range of sensitive topics (e.g., financial aid, parking, disabilities resource centers, judicial affairs, residence hall behavior). This book may

provide you with ideas for how to use mindfulness and acceptance within yourself in interacting with distress and distressing
students, or with the students themselves.

Other Readers

University administrators, parents of college students, or college students themselves, may find this book informative.

- If you are a university administrator, you may find sections of
  this book enlightening. It may help you obtain an overview of
  the breadth and effectiveness of mindfulness and acceptance-
  based approaches with college students and/or campuses, and
  allow you to make informed decisions about when/how/whether
  to implement mindfulness-based approaches on your campus.

- If you are a parent (or guardian) to a college student, and are
  interested in learning about how mindfulness and acceptance
  can be, or have been, applied to college students, this book may
  be handy. Although no one chapter is directly addressed to
  parents, your improved knowledge about these methods may
  help you advocate for your child if/when she is in need.

- Finally, if you are a college student either in distress or hoping to
  help a friend in distress, this book may help you learn about
  cutting edge approaches being utilized at counseling centers.

Limitations of This Book

- This book is not meant as a comprehensive description of any
  one approach. It has enough of a "how to" element to give the
  novice reader a flavor of a particular approach in practice.
  However, it cannot substitute for careful training, or at least
  more detailed reading, on any given approach. References will be
  provided at the end of each chapter for the original work on
  each approach.

- This book is not meant as a self-help book. Although readers may derive some personal benefit from some of the chapters, there are several self-help books that would be better suited for actually working on oneself. See Appendix 1A: Self-Help Books, for a list of these titles.

In conclusion, although this book is most directly relevant to mental health professionals, professors, other student affairs staff, medical personnel working at student health centers, parents, and even college students themselves, may find the book useful.

References

Hayes, S. C., Strosahl, K., & Wilson, K. G. (2011). *Acceptance and Commitment Therapy: The process and practice of mindful change* (2nd edition). New York: Guilford Press.

Kabat-Zinn, J. (1990). *Full Catastrophe Living*. New York: Delta.

Langer, E. J. (1997). *The power of mindful learning*. Reading, MA: Addison Wesley.

Linehan, M. M. (1993). *Cognitive-Behavioral Treatment of Borderline Personality Disorder*. New York: Guilford Press.

Segal, Z. V., Williams, J. M. G., & Teasdale, J. D. (2002). *Mindfulness-Based Cognitive Therapy for depression: A new approach to preventing relapse*. New York: Guilford Press.

CHAPTER 1

Mindfulness and Acceptance in College Students: Why it Matters

Steven C. Hayes

Jacqueline Pistorello

Michael E. Levin

University of Nevada, Reno

George dashes across campus, late for his economics class, after stopping for a "decaf, skinny, vanilla, venti latte, with cinnamon on top"—said with machine-gun precision—at Starbucks. Holding his cell phone to his right ear with his hunched-up right shoulder, he talks to his bank about a mix-up while checking for his iPad charger in his backpack. Whew, it's there, otherwise he wouldn't be able to Skype his family later. He wants to find out if everything is OK back home, given the TV scenes he has witnessed of the latest devastation in the Midwest. The images of houses reduced to a pile of boards, a few bricks, and debris, make him wonder if all his high school classmates are OK. These images don't last long, as he next starts making a mental note to check all of his e-mail accounts—why can't his parents and professors just text like everybody else? As he approaches the building where his class is taught, his heart rate jumps and a wave of hot sensations course through his body as he sees his ex-girlfriend heading toward the class they had originally signed up for together—now hand in hand with her new boyfriend, whose photo he's seen already on Facebook. George thinks they haven't seen him; he turns around and heads back to the dorm. He can always get the notes from someone else later and he does feel a touch of a cold, after all.

Many adults look back to their college years and remember them as relatively carefree—a time before full adult responsibilities needed to be carried out. If psychological help was relevant, it was for things like picking a major, or learning to manage time, or just getting along with a roommate. George, the student described above, as a representative of the college student of today, may beg to differ.

The Problem

If that myth of the carefree college years was ever actually true, it appears to be true no longer. Suicide is one of the leading causes of death among college students (Suicide Prevention Resource Center, 2004). Nearly 20% of college students have seriously considered suicide and over 7% have attempted it in their lifetime (American College Health Association [ACHA], 2011). Non-suicidal self-injury (NSSI) has been found to have 15.3% lifetime and 6.8% past-year prevalence rates among college students (Whitlock et al., 2011). Nearly 50% of college students have a diagnosable psychiatric disorder (Blanco et al., 2008); nearly one-fifth have suffered from depression and two-thirds experienced overwhelming anxiety in their lifetime (ACHA, 2011). Severe drinking problems are common, with over 45% engaging in binge drinking (Wechsler & Kowalik, 2005) and 20% experiencing an alcohol use disorder (Blanco et al., 2008); 600,000 college students are injured and 1,800 die each year from alcohol-related accidents (Hingson, Zha, & Weitzman, 2009). Approximately 14% of undergraduate females and 4% of undergraduate males receive a positive screen for a current eating disorder (Eisenberg, Nicklett, Roeder, & Kirz, 2011). The list could go on, and not only in this country. Several of the chapters in this book describe similar trends in countries around the world, such as Australia, Italy, and the United Kingdom (see chapters 5, 8, and 11).

Part of the reason for such horrid statistics is that college is a time of transition, and transitions are not easy. People become full adults in the college years. These are the years that young adults learn to individuate from parents, to establish social relations, to settle into their sexuality, to decide how they will deal with drugs and alcohol, and to rise to financial, intellectual, and social demands (Kadison & DiGeronimo, 2004). Students are adjusting to newfound freedom, with more control over their schedules, selection of activities, choice of friends, food consumption, and myriad similar choices large and small. At the same time, there is often a loss of family contact, and exposure to religious, racial, sexual, or cultural differences that may be disconcerting. For some large groups, such as international students, these stressors can be almost overwhelming (Matsumoto et al., 2001; Muto, Hayes, & Jeffcoat, 2011). Failures in adjustment and mental health problems that occur during this time can have long-lasting consequences (Eisenberg, Golberstein, & Hunt, 2009; Seeley et al., 2011; Zivin, Eisenberg, Gollust, & Golberstein, 2009).

The Opportunity

Bleak statistics like this are a challenge, but they also represent an opportunity. College is a pivot point. The mental health problems that emerge during this time of transition may last for years (Zivin et al., 2009) or even a lifetime (Kessler et al., 2005). Fortunately, the reverse is also true. Skills obtained, and problems prevented or ameliorated, can *also* last for years or a lifetime. And that realization leads to another exciting one: Higher education is *designed* to create life-changing experiences.

An infrastructure exists on campuses to educate and mold human beings. In a sense, colleges are all about providing potentially life-changing interventions. That is true not only of college counseling centers, but also of student orientation and success programs, health centers and wellness programs, or college classes, clubs, talks, and internet sites. College is about learning, and learning how to live a vital, committed human life is in a deep sense the whole purpose of psychological intervention. Furthermore, college is often intensely social, in a way that life later may not be. That allows the use of social processes to produce change that might not be as possible just a few years later. Not only that, but in the Western world a large portion of the adult population touches higher education and the proportion is still rising. In the United States, 41% of the adult population will spend at least some time in college (Snyder & Dillow, 2011).

This helps frame what is exciting about the present volume. The college years are critical to healthy development. College students are a wonderfully rich population with real psychological needs, not just help in picking careers or learning to study. The college setting offers special opportunities for change that could make a real difference to important behavioral domains of a large portion of the entire population over time. Psychologically speaking, college students matter.

The Challenge

It is one thing to see an opportunity. It is another to be able to seize it. Colleges and universities are overwhelmed, and no area of college more so than college counseling centers. The severity of clinical problems on campus appears to be on the rise (Twenge et al., 2010), along with the demand for counseling services (Gallagher, 2011). This is occurring at the same time that colleges and universities are strained as institutions and are being asked to do more with less.

Resources or no resources, however, colleges cannot walk away from these problems even if they wanted to do so. The public relations and legal effects of mental health problems have taught campuses that they have no choice but to expand their mental health efforts since the public and the courts will not let them off the hook if they try to shift these responsibilities elsewhere. A sad but telling example exists in mass killings and suicides. For example, in the spring of 2007, a single undergraduate student at Virginia Polytechnic Institute and State University in Blacksburg, Virginia, killed 32 people and wounded 25 others before committing suicide. Investigations questioned the roles of the college counseling center and the campus police, among other entities. In the years since, Virginia Tech has paid millions upon millions of dollars to victims, and the drip-by-drip succession of awards continues with no clear end in sight. For example, in spring 2012 yet another award for $4 million was granted to two more families (CNN, March 14, 2012). The incident is hardly unique. In 2011 Yale University was accused of negligence in a lawsuit by the family of a graduate student murdered in a school laboratory five days before she was to be married (McMullen, 2011). In July of 2012, a student withdrawing from the University of Colorado allegedly killed twelve people at a movie theater, and the role of the psychiatrist who had been treating the student on campus was put under a magnifying glass by the media. Any college administrator looking at such situations realizes that in the modern day it risks the entire institution, not just the health of students in need, to pretend that campus mental health efforts do not matter.

Unfortunately, it is not enough just to have a well-staffed counseling center because treatment seeking can be low among college students (Hunt & Eisenberg, 2010). For example, in the United States, only 34% of those with a mood disorder and 16% of those with an anxiety disorder seek treatment in a given year (Blanco et al., 2008). Students report not seeking services partly because they lack time, want to try to handle these issues on their own, or are not convinced of the seriousness of their problems (Eisenberg et al., 2011).

The Context

All of this can explain why efforts to improve the mental health of students are important, but it does not yet explain why the acceptance, mindfulness, and values work such as that described in this volume is particularly important. There are at least five reasons to think that it is.

The Practical Benefits of a Transdiagnostic, Common Core Process Approach

The very diversity of problems faced by college students as they transition into full adulthood is stunning. When combined with the extent of need, it is hard to imagine how institutions can successfully mount programs that will make a real difference across the board. There are existing efficacious prevention programs that can be used on campus, for example, in areas such as eating disorders (Stice, Shaw, & Marti, 2006), harmful alcohol use (Carey et al., 2007), and depression and anxiety disorders (Christensen et al., 2010). Many of these programs are underutilized, however. If a college has a program in harmful alcohol use, for example, the cost and complexity of adding another for suicidality, another for eating disorders, and yet another for anxiety and so on, just becomes overwhelming. Even if a campus took that approach, students generally are not jumping at the chance to participate in programs at all, never mind several. What the work on acceptance and mindfulness offers is the possibility of a transdiagnostic common core process approach that can develop resilience skills that are applicable to the prevention of a wide range of problems and difficulties, and at the same time ameliorate a wide range of current problems.

While the days are still early, that possibility seems real. An example is a study by Muto et al. (2011) that applied a self-help program in Acceptance and Commitment Therapy (ACT; Hayes, Strosahl, & Wilson, 2011) to more than half of the Japanese international students at a Western university campus. This student group was recruited simply because of their international status, not their level of distress. In that context, the number of clinical problems was stunning: 80% exceeding clinical cutoffs on one or more measures of anxiety, depression, stress, or general mental health. Very few had sought treatment for these difficulties, nor were they likely to, given that Japanese international students in the United States see psychological difficulties as being more shameful and stigmatizing than do either Caucasian students or non-Asian ethnic minority students (Masuda, Hayes, Twohig, Lillis, Fletcher, & Gloster, 2009). What was important in this context is that in a randomized comparison, the program reduced depression, anxiety, and stress relative to a waitlist for those in the clinical range, with generally large between-group effect sizes; and at the same time the program significantly reduced the emergence of mental health problems over time for those who were not initially distressed with a medium effect size. Mediation analysis showed that these effects came due to changes in acceptance and mindfulness processes. Thus, focusing on acceptance and mindfulness a single program both prevented and ameliorated multiple problem areas. That kind of practicality is part of the hope offered by work in this area due to the transdiagnostic and common core processes nature of these methods.

The Scalability and Flexibility of Acceptance and Mindfulness Work

College students are important not just because these years are a time of transition—the importance of transition is equally true of those in the same age range who do not go to college (Kessler at al., 2005).

What is exciting in part is that the college setting presents so many different ways of reaching people. College students generally have access to counseling, but they also take classes, join clubs, use the Internet, listen to podcasts, and so on. Work in acceptance and mindfulness has proven to be extremely flexible in format. It can be done individually or in groups; in classes or in therapy; over the Internet or in person; via peer support or professional intervention. A glance at the table of contents of this book shows that readers will be exposed to that sense of scalability and flexibility. It is one of the most exciting aspects of this work—maybe really useful skills can be acquired through multiple channels if a common set of sensibilities infuses a campus.

The Benefits to Staff

A third reason to think that acceptance and mindfulness work fits especially well into the college campus setting is that these programs can be of benefit to staff themselves. This can be true of deliberate programs such as classes in Mindfulness-Based Stress Reduction (MBSR; Kabat-Zinn, 1990), which is frequently used for staff as well as students on campus, or through employee assistance programs. It is true in a broader way as well. As mindfulness, acceptance, and values enter into schools and organizations, they bring benefits for students and staff alike, perhaps because they soften and humanize the interactions between people (Biglan & Hinds, 2009; Meiklejohn et al., 2012; Noone & Hastings, 2010).

Some of the rise of acceptance and mindfulness may be a cohort effect linked to staff. The children of the 1960s and '70s were exposed to Eastern methods as a result of the popularity of authors such as Allan Watts or D. T. Suzuki, or the popularity of the Beatles and their interest in the Maharishi Mahesh Yogi. To express this idea in a slightly silly way: the hippies grew up and now they are driving the bus. Fortunately, work in acceptance and mindfulness is arriving as part of evidence-based practice, which allows excesses to be trimmed back and what is useful to survive. There is something useful to teachers and providers inside this work that seems to prevent burnout and enhance the mental health and sense of personal accomplishment of professionals and clients alike. These effects have been shown with psychotherapy providers (Brinkborg,

Michanek, Hesser, & Berglund, 2011; Hayes et al., 2004), as well as with teachers (Bethay, Wilson, Schnetzer, & Nassar, in press; Biglan et al., in press).

Cultural Changes: Mindfulness is Especially Needed Now

The final reason to think that acceptance and mindfulness work is particularly relevant to the campus now is that the world has changed. The world has become far, far more verbal.

As illustrated by the opening vignette in this chapter, the college student of today grew up with computers, the internet, e-mail, text messages, cell phones, MP3 players, and a raft of similar technologies. They are the first connected generation, but they were connected not just to each other but also to pain, horror, and judgment as a daily diet. George, the student described in our opening vignette, not only kept in contact with family and friends in a supportive sense, but also got to witness through simultaneous broadcast the devastation of his neighbors' houses in the Midwest and witness in a painfully public way his being replaced by a new boyfriend due to Facebook.

If anything terrible happens anywhere in the world, we can know about it minutes later. We can watch tsunamis live—seeing the walls of water swallow cars, homes, and people before our very eyes. If a bomb goes off or a rocket falls, we can see the video as people are killed. If a person is beaten by police, a local bystander will upload the iPhone video to YouTube.

This is not all to the bad. Technology is creating a sense of community and common action. A dictator was overthrown in Egypt in part because it is difficult to control social media (Naughton, 2011). Students arrive at college being part of a social network, and with the ability to access information and to multitask. But it is also increasing exposure to judgment, criticism, shame, and blame. A quick visit to any news portal on the Internet will show the phenomenon. After a news story, readers are allowed to post comments. Inevitably, these comments will be filled with hateful criticism and judgments, often not just of the story but also of other people making comments. Students may be on the receiving end of such things, with over a quarter of college students saying they have been the victims of cyberbullying (Held, 2011). Students have committed suicide after college roommates have posted secret recordings of them and other students have been put in jail for doing so (Zernike, 2012). There is a harsh edge to being part of the connected generation.

The cacophony of horror, pain, and judgment is overwhelming students' ability to find peace and purpose. The human mind did not evolve for such a situation. Language evolved in a cooperative context, but its usefulness as a problem solving tool has so fed prediction, categorization, and judgment that people are beginning to think of life itself as a problem to be solved rather than a process to be lived (Hayes, Strosahl, & Wilson, 2011).

This book will present various approaches to mindfulness, acceptance, and values clarification drawn largely from Acceptance and Commitment Therapy (Hayes, Strosahl, & Wilson, 2011), but also from Dialectical Behavior Therapy (DBT; Linehan, 1993), Mindfulness-Based Stress Reduction (MBSR; Kabat-Zinn, 1990), Mindfulness-Based Cognitive Therapy (MBCT; Segal, Williams, & Teasdale, 2002), and Mindful Learning (Langer, 1997). While the exact approaches differ, all of these methods emphasize at least three key targets: learning to be more psychologically open and flexible, to be more centered in consciousness and in the now, and to be more actively engaged in meaningful, values-based action (Hayes, Villatte, Levin, & Hildebrandt, 2011).

Being more open, aware, and active is an antidote to the cultural changes that are making peace of mind more difficult. The early and frequent exposure to pain and judgment has encouraged more avoidant and entangled approaches to psychological experiences. Openness and flexibility help tamp down these excesses. The rise of judgment and problem solving has caused people to drift away from the present moment and to become more focused on maintaining their story about themselves. Being centered in consciousness and in the now helps bring people's feet back to the ground. As people have been drawn into an unhealthy self-focus, they have put life on hold, or have responded impulsively rather than in ways that create a sense of purpose and direction. Being actively engaged in living out one's values allows consciousness to be linked to purpose. For most of us, that is the bottom line of most importance.

Connecting Deep Human Concerns with Evidence

Finally, it is not just that acceptance, mindfulness, and values fit the practical and cultural need; it is also that this work has become vigorously evidence-based. In the modern era, nothing less will do. Administrators, clinic directors, professors, staff, and students themselves rightfully expect to see the data showing that methods are useful. We have learned that these methods are effective, not just at the level of overall outcome, but also at the level of their components and putatively important change processes (Hayes, Villate, et al., 2011). In fact, this field, even within the context of working specifically with college students, has just in the last few years become so prolific that the chapters in this book represent only a fraction of the work being conducted on campuses. In the Thomson Reuters portal *Web of Science,* if one enters "college students" crossed with just a few key terms such as mindfulness, meditation, psychological flexibility, personal values, and experiential avoidance, over 100 studies have been published *in the last decade* (compared to almost none in the decade before), already garnering over 1,000 citations in the literature, despite their recent appearance (see Figure 1).

Final Words

The problems, opportunities, challenges, and larger context of college have led to a moment in which acceptance, mindfulness, and values are arriving on campus. It seems very unlikely that these trends will reverse anytime soon. The fit is too useful, the need is too great, and the data are too supportive. This book is the first to focus exclusively on this exciting frontier. It will walk the reader through the developments that are increasingly taking college campuses by storm. If we embrace and guide these developments, they have a chance to make a profound difference in the lives of millions.

References

American College Health Association (ACHA, 2011). ACHA-National College Health Assessment II: Reference group executive summary Spring 2011. Hanover, MD: American College Health Association.

Bethay, S., Wilson, K. G., Schnetzer, L., &Nassar, S. (in press). A controlled pilot evaluation of Acceptance and Commitment Training for intellectual disability staff. *Mindfulness.*

Biglan, A., & Hinds, E. (2009). Evolving prosocial and sustainable neighborhoods and communities. *Annual Review Of Clinical Psychology, 5,* 169-196. doi:10.1146 /annurev.clinpsy.032408.153526

Biglan, A., Layton, G. L., Backen Jones, L., Hankins, M. & Rusby, J. C. (in press). The value of workshops on psychological flexibility for early childhood special education staff. *Topics in Early Childhood Special Education.*

Blanco, C., Okuda, M., Wright, C., Hasin, D. S., Grant, B. F., et al. (2008). Mental health of college students and their non-college-attending peers: Results from the national epidemiologic study on alcohol related conditions. *Archives of General Psychiatry, 65,* 1429-1437.

Brinkborg, H., Michanek, J., Hesser, H., & Berglund, G. (2011). Acceptance and commitment therapy for the treatment of stress among social workers: A randomized controlled trial. *Behaviour Research and Therapy, 49,* 389-398.

Carey, K. B., Scott-Sheldon, L. J., Carey, M. P., & DeMartini, K. S. (2007). Individual-level interventions to reduce college student drinking: A meta-analytic review. *Addictive Behaviors, 32,* 2469-2494.

Christensen, H., Pallister, E., Smale, S., Hickie, I.B. & Calear, A. L. (2010). Community-based prevention programs for anxiety and depression in youth: A systematic review. *Journal of Primary Prevention, 31,* 139-170.

CNN (March 14, 2012). Jury finds for two Virginia Tech victims' families in lawsuit. *CNN.* http://articles.cnn.com/2012-03-14/justice/justice_virginia-virginia-tech _1_colin-goddard-virginia-tech-mark-owczarski?_s=PM:JUSTICE

Eisenberg, D., Golberstein, E. & Hunt, J. B. (2009). Mental health and academic success in college. *The B.E. Journal of Economic Analysis & Policy, 9,* 40.

Eisenberg, D., Nicklett, E. J., Roeder, K., & Kirz, N. E. (2011). Eating disorder symptoms among college students: Prevalence, persistence, correlates, and treatment-seeking. *Journal Of American College Health, 59*(8), 700-707.

Gallagher, R. (2011). *National Survey of Counseling Center Directors.* Pittsburgh, PA: University of Pittsburgh.

Hayes, S. C., Bissett, R., Roget, N., Padilla, M., Kohlenberg, B. S., Fisher, G., Masuda, A., Pistorello, J., Rye, A. K., Berry, K., & Niccolls, R. (2004). The impact of acceptance and commitment training and multicultural training on the stigmatizing attitudes and professional burnout of substance abuse counselors. *Behavior Therapy, 35,* 821-835.

Hayes, S. C., Strosahl, K., & Wilson, K. G. (2011). *Acceptance and Commitment Therapy: The process and practice of mindful change* (2nd edition). New York: Guilford Press.

Hayes, S. C., Villatte, M., Levin, M. & Hildebrandt, M. (2011). Open, aware, and active: Contextual approaches as an emerging trend in the behavioral and cognitive therapies. *Annual Review of Clinical Psychology, 7,* 141-168.

Held, E. (December 9, 2011). 27 percent of college students say they have been cyber-bullied. *USA Today College.* http://www.usatodayeducate.com/staging/index .php/ccp/27-percent-of-college-students-say-they-have-been-cyber-bullied

Hingson, R. W., Zha, W., & Weitzman, E. R. (2009). Magnitude of and trends in alcohol-related mortality and morbidity among U.S. college students ages 18–24, 1998–2005. *Journal of Studies on Alcohol and Drugs, 16,* 12–20.

Hunt, J., & Eisenberg, D. (2010). Mental health problems and help-seeking behavior among college students. *Journal of Adolescent Health, 46,* 3-10.

Kabat-Zinn, J. (1990). *Full Catastrophe Living.* New York: Delta.

Kadison, R., & DiGeronimo, T. F. (2004). *College of the overwhelmed: The campus mental health crisis and what to do about it.* San Francisco, CA: Jossey-Bass.

Kessler, R., Berglund, P., Demler, O., Jin, R., Merikangas, K.R., & Walters, E. E. (2005). Lifetime prevalence and age-on-onset distributions of DSM-IV disorders in the National Comorbidity Survey Replication. *Archives of General Psychiatry, 62,* 593-602.

Langer, E. J. (1997). *The power of mindful learning.* Reading, MA: Addison Wesley.

Linehan, M. M. (1993). *Cognitive-Behavioral Treatment of Borderline Personality Disorder.* New York: Guilford Press.

Masuda, A., Hayes, S. C., Twohig, M. P., Lillis, J., Fletcher, L. B., & Gloster, A. T. (2009). Comparing Japanese international students and U.S. college students' mental health related stigmatizing attitudes. *Journal of Multicultural Counseling and Development, 37,* 178-189.

Matsumoto, D., LeRoux, J. A., Ratzlaff, C., Tatani, H., Uchida, H., Kim, C., & Araki, S. (2001). Development and validation of a measure of intercultural adjustment potential in Japanese sojourners: The Intercultural Adjustment Potential Scale (ICAPS). *International Journal of Intercultural Relations, 25,* 483–51.

McMullen, T. (September 7, 2011). Annie Le family files lawsuit against Yale. *ABC News.* http://abcnews.go.com/US/annie-le-family-files-lawsuit-yale/story?id=14464 186#.UCmWp8hYuKU

Meiklejohn, J., Phillips, C., Freedman, M. M., Griffin, M., Biegel, G., Roach, A., et al. (2012). Integrating mindfulness training into K-12 education: Fostering the resilience of teachers and students. *Mindfulness, 2,* 1-17.

Muto, T., Hayes, S. C., & Jeffcoat, T. (2011). The effectiveness of Acceptance and Commitment Therapy bibliotherapy for enhancing the psychological health of Japanese college students living abroad. *Behavior Therapy, 42,* 323-335.

Naughton, J. (February 5, 2011). How Twitter engineers outwitted Mubarak in one weekend. *The Guardian.* http://www.guardian.co.uk/technology/2011/feb/06 / twitter-speak-tweet-mubarak-networker

Noone, S., & Hastings, R. (2010). Using acceptance and mindfulness-based workshops with support staff caring for adults with intellectual disabilities. *Mindfulness, 1,* 67-73.

Segal, Z. V., Williams, J. M. G., & Teasdale, J. D. (2002). *Mindfulness-Based Cognitive Therapy for depression: A new approach to preventing relapse.* New York: Guilford Press.

Seeley, J. R., Kosty, D. B., Farmer, R. F., & Lewinsohn, P. M. (2011). The modeling of internalizing disorders on the basis of patterns of lifetime comorbidity: Associations with psychosocial functioning and psychiatric disorders among first-degree relatives. *Journal of Abnormal Psychology, 120,* 308-321.

Snyder, T. D., & Dillow, S. A. (2011). *Digest of Educational Statistics: 2010.* Washington, DC: U. S. Department of Education, National Center for Educational Statistics. Retrieved from http://nces.ed.gov/pubsearch/pubsinfo .asp?pubid=2011015

Stice, E., Shaw, H., & Marti, C. N. (2006). A meta-analytic review of eating disorder prevention programs: Encouraging findings. *Annual Review of Clinical Psychology, 3,* 207-232.

Suicide Prevention Resource Center. (2004). *Promoting mental health and preventing suicide in college and university settings.* Newton, MA: Education Development Center, Inc.

Twenge, J. M., Gentile, B., DeWall, C. N., Ma, D., Lacefield, K., & Schurtz, D. R. (2010). Birth cohort increases in psychopathology among young Americans, 1938-2007: A cross-temporal meta-analysis of the MMPI. *Clinical Psychology Review, 30,* 145-154.

Wechsler, R. L., & Kowalik, S. C. (2005). Adolescent substance abuse treatment in the United States: Exemplary models from a national evaluation study. *Journal of Child and Adolescent Psychopharmacology, 15,* 835-838.

Whitlock, J., Muehlenkamp, J., Purington, A., Eckenrode, J., Barreira, P., Baral Abrams, G., & … Knox, K. (2011). Nonsuicidal Self-injury in a College Population: General Trends and Sex Differences. *Journal Of American College Health, 59*(8), 691-698. doi:10.1080/07448481.2010.529626

Zernike, K. (May 21, 2012). Rutgers webcam-spying defendant is sentenced to 30-day jail term. *The New York Times.* http://www.nytimes.com/2012/05/22/nyregion /rutgers-spying-defendant-sentenced-to-30-days-in-jail.html?pagewanted=all

Zivin, K., Eisenberg, D., Gollust, S. E., & Golberstein, E. (2009). Persistence of mental health problems and needs in a college student population. *Journal of Affective Disorders, 117,* 180-185.

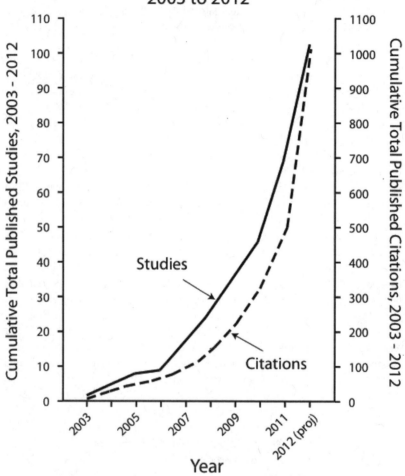

Figure 1. Growth and Impact of Acceptance, Mindfulness, and Values Research with College Students 2003 to 2012

CHAPTER 2

Dialectical Behavior Therapy (DBT) Applied to Severely Distressed College Students

Jacqueline Pistorello

Chelsea MacLane

Alan Fruzzetti

Karen Erikson

University of Nevada, Reno

Carrie Guthrie

Holly Landsbaum

Abby Bjornsen

University of California, Berkeley

Amy, a Japanese international student who is a sophomore in nursing, cut her wrists in her residence hall room, which she shares as part of a suite with three other female students. One of her roommates saw a red substance on the bathtub and soon realized it was blood. She discussed this with two of the other roommates and the three of them confronted Amy, who acknowledged that she had indeed cut her wrists but "chickened out." The roommates also noted that Amy hardly ever eats, is already very thin, and sometimes goes on drinking binges. Surprisingly, she usually seems "together" (well groomed, with makeup), although the roommates noted that they walk on eggshells around her because she is quick to anger. Amy refused to go to the ER, stating that the cut was just a scratch. She did agree to go to the university health center, where medical staff also referred her for counseling. She had been reluctant to go, but the Resident Director (RD) said that unless she attended counseling, she could not remain in the residence halls. Amy then attended an assessment at the counseling center accompanied by her RD. Amy's story illustrates an increasingly common situation in college counseling centers (CCCs) these days: students presenting for treatment with multiple complex problems, whose psychological struggles have ripple effects on the entire university community and who may or may not be doing well academically and may or may not seek treatment.

The purpose of this chapter is to describe the use of Dialectical Behavior Therapy (DBT; Linehan, 1993a, 1993b) with college students presenting with severe, complex profiles, such as Amy. The chapter will begin with a review of trends among college students that support the need for DBT in CCCs, along with a description of comprehensive DBT. We will then illustrate the potential application of DBT at a CCC through two different projects: 1) Project 1 is the first randomized controlled trial (RCT) showing the effectiveness of comprehensive DBT, relative to an optimized control condition, with college students; 2) Project 2 describes the clinical experience of offering DBT skills training alone as an adjunctive treatment at a CCC. The chapter will end with a discussion of empirical considerations and challenges/recommendations in applying DBT, either in its comprehensive format or as a skills-group only approach, to college students.

Why We Need DBT at College Counseling Centers

CCCs across the nation are treating students with increasingly higher levels of psychopathology, such as suicidality, non-suicidal self-injury (NSSI), personality disorders (particularly borderline personality disorder [BPD]), and complex issues (e.g., Kitzrow, 2003). Data collected from a survey of CCC directors (Gallagher, 2011) paints a picture of increased severity, complexity, and acuity. Approximately 90% of counseling center directors noted an increase in overall psychopathology, but the greatest stress on the resources of CCCs appears to come from an increase in the number of extremely distressed students presenting with complex profiles: 78% of directors noted an increase in crises requiring immediate attention and a threefold increase in number of hospitalizations since the mid-1990s (Gallagher, 2011). Furthermore, directors estimate that 37% of students seeking services have severe psychological problems, 6% with problems that are so severe that they cannot remain in school and 31% with problems that can be managed while still in school (Gallagher, 2011). Most directors reported that their jobs are more stressful than they used to be, partly because of the pressure to manage students with increasing complexity (73%) and to prevent tragic events from occurring on campuses (51%; Gallagher, 2011).

Even when data are not collected by retrospective self-report, this pattern prevails: the percentage of students presenting with depression, suicidality, and personality disorders appears to have at least doubled within a decade (Benton, Robertson, Tseng, Newton, & Benton, 2003). Recent data collected from students seeking services tells a similar story. A survey from the Center for Collegiate Mental Health (CCMH, 2012) found that approximately 32% of students presenting to treatment at counseling centers nationwide are experiencing some level of suicidal ideation, 30% have taken a psychotropic medication, and 7.1% have been previously hospitalized for psychiatric reasons.

The definition of "severe or complex" cases presenting to counseling centers often includes borderline personality disorder (BPD) features or correlates (e.g., Lippincott, 2007). These features include: suicidality and self-injury, dissociative or psychotic symptoms, uncontrolled anger, intense relationships, comorbid eating disorders, comorbid substance abuse, trauma, dysfunctional family of origin issues, difficulty forging a working therapeutic alliance, prior hospitalizations, and a history of treatment failures (e.g., Gilbert, 1992).

Although staff report that there are increasing numbers of students presenting with BPD or significant BPD features to CCCs (e.g., Tryon, DeVito, Halligan, Kane, & Shea, 1998), the prevalence rate of BPD among treatment-seeking college students is unknown. The absence of clear prevalence rates may be due to several factors: many counseling centers do not typically diagnose (e.g., Kitzrow, 2003), some of the cases may be at a "subclinical" level (Tryon, DeVito, Halligan, Kane, & Shea, 1998), and due to "apparent competence" (Linehan, 1993a), these students may initially present with a more functional profile than they maintain in general. Although some CCCs quickly refer such cases to off-campus providers, BPD is regularly treated on campuses (Tryon, DeVito, Halligan, Kane, & Shea, 1998). Leaving these individuals untreated may result in "disruptive or disturbing behavior, potentially affecting numerous people on the college campus, including roommates, classmates, faculty, and staff" (Kitzrow, 2003, p. 287).

Clearly the severity and complexity of cases presenting for treatment at CCCs is increasing, and DBT is one of the few empirically validated approaches that can treat severe multi-problem presentations including suicidality, non-suicidal self-injury, and BPD features.

Dialectical Behavior Therapy (DBT): A Brief Overview

Developed by Marsha Linehan and colleagues (Linehan, 1993a, 1993b), DBT is designed to treat problems associated with emotion dysregulation and is supported by dozens of controlled studies (see Empirical Considerations section below). DBT is built around a biosocial or transactional model for the development of BPD and other disorders of emotion dysregulation (Fruzzetti, Shenk, & Hoffman, 2005; Linehan, 1993a). The key transaction is between an emotionally vulnerable individual and social invalidation in his or her family and environment, which mutually affect each other. Vulnerability to becoming dysregulated includes sensitivity and high reactivity to emotional stimuli in a person's social environment, as well as a slow return to emotional baseline. Invalidating responses from others convey that the person's private experiences (emotions, desires, opinions, etc.) are illegitimate, wrong, or incomprehensible. In this ongoing transaction, a person's vulnerabilities make her more susceptible to being invalidated, and being invalidated increases her vulnerabilities, ultimately leading to chronic emotion dysregulation (Fruzzetti & Worrall, 2010).

Treatment targets in DBT are arranged hierarchically, by stages of disorder (Linehan, 1993a). Stage One refers to severe problems that sometimes include out-of-control overt behaviors, such as severe suicidality, self-harm, severe substance use, inability to attend or participate effectively in treatment, being too depressed to go to school or work, binge-eating or purging, and so on. Within Stage One, targets are arranged hierarchically as well, with life-threatening behaviors at the top of the hierarchy, followed by behaviors that interfere with treatment, then behaviors that severely interfere with quality of life (severe depression, eating disorders, substance use, etc.). In Stage Two, the focus moves to misery and severe emotional suffering, but in the context of some control over action. Here, a person may be able to engage in the structure of her life (e.g., go to school, stay safe) but still has moderate to severe clinical problems such as depression, anxiety, or PTSD. Stages Three and Four are less clinical, focusing on problems in living and a mindful capacity for happiness and close relationships, respectively.

Comprehensive DBT differs from traditional psychotherapy interventions in a variety of ways. First, outpatient DBT is a comprehensive program of treatment that includes five different functions (Linehan, 1993a): 1) psychological skill training, typically in groups, to help clients learn specific psychological skills; 2) individual therapy, to address client motivation (targeting, doing chain analyses of problems, developing and pushing for solutions, and providing support and validation); 3) planning and coaching to help clients generalize their new skills to difficult situations in their lives; 4) a therapist consultation team meeting to help therapists improve their treatment skills and maintain motivation to treat effectively; and 5) couple, parent, family, or other social interventions to help people in the social environment support the client's progress.

DBT therapists teach clients, usually in a group format, the following skills to help them master tasks related to emotion modulation and self-management (Linehan, 1993b): 1) mindfulness (to facilitate attention control, reduce judgments toward self and others, and to build self-awareness and self-management skills); 2) interpersonal effectiveness (to help reduce chaos and invalidation and help build social support); 3) emotion regulation (to reduce emotional vulnerability, reactivity and misery, and to facilitate emotion modulation and self-management); and 4) distress tolerance (to interrupt negative emotion escalation and urges to engage in out-of-control behavior and to "accept" things in life that are very undesirable but unchangeable).

In addition, DBT employs a dialectical epistemology across all aspects of the treatment. In practice, this means utilizing principles of both acceptance (understanding, validating) and change (behavior therapy and problem solving) in the treatment (Linehan, 1993a). It also means that every dimension of the treatment can be conceptualized within a dialectical framework. For example, the therapist communicates dialectically with the client, using *both* a warm, supportive, genuine communication style *and* an unorthodox, pushy, matter-of-fact or irreverent communication style. Similarly, the therapist typically consults with the client on how to solve his or her problems, but sometimes intervenes directly to solve them. In terms of solutions, *both* more acceptance-oriented solutions (mindfulness, distress tolerance, accepting emotions and situations) are developed *and* more traditional change-oriented solutions (changing the situation, others, or, in some situations, emotions) are implemented.

Project 1: Comprehensive DBT in a CCC Setting and Adaptations (University of Nevada, Reno)[1]

Jacqueline Pistorello, Chelsea MacLane, Alan Fruzzetti, and Karen Erikson

1 The project described was supported by grant R34MH071904 from the National Institute of Mental Health (P.I.:J. Pistorello). The content is solely the responsibility of the authors and does not necessarily represent the official views of the National Institute of Mental Health or the National Institutes of Health.

Comprehensive DBT (Linehan, 1993a, 1993b) has been utilized as part of a federally funded randomized controlled study in a mid-size Western university. The results of this study are reported in detail elsewhere (See Pistorello, Fruzzetti, MacLane, Gallop, & Iverson, 2012) and summarized briefly below, but first we will describe some of the modifications and adaptations of comprehensive DBT utilized in this study. We have found certain modifications of DBT helpful when applying it to college students.

Skills Training Modifications

In terms of changes in skills training, we added a 3-week module in validation skills training utilized in other studies (e.g., Iverson, Shenk, & Fruzzetti, 2009) and shortened the distress tolerance module to three weeks. Linehan enumerates six levels of validation, starting with listening skills and evolving into increasingly more sophisticated and hypothetically more powerful levels of validation (Linehan, 1998). The validation skills taught as part of this study were gleaned from two modules of validation: self-validation (Fruzzetti, 2011) and relational validation (Fruzzetti, 2009). Self-validation pertains to "taking yourself seriously, allowing yourself to feel what you feel (primary emotions), think what you think, want what you want, with acceptance *and* without judgments, second-guessing, self-loathing, or self-contempt" (Fruzzetti, 2011, p. 3). The areas taught included: understanding what self-validation is, outlining the steps in self-validation, and sustaining self-validation in the context of invalidation by others. Relational validation (Fruzzetti, 2009) included skills in relational mindfulness and accurate expression as necessary precursors to relational validation, as well as specific steps in being able to validate others. A key concept imparted is that "in order to be understood, or for another person to respond in the way you want, you first must be able to identify accurately what you want (or feel, think, etc.) and tell the other person in a way he or she can understand" (Fruzzetti, 2009, p.7).

In order to add validation, we also shortened some of the other skills from DBT (Linehan, 1993b). During our pilot work, college students who had participated in DBT skills training groups reported finding parts of the distress tolerance module less helpful to them than skills in the area of emotion regulation and interpersonal effectiveness, and somewhat repetitive (e.g., soothing with five senses mostly overlapping with mindfulness skills). This feedback stands in contrast of work with adolescents, where distress tolerance was rated highly (Miller et al., 2000). This difference between adolescents and young adults in college could simply reflect idiosyncratic factors of these samples (e.g., how the skills were taught or the composition of the group), or could possibly be because students who are able to remain in college may have already mastered some of the distress tolerance skills in the module, given that the distress tolerance module was originally designed for a severe community sample (Linehan, 1993b).

Thus, in our study, there were three DBT skills areas (emotion regulation, interpersonal effectiveness, and distress tolerance/validation), each lasting six weeks and immediately preceded by two weeks of mindfulness training, for a total of three modules, lasting eight weeks each. Additionally, skills training was adjusted to students' schedules. We shortened the length of skills groups to 1.5 hours a week instead of 2.5 hours (Linehan, 1993b) in order to better accommodate students' busy class schedules. One of the challenges in running any group on a college campus is finding a time that everyone can attend. We also only conducted one group per semester, starting a few weeks into the semester, when everyone's class schedules were finalized and ending before finals, as students often miss group sessions during finals. Therefore, in an academic year, the three eight-week skills modules followed the campus schedule with one module taught in the spring, one in the fall, and one in the summer.

DBT Attendance Requirements and Therapeutic Contact Modifications

The campus setting necessitated a few other modifications to DBT, including attendance issues. As is typical of DBT, CCC counselors relentlessly encouraged attendance and followed up on missed sessions through phone calls, e-mails, and texting. Because students generally left town for extended periods of time, participants had to miss at least four scheduled consecutive individual appointments without making contact with the therapist to be considered to have dropped out of therapy, even if they were away for three months.

The definition of therapy attendance was broadened. For example, students often leave campus or town during holiday closures. With this knowledge, we reduced the chance that students would miss appointments by offering sessions conducted via phone or Skype during school vacations. College students often use text messaging and e-mail, in addition to phone, to communicate. Thus, traditional coaching methods (Linehan, 1993a) were modified to accommodate the student's preferred method of communication. While it is preferable to assess lethality in person, the phone, texts, and e-mails can serve as an effective tool for skills coaching.

Finally, comprehensive DBT was originally empirically validated to last one year (Linehan, 1993a), although studies have used different treatment dosages as well with great success (e.g., Koons et al., 2001). For the purposes of the study, we emulated the original empirical studies by offering one year of comprehensive DBT treatment to college students who needed it. However, we also recognized that not all students presenting with BPD features, suicidality, and complex behaviors would require as much treatment, given that college students presenting with BPD features differ from community samples (Trull, 1995). Yet, we wanted students to have the opportunity to complete at least one skills group, and to be seen after a semester break, therefore we required attendance of at least seven months, but treatment could last as long as 12 months.

Additional DBT Strategies: Some Considerations

Traditional-age college students (18-22) are a unique population, in that they are no longer children, but many are still being financially supported by, and during the breaks living with, their parents. Comprehensive DBT with college students does not automatically involve parents the way DBT with adolescents might (Miller, Rathus, & Linehan, 2006). However, parents remain a very important aspect of college students' lives. A recent study showed that 30% of all college students speak to at least one of their parents every day, that when distraught, they often prefer to speak to their parents, and that not having a parent as a confidant was a key factor in predicting students who progressed from NSSI into suicidal ideation (Whitlock, in preparation). Thus, as needed, we relied on family interventions during the DBT treatment, utilizing available DBT protocols (Fruzzetti, Santisteban, & Hoffman, 2007). These interventions involved sporadically conducting in-person and over the phone sessions with parents, always in the presence of the student client. The purpose of such sessions varied greatly, but often included psychoeducation about the biosocial model, which was often discussed with non-abusive parents as a function of "incompatibility" as opposed to invalidation (Hoffman, Fruzzetti, & Swenson, 1999). This nonjudgmental way of explaining to parents their child's pattern of escalation can help parents develop some perspective taking skills without inviting defensiveness (Hoffman, Fruzzetti, & Swenson, 1999). At other times, these sessions focused on agreements between student and parents on how parents can respond during suicidal crises periods, as a way of reducing inadvertent reinforcement of escalation.

In DBT, we may irreverently say "I can't treat you if you are not alive" (Linehan, 1993a). In DBT with some college students, we may say "I can't treat you if you are not in school." Although dropping out of school may be the most effective behavior for a student, sometimes, the shame and feelings of failure that dropping out of school evokes may offset any benefits of leaving a stressful environment. In a way, leaving school for some students exhibiting BPD features may function like hospitalizations for chronically suicidal individuals: it may provide temporary relief to all involved but the problems are likely to persist or even worsen after discharge (Chiles & Strosahl, 1995). Many students may face additional challenges, as well as a sense of lack of direction, upon dropping out of school—not to mention the fact that the underlying suicidality, depression, or whatever else was going on back in college will still be present. Conversely, sometimes dropping out of school temporarily may provide a much needed respite for a distressed student. Typical DBT conceptualizations are very important in figuring out the *function* of the behavior of dropping out of school. In our study, we made concerted efforts to keep students enrolled if the student so wanted when in "wise mind" (Linehan, 1993b). For example, Amy, the student discussed at the beginning of the chapter, feared going back to Japan and being faced with a lot of criticism and ostracism by her family for "wasting so much money" if she returned without a terminal degree. Her family had always been a trigger for her suicide attempts and coming to the U.S. to study had been her "last resort." Her suicidality, as it turns out, had been triggered by her not doing well in a couple of classes and fearing having to drop out of school and return home. In this instance, we worked with Amy to request special dispensation to take fewer credits and remain enrolled (international students have to remain full-time at most schools).

The above situation with Amy also illustrates a more direct impact on the environment by the therapist than a typical "consultation to the patient" approach in DBT (Linehan, 1993a). Similar to DBT in general, the preference is always to coach the student to initiate interactions with the university instead of relying on therapist-initiated contacts. In this context, however, the CCC counselor actually does have the power to effect some changes in the environment that the student does not have on her own. A letter from a counselor may help students be able to drop a class after the drop out date, reduce their credit load and stay enrolled, and so on. During our study, we wrote many letters to the university on behalf of the students; however, this had to be done carefully, making sure that the focus was always on the function of the behavior. For example, in Amy's case, helping her stay enrolled and eventually graduating helped her build a life worth living. However, situations that seem to be functioning as avoidance or "emotion-mind" choices, the DBT therapist would be less likely to comply (e.g., allowing a student to break an agreement with the residence halls in order to give money to a substance-abusing boyfriend).

Sometimes, DBT therapists may be put in a situation similar to conducting mandated therapy. One of the very first issues to consider is "Who is the client?" For example, in Amy's case, the residence hall contacted the CCC and had a vested interest in her remaining in treatment. Students may indeed be kicked out of residence halls after attempting suicide. Although commitment strategies from DBT can be useful in helping a reluctant student agree to treatment (Linehan, 1993a), it is important that these issues be discussed up front with the student and the referral source, and that all roles be clarified. In Amy's situation, for example, we agreed that the only information to be shared with the RD was confirmation that the student was in therapy.

This study's results are briefly summarized below under Empirical Considerations.

Project 2: Providing DBT Skills Training Groups as Adjunctive Treatment for College Students

Carrie Guthrie, Holly Landsbaum, and Abby Bjornsen

Individuals like Amy are presenting to CCCs across the nation with a pattern of hospitalizations, crises, and/or frequent NSSI or suicide attempts, and CCCs are actively trying to find an approach that is effective in clinical impact and costs. The current CCC context is marked by a lack of resources and a brief therapy mandate due to high demand for services, coupled with a clear need for treatments designed for complex presentations (Gallagher, 2011). Despite the lack of clear empirical guidelines, CCCs (as well as many other clinical settings) have begun providing DBT skills training groups alone as adjunctive treatment (Dimeff & Koerner, 2007). This is most often due to limited financial resources and sometimes the assumption that for many clients, the comprehensive DBT package may not be required (Dimeff & Koerner, 2007). In the next few paragraphs we will describe one approach to conducting DBT skills training as an adjunctive treatment in a CCC.

Development of Skills Group

At the University of California, Berkeley, the CCC is highly utilized and largely successful in meeting the needs of the student population. However, there are a few sub-sets of the population, including students who present with features or a diagnosis of BPD, who are seeking or are in need of more comprehensive, longer-term services that are not consistent with our brief CCC model. While there are a few DBT resources in the community surrounding the CCC, most do not accept the student health insurance and are thus financially prohibitive.

In 2010 we initiated an in-house task group (TG) to explore the possibility of providing DBT in the CCC as a way to address the needs of students presenting with BPD. The TG ultimately determined that it was beyond the CCC scope to provide a comprehensive CBT program and recommended that we offer a pilot DBT Skills Group alone (see "Appendix 2A: DBT Task Group Recommendations," at www.newhar binger.com/22225). To ensure that skills group members will have adequate treatment, the TG recommended that all participants must be in concurrent weekly individual psychotherapy throughout the duration of the group. Most students must commit to seeing a therapist off-campus since the group runs beyond the 8-session limit in the CCC. Although the TG had recommended that students see an individual DBT or DBT-informed therapist, this was not required due to the limited number of DBT therapists available in the community.

Group Selection Criteria

To guide our colleagues in making appropriate referrals, we developed referral guidelines based on the DBT goals for behaviors to decrease (interpersonal chaos, labile emotions, impulsiveness, confusion about self, cognitive dysregulation; see "Appendix 2B: Referral Guidelines for Managing Emotions Skills Group"). We do not require that students meet the full diagnostic criteria for BPD in order to be considered. The group screening process focuses on assessing the following: frequency and severity of self-injury/parasuicide and other impulsive behavior; frequency and acuity of suicidal ideation; recent suicide attempt(s) and severity; recent hospitalization(s); and co-occurring issues such as substance abuse, disordered eating, Axis I diagnoses, and severe interpersonal problems. Based on the group leader's assessment and consultation with the student's other providers, a student who is determined to need a higher level of care (e.g. full DBT, partial hospitalization, inpatient hospitalization) will be excluded. Other specific exclusion criteria include students who are in current and acute crisis, actively psychotic, medically unstable due to an eating disorder or other condition, overtly hostile or violent in a group setting, unable to participate in a 1½ hour group or complete homework, and unable to commit to group for the semester.

Pre-Group Meetings

In order to assess for fit and build motivation, every student referred, including returning group members, is required to meet with the group leaders for a 1-hour pre-group screening. We include both group leaders in these meetings in an effort to build rapport with the student and to establish the co-leadership structure. During the screening meetings we review consent for treatment, provide brief psychoeducation regarding DBT, and clearly inform students that we are offering a DBT skills group only, not a comprehensive DBT program. We review our Group Agreement (see "Appendix 2C: Agreements for Students in Managing Emotions (DBT) Skills Group"), which identifies the reduction of life-threatening behavior as a primary treatment goal. In addition we explore the student's goals, highlight the attendance policy, specify the requirement for concurrent individual therapy, and discuss an explicit safety plan that she will commit to with her individual therapist for emergencies. Students are asked to review the entire Group Agreement with their individual therapists. We also discuss our collaborative treatment team approach and the necessity of consulting with their individual therapists and psychiatrists.

Running the Group

Currently we run two 12-week closed groups each semester. Group size has ranged from 7-11 students. Groups have been led by two senior clinicians, one intensively trained in DBT, or a senior clinician and a post-doctoral or post-Master of Social Work fellow. The groups include undergraduate and graduate students. Of the 15 students currently participating in the groups, all but two are female. We work directly from Linehan's DBT *Skills Training Manual* (Linehan, 1993b) but have made some adaptations to the structure and time frame due to issues specific to working within our academic schedule. A primary goal is to offer all of the DBT skills modules over the course of the academic year—fall and spring semesters. We encourage students to participate for at least two semesters so that they receive all skills, ideally consecutively. However, due to the nature of students' ever changing schedules, this is not always possible. Students are invited to return subsequent semesters to receive all of the skills training and to repeat if desired and as space is available.

Based on feedback from our initial group members to cover the Distress Tolerance Skills early in the group, we decided to offer both Mindfulness and Distress Tolerance Skills each semester. Therefore, in each group we cover Mindfulness and Distress Tolerance Skills in the first 5-6 weeks, followed by Interpersonal Effectiveness Skills in the fall and Emotion Regulation Skills in the spring for the remaining 6-7 weeks. As a result of this schedule we also reduced the length of the Distress Tolerance Skills module to 3 weeks (see Project 1 above).

Consultation and Managing Crises

The three group leaders meet weekly for two hours as an informal DBT consultation team for group planning and consultation. We routinely make phone contact with the individual psychotherapist once the student has been accepted into the group and again once the group has terminated. A large majority of our referrals come from our CCC psychiatrist colleagues, with whom we consult both at the time of referral and as questions or concerns arise. Establishing collaborative relationships with the other treatment providers has become a high priority. Functioning as a treatment team with weekly phone or in-person consultation has been essential for our work with some group members, specifically those who have made suicide attempts, are engaging in potentially lethal self-harm, and for whom significant therapy-interfering behavior is impacting treatment. While our underlying assumption has been that it would be ideal for group members to be in concurrent individual DBT therapy, we have found that it may be most important for them to work with a highly skilled psychotherapist who is motivated to collaborate across theoretical orientations and who has the experience and ability to maintain a positive working alliance with her client through periods of very difficult and high-risk behavior and interpersonal dynamics.

We have also learned from experience the importance of being explicit with group members and their other providers that group leaders are unable to provide crisis counseling outside of group time. It seems clinically important to maintain these boundaries in terms of limiting the amount of time group leaders spend interacting with students and other parties outside of group. For a few group members, it appears that significant therapeutic progress has been attained across several semesters of their group participation. The cohesive treatment team approach with frequent consultation has potentially been a key ingredient in these gains. While this perceived progress is encouraging, it remains a continued area for analysis in regards to the cost to the CCC in terms of the amount of time and resources we are investing in a small number of students.

Empirical Considerations: DBT with College Students

DBT is supported by dozens of controlled trials and other studies (See Feigenbaum, 2007 for a review and Kliem, Kröger, & Kosfelder, 2010 for a recent meta-analysis). Initial studies focused on treating BPD and suicidal and self-harming behaviors, and more recently DBT has been applied successfully to a variety of severe problems including aggression, depression, PTSD, eating disorders, substance abuse and family and relationship problems (cf. Feigenbaum, 2007; Robins & Chapman, 2004). Originally developed as an outpatient treatment program, DBT has also been shown to be effective in day treatment, residential, inpatient, and forensic settings (cf. Feigenbaum, 2007).

Project 1 described above is the first RCT of DBT with college students. The sample was composed of a total of 63 college students between the ages of 18 and 25 who were suicidal at baseline, reported at least one lifetime NSSI act or a suicide attempt, and exhibited significant BPD features. Treatment was provided by mental health trainees (i.e., doctoral students, postdoctoral fellows, or psychiatry residents), and, emulating the approach taken in a recent study where DBT was compared to treatment by experts nominated from the community (Linehan, Comtois et al., 2006), supervision was conducted by a locally nominated expert. Participants were randomly assigned to either DBT ($n = 31$) or an optimized Treatment as Usual (O-TAU) control condition ($n = 32$). Treatment was provided by doctoral or post-doctoral trainees, supervised by experts in both treatments, with the locally nominated O-TAU supervisor relying on a non-cognitive behavioral approach. Both treatments lasted between 7 and 12 months and included both individual and group components. Assessments were conducted at pretreatment, 3-months, 6-months, 9-months, 12-months, and 18-months (follow-up).

Analyses revealed that DBT, compared to the control condition, showed significantly greater decreases in suicidality, depression, number of NSSI events (if a participant had in fact self-injured), and BPD features, and significantly greater improvements in social adjustment and global assessment of functioning—the latter as rated by a blind assessor, the therapist, and the supervisor. Most of these treatment effects were observed at follow-up. Figure 1 below (reprinted here by permission of the American Psychological Association) illustrates some of these findings. Academic performance factors, such as GPA and retention, obtained from the university did not show an effect for treatment; however, these were difficult to measure. For example, freshmen students did not have a baseline value and therefore were discarded from the analyses, and students often took classes at, or temporarily transferred to, a local 2-year college, and we did not collect data from other institutions. Interestingly, the DBT treatment dropout rate (before seven months of treatment were completed) was slightly higher than expected (35%, or 11/31), and higher than that reported in other studies (Linehan et al., 2006). However, this was not significantly different from that obtained in the O-TAU group (47% or 15/32). Approximately half of the DBT (14/31) and the O-TAU (13/32) groups stayed in treatment for 12 months. The average DBT completer attended 34 ($SD=10.46$) individual and 17 ($SD=9.38$) skills group sessions—a dosage considerably lower than what would be obtained for weekly participation in a 12-month treatment, as proposed in comprehensive DBT (Linehan, 1993a). Yet, the impact of the treatment provided remained quite significant, despite the lower dosage.

Moderation analyses showed that DBT was particularly effective for suicidal students who were lower functioning at pretreatment (i.e., Global Assessment of Functioning lower than 50). This latter finding is relevant to CCCs, as it suggests that a more labor-intensive approach such as comprehensive DBT could be reserved for a smaller percentage of "severe" students—those who are lower in functioning.

The efficacy of DBT group skills training as a stand-alone or adjunctive intervention in a CCC setting remains to be studied. However, these attempts (See Project 2 above) are partly justified, given preliminary findings that if carried out competently, DBT skills training alone in other settings may be efficacious (e.g., Feldman, Harley, Kerrigan, Jacabo, & Fava, 2009; Harley, Baity, Blais, & Jacobo, 2007).

Final Words

Currently there is a clear need for DBT at CCCs. Data from Project 1 above indicates that comprehensive DBT, even when compared to a strong control condition, is effective with college students presenting with a complex profile. At this time, this is the only empirically validated application of DBT with college students, and thus comprehensive DBT is the most indicated treatment option for this population.

Project 1 provided some guidance for reducing costs while applying comprehensive DBT. Given our findings that DBT was particularly effective with lower functioning students, CCCs with limited resources might consider offering comprehensive DBT only to those students. Project 1 also showed that perhaps treatment duration can be titrated according to the student's needs. Our data indicated a fair amount of stabilization after only a few months of treatment for a portion of students. Some students who stopped treatment before seven months (and therefore were technically dropouts in the study) were doing quite well and noted that they did not feel they needed such intensive treatment (group and individual). Conversely, half of the students remained in treatment for the entirety of the 12-month program, and some were referred for continued treatment immediately following the conclusion of the study.

The use of DBT skills training as a stand-alone or adjunctive treatment, such as in Project 2 above, will need to be empirically validated. An important next step in the application of DBT to CCCs is to conduct a stepped care study, where students are assigned to different levels of DBT care (e.g., skills group only vs. comprehensive). We question the efficacy of providing a DBT skills group alone with concurrent individual therapy of any orientation to this complex and high-risk population. Crucial aspects of comprehensive DBT are missing, including individual DBT, 24-hour skills coaching, and a formal consultation team. On the other hand, given the lack of affordable comprehensive DBT treatment available off campus in most areas of the country and some promising findings in terms of skills training alone in other settings (Feldman et al.,

2009; Harley et al., 2007), this practice is routinely followed across a number of other clinical environments (Dimeff & Koerner, 2007) and may be cautiously justified.

When utilizing DBT skills training alone as an adjunctive treatment, we recommend considering the following factors:

a. Criteria for participation in DBT skills group alone needs to be evaluated with great care taking into consideration issues related to safety, needs of specific students, and group leader limits.

b. The individual therapist matters, particularly if she is not a DBT clinician. Therapists who are open to DBT and flexible in their approach, have a strong therapeutic relationship with the student, have a thorough and specific safety plan, are available between sessions for managing crises, and are willing to access consultation when needed appear to be associated with positive treatment outcomes in anecdotal observations. We recommend providing detailed DBT psychoeducation to individual therapists who are not familiar with the approach.

c. Communication and collaboration with individual therapists is essential. This requires time, flexibility, and willingness on the part of group leaders and individual therapists. We have noticed that some students' motivation and consistent attendance decline around mid-semester, which we hypothesize may correlate with the increase in academic stress as the semester proceeds. We also wonder if this may be related to the fact that most students are not in individual DBT and thus are not receiving individualized skills coaching and attention to issues of motivation for practice of skills. Therefore, a weekly group consultation time by conference call or in person with all those involved in the student's treatment (e.g., skills group leaders, individual therapist in the community, psychiatrists) may be beneficial. Additional administrative time within the CCC to support the group leaders in managing the infrastructure of the program is essential.

d. Establishing and maintaining strong collaborative relationships with and between the group members, CCC, and community therapists provides more containment for students and therapists alike. For therapists, this may facilitate their capacity to manage extreme emotion dysregulation and high-risk behaviors. In order to effectively provide a DBT Skills Group alone concurrent with individual therapy of any orientation, we believe it is essential to maintain these connections as a way to emulate the structure and support of a full DBT program. Of course, this requires additional time for skills group leaders and thus has a cost. However, we believe this approach may significantly contribute to reducing therapist burnout and the pressure on CCC therapists and psychiatrists to manage crises without adequate clinical relationships.

e. Without DBT individual therapists, the task of maintaining motivation and commitment will fall on the group leaders. Perhaps closer collaboration and communication with individual therapists will help to address this issue. Asking individual therapists to sign a Group Agreement outlining their role and responsibility in collaborative treatment could be considered.

f. Treating students with BPD is difficult. It is for this reason that Marsha Linehan designed DBT to be a team-driven treatment (Linehan, 1993a). In practice, many skills groups offered alone do not incorporate teams due to lack of support or knowledge on the part of other involved providers. Therefore, we highly recommend creating a team of involved, DBT-informed treatment providers. Without a team, CCC treatment providers and clients can easily slide into therapy-interfering behaviors, or therapists can burn out. Without all of the elements of a comprehensive DBT program, group leaders become treatment team coordinators and crisis managers.

In review, comprehensive DBT has been shown to be effective with college students. This chapter described some of those data. It also highlighted issues to consider in adapting comprehensive DBT or implementing DBT skills training alone as an adjunctive form of therapy at a CCC.

References

Benton, S. A., Robertson, J. M., Tseng, W. C., Newton, F. B., & Benton, S. L. (2003). Changes in counseling center client problems across 13 years. *Professional Psychology: Research and Practice, 34(1)*, 66–72.

Center for Collegiate Mental Health (CCMH, 2012). *2011 Annual Report* (Publication No. STA 12-59).

Chiles. J., & Strosahl, K. (1995). *The suicidal patient: Principles of assessment, treatment and case management.* Washington. DC: American Psychiatric Press.

Dimeff, L. A., & Koerner, K. (2007). *Dialectical Behavior Therapy in practice: Applications across disorders and settings.* New York: Guilford Press.

Feigenbaum, J. (2007). Dialectical behaviour therapy: An increasing evidence base. *Journal of Mental Health, 16,* 51-68.

Feldman, G., Harley, R., Kerrigan, M., Jacabo, M., & Fava, M. (2009). Change in emotional processing during a dialectical behavior therapy-based skills group for major depressive disorder. *Behavior Research and Therapy, 47,* 316-321.

Fruzzetti, A. (2009). *Self-Validation skills to be used in DBT skills groups.* For more information, contact Dr. Fruzzetti at aef@unr.edu.

Fruzzetti, A. (2011). *Family Skills Module to be used with DBT Family Skills Training.* For more information, contact Dr. Fruzzetti at aef@unr.edu.

Fruzzetti, A. E., Santisteban, D. A., & Hoffman, P. D. (2007). Dialectical Behavior Therapy with families. In L. A. Dimeff & K. Koerner (Eds.), *Dialectical behavior therapy in clinical practice: Applications across disorders and settings* (pp. 222-244). New York: Guilford.

Fruzzetti, A. E., Shenk, C., & Hoffman, P. D. (2005). Family interaction and the development of borderline personality disorder: A transactional model. *Development and Psychopathology, 17,* 1007-1030.

Fruzzetti, A. E., & Worrall, J. M. (2010). Accurate expression and validation: A transactional model for understanding individual and relationship distress. In K. Sullivan & J. Davila (Eds.), *Support processes in intimate relationships* (pp. 121-150). New York: Oxford University Press.

Gallagher, R. P. (2011). *National survey of counseling center directors.* Alexandria, VA: International Association of Counseling Services.

Gilbert, S. P. (1992). Ethical issues in the treatment of severe psychopathology in university and college counseling centers. *Journal of Counseling and Development, 70,* 695-699.

Harley, R. M., Baity, M. R., Blais, M. A., & Jacobo, M. C. (2007). Use of dialectical behavior therapy skills training for borderline personality disorder in a naturalistic setting. *Psychotherapy Research, 17,* 351-358.

Hoffman, P. D., Fruzzetti, A. E., & Swenson, C. R. (1999). Dialectical Behavior Therapy—Family skills training. *Family Process, 38,* 399-414.

Iverson, K., Shenk, C., & Fruzzetti, A. E. (2009). Dialectical Behavior Therapy for women victims of domestic abuse: A pilot study. *Professional Psychology: Research and Practice, 40,* 242-248.

Kitzrow, M. A. (2003). The mental health needs of today's college students: Challenges and recommendations. *NASPA Journal, 41,* 167-181,

Kliem, S., Kröger, C., & Kosfelder, J. (2010). Dialectical behavior therapy for borderline personality disorder: A meta-analysis using mixed effects modeling. *Journal of Consulting & Clinical Psychology, 78,* 936-951.

Koons, C. R., Robins, C. J., Tweed, J., Lynch, T. R., Gonzalez, A. M., Morse, J. Q., & ... Bastian, L. A. (2001). Efficacy of Dialectical Behavior Therapy in Women Veterans with Borderline Personality Disorder. *Behavior Therapy, 32*(2), 371.

Linehan, M. M. (1993a). *Cognitive-Behavioral Treatment of Borderline Personality Disorder.* New York: Guilford Press.

Linehan, M. M. (1993b). *Skills Training Manual for Treating Borderline Personality Disorder.* New York: Guilford Press.

Linehan, M. M. (1998). Validation and psychotherapy. In A. Bohart & L. S. Greenberg (Eds.), *Empathy and psychotherapy: New directions to theory, research, and practice.* Washington, DC: American Psychological Association: 353-392.

Linehan, M. M., Comtois, K. A., Murray, A. M., Brown, M. Z., Gallop, R. J., Heard, H. L., et al. (2006). Two-year randomized controlled trial and follow-up of Dialectical Behavior Therapy vs. therapy by experts for suicidal behaviors and borderline personality disorder. *Archives of General Psychiatry, 63,* 757-766.

Lippincott, J. A. (2007). When psychopathology challenges education: Counseling students with severe psychiatric disorders. In J. A. Lippincott & R. B. Lippincott (Eds,), *Special populations in college counseling: A handbook for mental health professionals* (pp. 287-296). Alexandria, VA: American Counseling Association.

Miller, A., & Rathus, J. H., Linehan, M. M., (2006). *Dialectical behavior therapy with suicidal adolescents.* New York: Guilford Press.

Miller, A. L., Wyman, S. E., Huppert, J. D., Glassman, S. L., & Rathus, J. H. (2000). Analysis of behavioral skills utilized by adolescents receiving Dialectical Behavior Therapy. *Cognitive and Behavioral Practice, 7,* 183-187.

Pistorello, J., Fruzzetti, A. E., MacLane, C., Gallop, R., & Iverson, K. M. (2012). Dialectical Behavior Therapy (DBT) applied to college students: A randomized clinical trial. *Journal of Consulting and Clinical Psychology, 80*(6), 982-994.

Robins, C. J., & Chapman, A. L. (2004). Dialectical behavior therapy: Current status, recent developments, and future directions. *Journal of Personality Disorders, 18,* 73–79.

Trull, T. J. (1995). Borderline personality disorder features in nonclinical young adults: 1. Identification and validation. *Psychological Assessment, 7*(1), 33-41.

Tryon, G. S., DeVito, A., Halligan, F. R., Kane, A. S., & Shea, J. J. (1998). Borderline personality disorder and development: Counseling university students. *Journal of Counseling and Development, 67,* 178-181.

Whitlock, J. L. (in preparation). Mental health trajectories and psychological and social antecedents: The role of emotion regulation, social connection, and meaning.

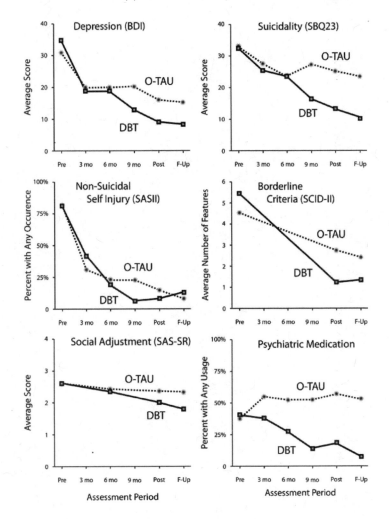

Figure 1. Results for Key Dependent Variables across Assessment Points in Both Conditions

Adapted from "Dialectical Behavior Therapy (DBT) Applied to College Students: A Randomized Clinical Trial," by J. Pistorello, A.E. Fruzzetti, C. MacLane, R. Gallop and K.M. Iverson, 2012, Journal of Consulting and Clinical Psychology, 80, p. 990. Copyright © 2012 by the American Psychological Association. Reprinted with permission.

CHAPTER 3

Acceptance and Commitment Therapy (ACT): Processes and Application

Matthew S. Boone
Cornell University

Imagine two college sophomores presenting for services at a college counseling center. Both are majoring in biology with the intention of going to medical school. Both have wanted to be doctors their entire lives. Both study in demanding academic programs and encounter a great deal of stress. For each, the stress takes a similar internal form: worries about not performing well, feelings of anxiety and irritability, and frequent physical tension. However, each student has a very different way of responding to these experiences. The first student studies constantly, rarely leaving the library or taking a break. Although she is often well-prepared for exams and finishes assignments before they are due, other parts of her life suffer. She feels disconnected from her friends, whom she rarely sees, and she is constantly sleep deprived, over-caffeinated, and underfed. Furthermore, despite her efforts, she does not feel she is really learning the material she studies, but rather absorbing it mechanically— enough to get the grades she wants, but not in a way that really supports a deeper knowledge of biology. She wonders if she is truly cut out for a career in medicine.

The second student usually leaves his work until the last minute. Every Sunday night he can be found in his dorm room furiously attempting to finish his physics problem set—due Monday morning—long after his roommate has gone to sleep. At other times, when he is hanging out with friends or trying to enjoy himself, a feeling of dread about the work he is putting off nags at him, sucking the pleasure out of everything he does. As a result, his relationships and health suffer: his friends notice he is barely present when he is with them, and he often plays videogames late into the night rather than going to bed, where he will inevitably encounter the worries that spring up as he is trying to fall asleep. Not surprisingly, his grades do not match his aptitude, and he also wonders if he is cut out for a career in medicine.

Though these patterns of behavior look very different, they have similar functions. The first pattern, which could be called "being driven," and the second, which could be called "slacking off," are both efforts to control worry, irritability, anxiety, and tension. For the first student, being driven keeps these thoughts and feelings at bay; if she slows down, they become more powerful. For the second, slacking off has the same purpose; the thoughts and feelings are most present when he begins to study, so he avoids studying as much as possible. Both patterns of behavior have similar consequences to the students' relationships, health, and, to some extent, academics (neither is getting much joy out of college). And despite the enormous time and effort devoted to "being driven" and "slacking off," either intentionally or (more likely) out of habit, neither has a significant overall effect on the thoughts and feelings it is intended to control. Instead, it is quite likely these attitudes perpetuate them.

Acceptance and Commitment Therapy: Opening Up and Doing What Matters

This chapter describes Acceptance and Commitment Therapy (ACT, said as one word) (Hayes, Strosahl, & Wilson, 2011), a mindfulness-based behavior therapy which seeks to unravel these patterns of responding. Rather than offering students a better way to control uncomfortable thoughts and feelings, however, ACT encourages students to develop a new relationship with them, one that is grounded in mindfulness. Using a variety of strategies, ACT helps students respond to thoughts and feelings with qualities that are either inherent in or follow closely from mindfulness. Painful experiences are encountered with openness and curiosity, welcomed with willingness and compassion, and observed without judgment or entanglement. At the same time, ACT encourages students to invest themselves in creating a vital and meaningful life based on what they care about most deeply, which oftentimes gets lost in the pursuit of struggling to control thoughts and feelings.

This chapter has two purposes: first, to provide an introduction for college counselors (or anyone working with college students) who are not familiar with ACT and, second, to offer mental health professionals who are familiar with ACT a guide for implementing it in individual counseling with college students. ACT theory and interventions are interwoven with case examples to highlight concepts and bring the reader into the consulting room.

The ACT Model of Psychopathology

The ACT model of psychopathology rejects the assumption, influenced by the medical model and some traditional psychologies, that psychological health is characterized by the absence of psychological pain (Hayes et al., 2011). Instead, ACT assumes that psychological pain is a normal part of living and that excessive efforts to avoid pain can paradoxically lead to greater suffering. ACT targets a core pattern of behavior: *experiential avoidance*. Experiential avoidance entails attempts to change the intensity, frequency, or duration of *private events* (anything in the subjective experience of an individual, such as thoughts, feelings, memories, and physical sensations), as well as efforts to avoid situations which give rise to those private events. Most college counselors are familiar with this process, if not these terms. A socially anxious student may avoid talking in class to prevent his peers from hearing his shaky voice and his mind from later ruminating about it. A depressed student may lie in bed to stave off feeling overwhelmed by the stress of classwork and extracurricular activities. An athlete suffering from panic attacks may avoid practicing with her team to prevent elevating her heart rate and possibly triggering another attack. In these examples, the student engages in a marginally effective but ultimately self-defeating effort to control aversive private events. Avoiding pain is necessary for survival: early humans would not have passed on their genes had they not worked to alleviate hunger or avoid danger. In the modern world, staying away from fearful situations keeps us from walking into traffic or wandering down dark alleys. Experiential avoidance becomes problematic when it grows to be a generalized and inflexible pattern of running from thoughts and feelings even when doing so interferes with problem-solving, relationship building, attending class, or anything else involved in living a full life.

Experiential avoidance is supported by *fusion* (Hayes et al., 2011), or the tendency shared by all people to allow mental events like thoughts, memories, meaning-making, and narratives about the world to dominate over lived experience. Examples of fusion can be seen in the way evaluations about the self and others, predictions about the future, rigid rules for living, and other products of the mind are treated as "truths," or favored in such a way that they have a self-defeating influence on behavior. Again, most college counselors will be familiar with this dynamic. A student may ruminate on the thought "I'm going to fail this test" so deeply that she barely studies. A depressed student may think "Nothing matters" and live the thought out by rarely going to class and never cultivating friendships. A socially anxious student may become so absorbed in monitoring his performance at a party that he misses half the conversation he is having.

Fusion often goes hand-in-hand with experiential avoidance. For example, the student who ruminates about failing may stay away from studying because the thoughts become more powerful and are accompanied by swells of anxiety as she sits down in front of her books. Fusion also has a role in framing private events (thoughts, feelings, memories, physical sensations, etc.) as "dangerous" or "bad," making experiential avoidance seem the only logical response. For example, a student with frequent panic attacks is more likely to be influenced by the thought "I'm in danger" than by what his experience tells him—that he is safe despite his rush of adrenaline. As a consequence, he may do everything he can to stay away from external circumstances, like open spaces and large classrooms, and private events, like thinking about an exam, which give rise to that adrenaline rush. Some degree of fusion is necessary for living: without the capacity to be both absorbed in and guided by our thoughts, treating abstractions as "real things," we could not plan for the future, learn from the past, or do any of the endless number of tasks that require thinking. But when fusion prevents living a life worth living, it is a problem worth addressing in counseling.

Experiential avoidance and fusion work in tandem with four other behavioral processes to create psychopathology and, more generally, human suffering (Hayes et al., 2011). *Attachment to the conceptualized self* is a special case of fusion in which a person attaches rigidly to narratives of identity, or who one *is*. Think of the student who believes deeply in the thought, "I am a bad test-taker," or the student who is so identified with her role as an athlete that she spirals into depression after an injury. *Inflexible attention* draws people into ruminating over the past or focusing excessively on the future. Think of the student who repeatedly recounts the same historical material over and over in counseling or the student who cannot stop worrying about an upcoming test long enough to take time to study. *Disconnection from personal values* leads people away from what truly matters to them, or prevents them from even identifying what matters; *inaction, impulsivity,* and *avoidant persistence* put this disconnection into practice. Think of the student who wants nothing more than a lasting relationship, and mitigates his loneliness by hooking up with a new partner each weekend. He fails to take the steps to cultivate a real relationship (inaction), allows his normal sexual attractions to exclusively guide his behavior (impulsivity), and persists with this pattern despite the fact that it leaves him even more lonely (avoidant persistence).

Because these processes are not always maladaptive, but become maladaptive in particular contexts, ACT encourages students to consider whether actions driven by them are "workable," both in terms of what they are intended to achieve and, more generally, in the service of living a fulfilling life. In the case of the pre-med students described in the introduction, the ACT counselor would likely explore with them whether efforts to control uncomfortable private events actually work: do the thoughts and feelings go away? Or do they fade into the background, only to emerge again? And do the students' efforts to control private events take them in the direction of what's important to them, like getting to know people, preparing for medical school, or having a rich college experience? If the answer is no, then ACT offers a model for encountering private events in a new way while at the same time pursuing what matters.

ACT Intervention Strategies

ACT enlists a variety of strategies to support students in the process of accepting what cannot be easily changed (e.g., private events like nervousness about finals and the pain of a breakup) and changing what can be changed (e.g., actions based on values, such as how one studies or behaves in a relationship). In addition to basic counseling skills like reflective listening and empathic attunement, as well as familiar cognitive behavioral modalities like psychoeducation and homework, the ACT counselor uses strategies that are less common in counseling, such as metaphors and experiential exercises, including mindfulness (Hayes et al., 2011; Strosahl, Hayes, Wilson, & Gifford, 2004; Luoma, Hayes, & Walser, 2007; Harris, 2010). In ACT, these strategies are used to convey knowledge and facilitate learning in a way that is less intellectual and language driven and more intuitive and experiential.

Metaphors are the primary teaching tool of the ACT counselor. Rather than simply telling a student that acceptance is a viable alternative to control, the counselor would introduce a metaphor that illustrates the difference. For example, the counselor might compare acceptance to how one survives in quicksand, noting that what seems "right"—thrashing one's body to get out—will inevitably lead to sinking deeper, and what is counterintuitive—leaning back with arms and legs spread to increase one's surface area—will keep one safely at the surface (Hayes et al., 2011).

Experiential exercises, which often incorporate both metaphors and mindfulness, are some of the most powerful tools in the ACT repertoire. To help a student notice thoughts as they occur in the moment, the counselor might encourage her to imagine her thoughts as leaves in a passing stream (Strosahl et al., 2004) during a mindfulness exercise. To help a student experience what it could be like to accept his anxiety, the counselor might have him visualize anxiety as an object and hold it gently with both hands, like something precious. To help a student understand what is most important to her, the counselor might ask her to visualize what she would like people to say about her at her funeral (Strosahl et al., 2004). These exercises, which can be woven throughout therapy, foster a kind of nonverbal knowing, one that is drawn more from experience and less from intellect. Experiential learning is important for all clients, but it is particularly relevant to students studying in a college or university environment where relying on one's intellect is more often rewarded.

The ACT Model for Intervention

Increasing Psychological Flexibility

The goal of these interventions, and ACT overall, is to increase the student's *psychological flexibility* – the ability to contact the present moment as it is and persist or change behavior in the service of chosen values (Hayes et al., 2011). Psychological flexibility can be thought of as the opposite of entrenched patterns of experiential avoidance, fusion, disconnection from personal values, and the other processes noted above. A student acting in a psychologically flexible way treats painful thoughts and feelings as a natural part of life (not experiences to be avoided at the cost of living fully), allowing them to influence her actions only when doing so is useful and acting in the service of what matters to her.

A helpful way to think about psychological flexibility is in terms of patterns of responding. Psychological flexibility means marshaling a broad, flexible repertoire of responses to whatever life affords, including painful private events (Wilson & DuFrene, 2009). Some of these responses may entail experiencing *more pain* if encountering that pain serves something meaningful. For example, a first-year student who fails her first calculus exam will likely feel disappointment and anxiety. In the face of these feelings, responding in a psychologically flexible way might entail a variety of responses, some productive, such as studying harder, seeking support from her parents and friends, or asking for help during her professor's office hours. Some responses might be unproductive, such as spending the day in bed or surfing the Internet when she could be studying. A psychologically flexible student would move between these responses with some fluidity, eventually settling on the ones that are most useful in the service of what's important to her. Thus, her repertoire of responding is both "broad"—she can respond in many ways—and "flexible"—she doesn't get stuck in any one response. Some of her responses, such as talking with her professor, might temporarily precipitate more anxiety in the form of worries about looking "dumb" or memories of the large, red "F" on her exam. A psychologically flexible student would choose this latter response (even though it would bring up more pain) in the service of something important, like succeeding academically.

This focus on acting in a way that may bring one into contact with internal pain is not evidence of a "no pain, no gain" philosophy within ACT. It simply reflects the philosophy that some pain is unavoidable, and constant efforts to avoid pain can make life unlivable. ACT makes an important distinction between pain and suffering (e.g., Follette & Pistorello, 2007). *Pain* (sometimes referred to as "clean pain") is a natural by-product of living: if we love, then we will inevitably feel loss; if we pursue what matters, then we will inevitably fear failing. Suffering (sometimes referred to as "dirty pain") is the result of efforts to stay away from pain when doing so takes us away from what matters. For example, if pain is feeling nervous upon meeting new people, then suffering is staying home on Friday night because of that fear. If pain is feeling sad when a relationship ends, suffering is drinking excessively to deaden the sadness of the loss.

In ACT, psychological flexibility is divided into six interrelated processes: acceptance (opening up to experience), defusion (getting distance from the mind), self as context (perceiving a self that is distinct from thoughts and feelings), contact with the present moment (flexibly attending to experience as it happens), values (choosing what matters), and committed action (acting in the service of what matters). Note that each process is the antithesis of one of the six processes in the ACT model of psychopathology described above. Readers familiar with mindfulness practice will notice that the first four (acceptance, defusion, self as context, and contact with the present moment) all closely relate to mindfulness. In fact, in ACT these are considered four components of mindfulness. More generally, each of the six psychological flexibility processes can be thought of as a stance, or a way of acting, in the face of what life offers, whether private events or external circumstances. The bulk of ACT treatment involves the counselor helping the student enact these processes in large and small ways, first in the counselor's office and, ultimately, in life. A detailed summary of each process follows the next section.

Beginning Therapy: Control Is the Problem

After the initial assessment is completed and informed consent is gained, but before approaching the six processes of psychological flexibility, ACT begins with helping students uncover the maladaptive patterns of experiential avoidance (often referred to informally as "avoidance and control") playing out in their lives. This is often called *drawing out the system* (Luoma, Hayes, & Walser, 2007). The counselor might say to a student who procrastinates, "You've told me that when you are working you feel antsy and bored and you worry that you won't finish in time. Tell me all the ways you deal with these thoughts and feelings." With the counselor's help, the student catalogs the variety of strategies he uses to avoid and control feeling antsy, worried, and bored. The list might be extensive: surfing the Internet, playing video games, hanging out in friends' dorm rooms, checking his preferred social networking website, asking for extensions from professors, using excessive caffeine, rationalizing to himself that he needs to "take a break," and waiting until the last minute so that his low motivation is overcome by the pressure of a deadline. The conversation then turns to the workability of these strategies for minimizing feeling antsy, bored, and worried. Do these thoughts and feelings stop occurring? The answer is usually no. Do they sometimes get worse? The answer is often yes. (See "Appendix 3A: Avoidance and Control," at www.newharbinger.com/22225) for a worksheet to help explore avoidance, control, and workability in a student's life.)

In ACT, uncovering the lack of workability in avoiding and controlling thoughts and feelings, as well as the consequences of trying to do so, is called *creative hopelessness* (Hayes et al., 2011). "Hopelessness" refers not to one's life being hopeless, but to a felt sense that continuing down the road of avoidance and control will lead nowhere. This hopelessness is "creative" in that it opens a vacuum into which new possibilities can enter. At this point, the student is usually a little puzzled and very curious about alternatives. This is where acceptance is first introduced.

Letting Go of the Struggle

The "Tug-of-War with a Monster" metaphor (Hayes et al., 2011) is useful to illustrate the difference between avoidance and control, on the one hand, and acceptance, on the other, and can be acted out experientially. The counselor first gets the student's consent to do an exercise in which both will hold onto either end of a "rope," which can be anything suitably rope-like, such as a scarf. The counselor then asks the student to imagine that he is playing tug-of-war with a monster which is made up of all the discomfort he feels when he studies. The rope stretches across a deep pit into which he would plunge should he lose, so the stakes are high. Actually enacting this tug-of-war, rather than just talking about it, brings those stakes into sharp relief: the student feels the pull of the rope in his hands and can imagine sitting face to face with his discomfort. The counselor helps the student contact, both experientially and intellectually, that there is no winning this game: the tug-of-war could go on forever because the monster is equally strong, if not stronger. The solution, which is really an anti-solution, is to drop the rope. Most students realize this without it being explained. As they literally drop the "rope," both the counselor and student feel a softness enter the room, and the student usually experiences, if only briefly, that he can be in the presence of his discomfort without having to change it.

The Six Core Processes of Psychological Flexibility

Figure 1, often called "The Hexaflex," depicts the six core processes of psychological flexibility.

ACCEPTANCE

Letting go of struggling with painful thoughts and feelings makes space for the possibility of acceptance. In ACT, acceptance means opening up to all of our experiences, whether painful or pleasant, welcoming both the fear we may be desperate to reject and the joy we may hope to prolong (Hayes et al., 2011; Luoma, Hayes, & Walser, 2007). Acceptance the *process* is very different from the qualities often associated with "acceptance" the *word*; it is not giving in, giving up, or tolerating. Most importantly, acceptance is directed toward the pain encountered in difficult circumstances, not the circumstances themselves. An ACT counselor would not encourage a student to resign herself to mediocre grades, unsatisfying friendships, or the fact of her depression. Instead, the counselor would support her as she encountered the fear and uncertainty of studying harder, taking risks in relationships, or creating a life that is not ruled by hopelessness and guilt.

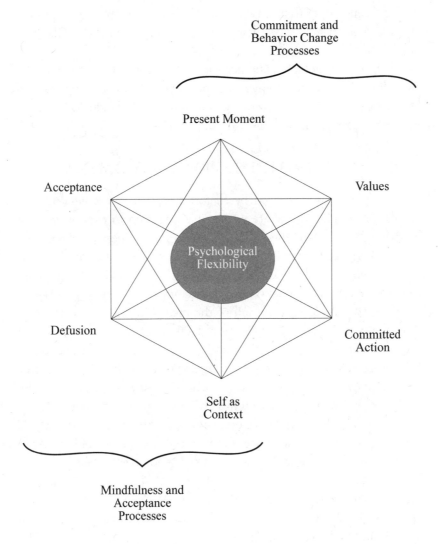

Figure 1. The ACT Model

A useful synonym for acceptance, one which more easily sidesteps associations with resignation, is "willingness." The counselor might ask a student who wants a romantic relationship but has never asked anyone out, "Would you be willing to have that fear of rejection and those butterflies in your stomach in return for the possibility of connecting more deeply with someone?" Or, the counselor might ask a student hoping to reduce the impact his binge drinking has on his life, "Would you be willing to encounter that sense of 'missing out on fun' you describe for a chance at better grades and fewer mornings when you don't remember anything?"

A variety of metaphors for acceptance are available throughout the ACT literature, many of which are included in "Pick a Metaphor," an experiential exercise that can be conducted with individuals or groups (see "Appendix 3B: Pick a Metaphor Exercise").

CONTACT WITH THE PRESENT MOMENT

Acceptance is supported by *contact with the present moment*, the process of bringing deliberate yet flexible attention to experience as it happens (Wilson & DuFrene, 2009). As in mindfulness practice, one's attention is placed squarely in the moment, neither ruminating about the past nor worrying about the future, dispassionately following the continuous stream of experiential input encountered as time passes– for example, the gentle rise and fall of the breath in one's body, the ever shifting texture of sounds in the aural landscape, or the play of light in the scope of one's vision. ACT counselors encourage students to encounter their pain in just this way by slowing down and noticing it as it occurs without judging it or becoming absorbed in it. For example, a counselor might encourage a student who has an urge to binge and purge during session to sit quietly with eyes closed and watch the urge play out in real time. The student might notice that it starts with an agitated feeling in her arms and legs, followed by racing thoughts about where she can binge in secret and images of binge/purge episodes flashing in her mind. She might also notice that these experiences are not fixed, but rather ebb and flow over time. The counselor could observe that the urge can come and go without her doing anything about it.

DEFUSION

Defusion, the antithesis of fusion, entails treating the products of one's mind, whether thoughts, images, memories, or meaning-making, as simply the products of one's mind—nothing more, nothing less (Hayes et al., 2011). Students are encouraged to engage thoughts only when they are useful in the service of something important, and to simply notice them when they are not. For example, a student with chronic depression might say to himself, "I'm no good at anything." The ACT counselor would encourage him to notice the thought as it occurs, get distance from it, and explore the consequences of allowing it to have undue influence on his behavior. The student might notice that when "I'm no good at anything" occurs, he tends to withdraw from friends and procrastinate on classwork. If engaging with others and getting things done is important to him, the counselor would help him encounter the thought mindfully, neither believing in it nor refuting it, while at the same time doing what matters.

Refraining from countering negative thoughts, repeating positive self-affirmations, and engaging in reappraisal is a unique feature of ACT, one that distinguishes it from many other therapies. In ACT, such strategies are considered further attempts to control private events, which risk making them more salient and reinforcing the belief that negative thoughts need to go away before the student can act differently. Instead, the counselor helps the student develop a different relationship with the thought, one that is more mindful and distant, one that becomes more about curious observation than automatic reactivity. In this context, a "negative" thought loses some of its power to direct a student away from meaningful living.

The counselor can enlist a wide variety of strategies to help facilitate defusion, some of which are playful and fun. A troublesome thought could be written on a 3x5 card and held closely or far away to illustrate the difference between being absorbed in a thought and simply noticing it (Hayes et al., 2011; Harris, 2010). The thought could be repeated quickly for a minute to illustrate that it is not only an evaluation or prediction which feels powerful and scary, but also a collection of sounds, many of which become absurd as they somersault through one's mouth (Hayes et al., 2011). The thought could be written on a piece of paper and carried in one's pocket between appointments to illustrate that it can be welcomed, no matter how aversive it seems, at the same time one goes about one's life (Hayes et al., 2011). Or, the student and counselor could imagine that their thoughts are like words passing across the bottom of the television screen on a news program and discuss what shows up on their respective "news crawls" (Hayes et al., 2011). Most simply, the counselor and student could cultivate a practice of creating distance from thoughts by prefacing what they say with "My mind says..." or "I'm having the thought...."

The following process excerpt illustrates a defusion exercise that is inspired by two standard ACT defusion techniques: repeating thoughts over and over (mentioned above) and saying them in different voices (Strosahl et al., 2004). It also incorporates a discussion about the lack of workability in trying to control thoughts:

Counselor: This thought, "I'm not good at anything," seems pretty powerful in your life.

Student: It's true. I'm not getting the grades I want, I have no idea how to talk to girls, and I'm always pissing off my friends.

Counselor: Maybe we can look at this thought from a different angle. When it's present and you're really entangled in it, how do you act?

Student: I sit in my room watching television shows online. It blocks it out a little.

Counselor: That makes sense. But if you're going to work on academics, talk to girls, or be a friend, I'm guessing that it's likely to show up.

Student: Yes.

Counselor: I don't think we could make it stop showing up right now—this pattern of thinking is pretty ingrained. One thing we could try to do is identify things you are actually good at. But I'm pretty sure you've tried that.

Student: Yeah, I've had long fights with myself about this.

Counselor: Did these fights make "I'm not good at anything" go away?

Student: Sometimes, but not for long.

Counselor: I'm not surprised. Often our efforts to change thoughts and feelings make them more of a problem. But if we were to "drop the rope" with this struggle, we might try something else. Would it be OK if we did something playful with "I'm not good at anything" today?

Student: I'll try anything at this point.

Counselor: OK. First, I want you to hold it in your mind for a few moments and really allow yourself to be affected by it.

Student: (Closes eyes for a moment) OK.

Counselor: Now, for the next few minutes let's have a conversation, but the only thing we get to say is "I'm not good at anything." We'll say it back and forth to each other in the cadences of a conversation, but if someone were listening from outside it would sound a little bit like we were speaking a different language, one in which the only words are "I'm not good in anything."

Student: Weird.

Counselor: It *is!* Are you willing to see what happens?

Student: Sure.

Counselor: (Stated matter-of-factly) I'm not good at anything.

Student: (Hesitantly) I'm not good at anything.

Counselor: (Stated as a question) I'm not good at anything?

Student: (Firmly) I'm not good at anything!

Counselor: (Conversationally) I'm not good at anything.

Student: (In an offhand manner) I'm not good at anything.

The counselor and student go on like this for the next few minutes as they continue to speak as if in conversation. After a few minutes, and inevitably some laughter, they stop and discuss the exercise.

Student: I've had that thought many times before, but it seems different now.

Counselor: Notice it's still the same thought. We haven't really changed it in any way. However, we could say that you

> are relating to it differently. You are not buying into it
> so much. Do you think that from this perspective you
> might be able to bring the thought with you as you do
> the things you need to do?

Student: Maybe. I'd like to try it out.

At this point, the counselor could give a homework assignment in which the student does something similar with the thought when it shows up. Or, the counselor could assign a writing assignment in which the student monitors troublesome thoughts and notices how they affect his behavior. (See "Appendix 3C: Noticing Thoughts that Hook You" for a worksheet useful for this purpose.)

Notice that the focus of this exercise is on changing the function of the thought, not the thought itself. When this thought (or other versions of it) occurs, it becomes dominant over everything else in his experience. The majority of the student's responses become organized around it: he is escaping it, arguing with it, or following its lead. Saying the thought repeatedly undermines its dominance: it becomes merely a collection of words, one of many sentences generated continuously by the mind. In this space, when the student is no longer "fused" to the thought, wedded to it and weighed down by it, he is more capable of making choices that are guided by something else, like his values and goals.

SELF AS CONTEXT

Self as context refers to a special case of defusion in which the counselor helps the student view the "self" as the container (i.e., context) of all of his experiences (Hayes et al., 2011; Harris, 2010). Whereas thoughts and feelings are always transient, coming and going throughout the course of one's life, this aspect of self is experienced as continuous, like a sturdy house whose furnishings and occupants change over time (Hayes et al., 2011). ACT does not suggest that this is a "true self," but rather a posture one can adopt to increase awareness and disidentify with private events. This posture can be contrasted with identifying with one's *conceptualized self*, described earlier, which is the constellation of narratives about who one *is*, such as "I'm a bad student" or "I'm not the kind of person who goes to parties." From the perspective of the conceptualized self, a "bad student" can't offer an insightful comment in a class discussion. But from the perspective of the self as context, a self which is bigger than "I'm a bad student," these narratives are simply more thoughts and feelings one *has*.

Self as context is introduced through metaphors such as the "Sky" metaphor (Harris 2010), which characterizes the self as the sky, unharmed and unchanged in the face of constantly shifting—and sometimes very scary—weather. Self as context is a sense of self from which all experiences are observed. The following excerpt shows a counselor introducing this concept experientially in session:

Student:	When I start thinking about all the work I have to do, that's when I start getting really anxious.
Counselor:	Is the anxiety showing up right now as we are speaking?
Student:	Yes.
Counselor:	Okay. Would you be up for doing something a little bit different with the anxiety today? Let's take a moment to break the anxiety down into its components. Let's start with what it's like physically. Notice where it manifests in your body and describe it to me.
Student:	(After a few moments) I feel it in my shoulders and my chest. It's like a big, heavy weight.
Counselor:	Interesting. Is that big heavy weight always there, or does it come and go?
Student:	It comes and goes, I guess.
Counselor:	Okay. Let's talk about the mental component of this anxiety. What goes on in your mind when it shows up?
Student:	I think, "What's wrong with me?"
Counselor:	Anything else come up?
Student:	I start imagining all the bad things that can happen.
Counselor:	So it's thoughts, but it's also images. Those thoughts and images—are they always here or do they come and go?

Student: I guess they come and go.

Counselor: Okay, finally, let's look at the emotions here. Would you describe anything inside you that is an emotion separate from these thoughts and physical sensations?

Student: I guess I would say I'm afraid.

Counselor: So let's ask that question again—are you always afraid?

Student: It comes and goes. But lately it comes around a lot!

Counselor: So these physical sensations, thoughts, memories, images, and emotions are here sometimes, but they are not here at other times. What about you: do you come and go?

Student: (Looking a little puzzled) Of course not. I'm always here.

Counselor: Right. Close your eyes for a second and just notice that: no matter what is going on inside of you, there is a part of "you" there that is unchanged. Take a moment to really notice that it is different from everything going on inside of you.

Student: (After a few moments) I guess you're right.

Counselor: It's kind of like our student union building: it stands there year after year, as a lot of things inside it change: furniture, the color of the walls, students, professors, ideas. These things shift over time—they come and they go. But the building basically stays the same. Just like you.

At this point, the counselor could suggest a homework assignment in which the student stops a few times a day and labels his thoughts, physical sensations, and emotions on paper. This exercise can provide at least two benefits: first, it objectifies the private events, which may provide a little freedom when they are especially powerful; second, monitoring over time highlights the transient nature of private events, because inevitably the student will have different experiences to write about at different points during the week. See "Appendix 3D: "A Functional Analysis" for a worksheet that also incorporates values and committed action.

VALUES

Values are chosen directions for living which are informed by what our experience tells us – and by what we imagine – brings meaning and vitality to life (Hayes et al., 2011). In ACT, students are encouraged to explore and articulate their values, which might include statements like "helping others," "doing the best I can in school," or "being open with the ones I love." Notice that these statements are framed as actions, or qualities of being, rather than feelings or "things." As such, values can be enacted in large and small ways in any given moment, regardless of the circumstances. A student who values "being thoughtful and honest" can enact these qualities with his boyfriend even during an argument. He could also be "patient and loving," even though he does not feel especially patient and loving. Obviously, this is not always easy. But enlisting the four mindfulness processes noted above – acceptance, contact with the present moment, defusion, and self as context – makes it more possible. If the student mindfully watches his feelings ebb and flow from the perspective of an observer, holding lightly the angry thoughts that will likely arise, he can more easily be patient and loving.

Values are directions one can return to over and over again, much as someone practicing mindfulness returns to the breath as the mind repeatedly drifts away (Wilson & DuFrene, 2009). A student who struggles with procrastination could write her academic values on a sticky note attached to her computer screen, reminding herself to be "curious, engaged, and hard-working" as the inevitable urge to surf social networking sites and the thought "this isn't any good" arise again and again. A student working to stop arguing with his father during their weekly phone calls could do his best to be "respectful and considerate yet firm in my convictions" as frustration rises to the surface when he hears once again that his choice of major is wrong.

COMMITTED ACTION

The two examples above are instances of *committed action*: doing what it takes to bring values to bear in one's life (Harris, 2010). The counselor supports the student engaging in a thoughtful pattern of committed actions – large and small – in the service of values. Committed action can involve outlining a series of values-based goals or identifying specialized skills to be learned. For example, a student with social anxiety could register for a public speaking class in the interest of becoming more capable in social situations and thereby better at building relationships. Committed action can also be a phase in counseling when traditional behavior therapy processes like exposure can be enlisted. For example, a counselor might spend a number of sessions helping a student with obsessive-compulsive disorder practice contacting the present moment, welcoming his anxiety in a variety of ways, and articulating his values as preparation for exposure and response prevention with a graded hierarchy of avoided situations.

Integrating ACT Processes

Discussing the six components of psychological flexibility separately can give the false impression that each is wholly distinct from the others. However, readers will notice that each process incorporates elements of the others. For example, enacting acceptance by holding an aversive feeling in one's awareness relies, at minimum, on both contact with the present moment and defusion (e.g., mindfully experiencing what the feeling is actually like without attaching meaning to it). The six-part model of psychological flexibility is best understood as a heuristic rather than a representation of what psychological flexibility *is*. As ACT counselors develop in their understanding and skill, the processes begin to flow more seamlessly into one another. The counselor begins to think less in terms of how to help students defuse or accept, and more in terms of assisting them in showing up to life willingly and openly, moving in the direction of what is most important to them.

The following exercise, "Getting to Work," incorporates all six processes and can be used with students who procrastinate. It involves "exposure" to avoided coursework, performed in vivo in the counselor's office. Just as in exposure therapy, where the counselor helps the client face a feared stimulus (e.g., an insect, dirt, or a physiological manifestations of anxiety), Getting to Work involves helping a student face an avoided assignment. However, in typical ACT style, and consonant with ACT variations on traditional exposure exercises (e.g., Eifert & Forsyth, 2005), the feared stimulus is approached mindfully with the help of acceptance, defusion, self as context, and contact with the present moment skills. Furthermore, approaching the feared stimulus is framed as a committed action in the service of values. The counselor dissuades the student from taking a controlling stance toward private events, such as "toughing it out" or "gritting one's teeth" through the anxiety. The following process excerpt provides an illustration:

Student: I still haven't gotten started on that assignment we discussed last time.

Counselor: What does your mind say has to change before you can get started?

Student: It says I just need more motivation. So I mess around on the Internet or do something else until I start feeling motivated. But motivation rarely comes.

Counselor: My guess is that there is something uncomfortable that you are staying away from by procrastinating. Take a moment to close your eyes and imagine what would happen if you were to suddenly begin working. What kinds of thoughts, emotions, physical sensations show up?

Student: (Closes eyes) I'm starting to get a little anxious just thinking about it. My mind starts saying, "I'm no good at this" and "I'm going to fail."

Counselor: So there is some anxiety, some evaluations of yourself, and some predictions about failure. What else?

Student: I'm getting antsy and getting the urge to get up and do something else.

Counselor: Go ahead and open your eyes. Is this what usually happens when you get started?

Student: Absolutely.

Counselor: I wonder if you might be willing to practice getting started right here in my office today. Usually your pattern is to avoid, avoid, avoid, until it becomes so late that you *have* to get started. What do you think about getting started right now and working on noticing and welcoming everything that shows up?

Student: Start my paper? Right now?

Counselor: Yes. Do you have some work with you?

Student: I have my laptop.

Counselor: Great. Before we do it, let's think for a second about why you would do your work. What values would be served by doing this work?

Student: Well, I really want to get a degree so that I can have a career that matters.

Counselor: So "having a career that matters."

Student: Yes, and gaining knowledge also. That's really important to me.

Counselor: In the service of having a career that matters and gaining knowledge, would you be willing to mindfully encounter all that stuff you just described?

Student: I can try.

(At this point, the student gets out her laptop and opens up a document.)

Counselor: (After about half a minute) Are your old friends showing up?

Student: Not all of them just yet, but I can feel that anxiety beginning to rise.

Counselor: Great. Can you welcome it in and bring it with you as you keep moving? Take a moment to observe it and breathe into it.

Student: Hello anxiety. (Pauses for a few moments and breathes deeply.) I'm going to start writing right now. (Begins typing for a few moments, then stops.)

Counselor: What just showed up?

Student: Those evaluations. My mind keeps saying that this is going to suck!

Counselor: Your mind is just doing what it is built to do: assess, predict, judge. Just notice all that with some compassion and keep writing.

(The student begins writing and the counselor backs off from the conversation for a few minutes.)

Counselor: How's it going in there?

Student: Well, I was really anxious and pretty distracted for a couple minutes, but I kept working. Then I lost track of the anxiety for a while as I hashed out an idea.

Counselor: That stuff is probably going to come and go as you work. It's only a problem when you let the thoughts and feelings be in charge.

Sometimes it is useful to do this exercise with objects representing private events. The counselor chooses objects from his or her office to represent the private events the student describes and places them next to her as she works. The counselor can also use 3x5 cards with thoughts and feelings written on them. As the conversation progresses, the student becomes surrounded by all of these "private events," showing that she can continue working while they are present.

Counselor: Notice that you are working. And at the same time you are surrounded by "This is going to suck," "I hate this," anxiety, and everything else. It's like you're saying, "OK all of you, come along with me. We're going to get some work done."

Notice that each of the six processes is represented in this conversation: acceptance (breathing into a difficult feeling, "Hello anxiety"), defusion (noticing thoughts as thoughts), self as context (talking as if there's a difference between the student and her private events), contact with the present moment (observing private events as they occur), values (naming "having a career that matters" and "gaining knowledge" as reasons for doing something uncomfortable), and committed action (starting the assignment). This exercise is also an example of the way ACT can be implemented creatively: it draws on the theory and techniques described in the ACT literature, but is uniquely tailored to college students.

Empirical Considerations

ACT has been subjected to over 60 randomized controlled trials and has proven effective for a range of problems, including depression, anxiety, obsessive-compulsive disorder, chronic pain, worksite stress, diabetes management, and a host of others, including several studies with college students (see Ruiz, 2010, for a recent review). ACT research focuses not just on treatment outcomes, but also on processes of change (e.g., psychological flexibility) and whether these processes mediate, or can account for, outcomes (Hayes et al., 2011). ACT is listed as an evidence-based treatment by the Clinical Psychology Division of the American Psychological Association (www.div12.org/psychological treatments/treatments) in a growing list of areas, including chronic pain, depression, obsessive-compulsive disorder, mixed anxiety disorders, and psychosis, with the strength of evidence varying from moderate to strong depending on the specific area. It is currently being considered in other areas as well, including substance use disorders. ACT is also recognized as evidence-based by the United States Substance Abuse and Mental Health Services Administration (174.140.153.167/viewintervention.aspx ?id=191).

In college students specifically, ACT has been studied in individual and group formats (e.g., Block & Wulfert, 2002), but this body of evidence is in its early stages. However, the strong empirical support for ACT, as well as its applicability to a number of diagnoses, suggests it might provide a promising transdiagnostic treatment model for college counseling centers.

Final Words

Counseling centers see an ever-increasing number of students with complex problems, yet resources are often limited, requiring session limits and brief treatment (Gallagher, 2011). ACT can be a good fit for these limitations. Most ACT protocols are brief, and in settings with even more limited resources, counselors can weave ACT concepts like values and acceptance into brief interventions. For example, a problem-solving conversation about a roommate conflict could be grounded in identifying what cannot be controlled, such as the roommate's personality and the student's reflexive irritation, and what can be controlled, such as how the student approaches conflict. Sometimes a single statement about acceptance and values can frame an entire conversation about "what to do." For example, a counselor working with a distraught student who has recently failed a test might say:

"It makes sense that you would feel bad. It's clear that academics are really important to you. Sometimes, in situations like this, we let feeling bad dictate our actions. We do things that make sense in the short term, like blowing off work or drinking alcohol, but that interfere with what matters to us. So if you were to let what's important guide your next step, rather than trying to make this feeling go away (because it will eventually pass anyway), what would that look like?"

Notice that many ACT elements are embedded in this statement: pain is normal, control can be problematic, acceptance is an alternative, and one can commit to actions based on values.

References

Block, J., & Wulfert, E. (2002, May). Acceptance or change of private experiences: A comparative analysis in college students with a fear of public speaking. In R. Zettle (Chair), *Acceptance and Commitment Therapy*. Symposium presented at the annual meeting of the Association for Behavior Analysis, Toronto, Ontario.

Eifert, G., & Forsyth, J. (2005). *Acceptance and Commitment Therapy for anxiety disorders*. Oakland: New Harbinger.

Follette, V. M, & Pistorello, J. (2007). *Finding life beyond trauma*. Oakland, CA: New Harbinger.

Gallagher, R. P. (2011). National survey of counseling center directors. The International Association of Counseling Services, University of Pittsburgh.

Harris, R. (2010). *ACT made simple*. Oakland, CA: New Harbinger.

Hayes, S. C., Strosahl, K., & Wilson, K. G. (2011). *Acceptance and commitment therapy: The process and practice of mindful change* (2nd edition). New York: Guilford Press.

Luoma, J., Hayes, S. C., & Walser, R. (2007). *Learning ACT.* Oakland, CA: New Harbinger.

Ruiz, F. J. (2010). A review of Acceptance and Commitment Therapy (ACT) empirical evidence: Correlational, experimental psychopathology, component and outcome studies. *International Journal of Psychology and Psychological Therapy, 10,* 125-162.

Strosahl, K. D., Hayes, S. C., Wilson, K. G., & Gifford, E. V. (2004). An ACT primer: Core therapy processes, intervention strategies, and therapist competencies. In S. C. Hayes and K. D. Strosahl (Eds.), *A practical guide to acceptance and commitment therapy* (pp. 31-58). New York: Springer.

Wilson, K. G., & DuFrene, T. (2009). Mindfulness for two: An acceptance and commitment therapy approach to mindfulness in psychotherapy. Oakland, CA: New Harbinger.

CHAPTER 4

Acceptance and Commitment Therapy (ACT) in Groups

Matthew S. Boone

Cornell University

James Canicci

University of Texas at Dallas

In a conference room on the campus of a northeastern university, eight students walk slowly and silently around the room. Each is covered head-to-toe with 20-30 adhesive name badge labels—the kind that usually say, "Hello, my name is." Written on the labels in various colors of permanent marker are words and phrases like "worry," "tension," "I'm no good," "nothing ever works for me," and "depression." The students pause briefly in front of signs posted around the room at eye level. Each sign has one word written on it in large letters: "work," "school," "family," "love," "fun," "the future," "community," "friends," or "health." Eventually, the two other people in the room, group counselors, ask the students to sit down and spend a few moments reflecting.

Counselor 1: As you look around you, take a moment to observe your fellow group members... Allow yourself to really become aware of their presence... Notice the variety of experiences they have labeled on their bodies... Look down and notice all the experiences *you* have labeled

on *your* body… Notice that we all encounter a variety
of experiences as we walk through life, including the
inevitable pain of living… And now, when you are
moved to speak, let's discuss what we've experienced in
this exercise.

Jennifer: Wow, it never occurred to me that everyone else here
is just as crazy as I am! (Everyone laughs.)

Angela: I knew we were all dealing with some kind of depression
and anxiety—that's what this group is about—but it
seems so normal now that I see it written on everyone's
bodies.

Lourdes: (Looking sad) I sure wish it wasn't so normal.

Troy: Me too, but as we were walking around I was really
beginning to understand this distinction between our
feelings and ourselves. It's like, here's *me*, and here are
my feelings. But I'm not my feelings. Now if I could just
remember that when I'm having a panic attack! (Laughs)

Jennifer: I feel kind of sad. I can tell everyone in here has a lot
of hurt.

Troy: Yeah, I felt the same way when we interviewed each
other at the beginning of the exercise. Lourdes, I realized
as I was asking you questions and writing your thoughts
and feelings on these labels that I never have conversations like this. I felt really connected. But I also felt kind
of sad—and mad also—that you have to go through
what you go through.

(The group members sit in silence for a few moments.)

Counselor 2:   Lourdes, what's it like to hear Troy say that?

Lourdes: I agree. People at this school don't really talk to each
other. So we don't really get to know one another. I
think people here are really self-centered. Like, this one
time, I was hanging out in my dorm when…

Counselor 2: Lourdes, if I may interrupt for a second. Can you pause and check in with yourself? See if you can observe what thoughts and feelings show up in response to what Troy said. What else could you put on the labels you are wearing?

Lourdes: (Pauses) It's hard to describe. It feels good but also kind of scary. I kind of want to run away. (Pauses) It's like when we walked around the room and I walked towards "friends": I got a knot in my stomach. Getting close to people is not something I really do.

This process excerpt illustrates a modified version of "Label Parade," an experiential exercise first described in Walser and Westrup (2007), conducted in Acceptance and Commitment Therapy (ACT: Hayes, Strosahl, & Wilson, 2011). The exercise is designed to facilitate self as context, one of the six processes of psychological flexibility (see chapter 3 for a description of all ACT processes). The exercise is usually conducted during the sixth session of a semester-long counseling group for depression and anxiety. The students begin by breaking into pairs and taking turns interviewing each other about situations in which difficult private experiences are likely to arise. Every time the speaker identifies a thought, feeling, or physical sensation, the interviewer writes it on a name badge and hands it to the speaker. The speaker then sticks it on his or her body. After 15-20 minutes of interviewing, the group members walk silently around the room, stopping in front of signs identifying domains of values posted on the walls.

Conducting this exercise in a group enhances its effectiveness. The students are able to observe not just the distinction between themselves and their private experiences, but also the distinction between the other members in the group and *their* private experiences. Participants can experience firsthand, albeit in a metaphorical way, that they can carry their pain with them as they move toward what is important. They can also reflect on the exercise with one another, thereby enhancing their learning, and observe, with the help of the counselors, what it stirs up *between* them. As a social microcosm (Yalom, 2005), and therefore a setting in which each member is likely to play out his or her habitual interpersonal behaviors and roles, a group is fertile ground where experiential avoidance, fusion, and disconnection from values—the targets of

ACT—are likely to take root. Notice that Lourdes's pattern of avoiding meaningful connections with others in her daily life shows up in her interaction with Troy. However, a group also provides rich opportunities for students to practice the processes encouraged by ACT– acceptance, defusion, contact with the present moment, self as context, values, and committed action—so that they may bring them to bear in their lives outside of the group.

This chapter describes ACT in a group format in college counseling. It uses chapter 3, which describes the ACT theoretical model and principles, as a starting point. It offers suggestions for structuring and facilitating ACT groups and describes a number of experiential exercises tailored specifically to college students.

The Benefits of ACT in Groups

Groups are an important part of the services college counseling centers provide (Eichler & Schwartz, 2010), and ACT is well suited to groups. The therapeutic factors unique to groups (Yalom, 2005) have the potential to both enhance and be enhanced by the six processes of psychological flexibility. For example, the sense of universality (Yalom, 2005)—of being "in the same boat" (Shulman, 2011)—that groups foster can have a powerful effect on acceptance; making space for one's panic symptoms can be easier when one becomes aware that others struggle with panic as well, and that fear is a human experience rather than something that marks one as different. Groups also offer social support (Yalom, 2005) for making changes; taking risks in the service of a meaningful life can seem more possible with the encouragement of fellow group members. Furthermore, groups allow students to learn by example as participants model new behaviors for one another, whether noticing one's self-defeating thoughts or committing to doing what it takes to perform better academically. Finally, as noted above, and perhaps most important for building patterns of psychologically flexible interpersonal behavior, groups offer a safe space where students can practice relating differently to others as they become aware of the influence of fusion and experiential avoidance on their relationships. Yalom (2005) calls this interpersonal focus "the engine of group therapy" (p. xvi).

ACT Groups and College Counseling Centers (CCCs)

College counseling centers (CCCs) have unique needs which influence what kinds of groups are offered and how groups are run. First, CCCs often have limited resources and enlist a time-limited treatment model, yet the problems students present with are becoming more severe and complex (Gallagher, 2011). Therefore, effective short-term interventions for students struggling with multiple problems are necessary. Second, because of the variety of presenting problems for which students seek help, it can be difficult to compose a group with members who share a common diagnosis; it is more common that group members will carry a variety of diagnoses, regardless of the "theme" of the group.

These factors make ACT groups a good fit for CCCs. ACT theory suggests that experiential avoidance is a core process operating in most psychological disorders (Hayes et al., 2011), and studies have shown that ACT can successfully reduce experiential avoidance and increase psychological flexibility across a variety of presentations (see Ruiz, 2010, for a recent review). Furthermore, ACT has shown efficacy as a short-term group intervention for a wide range of problems (e.g., Zettle & Rains, 1989; Bach & Hayes, 2002; Pearson, Heffner, & Follette, 2010), and ACT in a group format has been "road tested" with high satisfaction ratings in a busy CCC (See Empirical Considerations at the end of this chapter for a brief description of the pilot study for which many of the materials and exercises discussed here were created).

Facilitating ACT Groups: The Basics

We will outline below some factors to consider in running ACT groups at CCC.

Composition

Whether an ACT group should be composed of students who share a specific problem (e.g., procrastination) or students who present with a variety of problems depends on a number of factors, including the pool of students willing to participate in group, the CCC's resources, and the training and interests of the staff. Though composing a group for a single diagnosis—e.g., dysthymic disorder—can be difficult, composing a group for a broader category of diagnoses—mood disorders—can be much easier. Consider an ACT group composed entirely of students with anxiety disorders. The group could focus exclusively on the dynamics of anxiety, including manifestations (e.g., panic, worry, and physiological arousal) and the behaviors that sustain it (e.g., avoidance of anxiety-producing situations). The participants could provide encouragement for one another as they expose themselves to feared situations and private experiences while pursuing valued directions. Furthermore, the group could be structured around an existing 12-session ACT protocol for anxiety disorders (Eifert and Forsyth, 2005) that can be easily adapted to a group format. Indeed, one of the authors (J.C.) has done just that. However, as noted above, CCC groups may need to be heterogeneous, especially in small centers with limited resources. One benefit of hetero-geneous groups is that students can observe the role of experiential avoidance and fusion in a variety of problems and experiment with new behaviors with feedback from other students who represent the diversity of their social world.

Orienting Students to Group

Interested students can be oriented in an individual meeting with one of the group leaders, who might describe the group as follows:

"This group is based on Acceptance and Commitment Therapy, or ACT. ACT assumes that pain is a normal part of living and that excessive efforts to avoid pain can lead to greater suffering. You will have the opportunity to explore how your painful thoughts and feelings affect your life, experiment with different ways of relating to them, and learn how to pursue your values more fully."

Individual group orientation meetings can also provide preliminary opportunities to explore the role of unworkable avoidance and control in students' lives and introduce willingness as an alternative. It can be useful to facilitate a brief experiential exercise during orientation meetings, both to introduce potential group members to the experiential nature of ACT and to provide a window into what the group will be like. To these ends, both the "Butterfly" (see below) and the "Tug-of-War with a Monster" (see chapter 3) are useful, as is any ACT exercise with which the counselor is comfortable. A sample flyer advertising an ACT group, which can be given to students before or during an orientation meeting, is included as Appendix 4A at www.newharbinger.com/22225.

Group Norms

Readers familiar with group counseling will need no introduction to the necessity of confidentiality, regular attendance, and other group norms. Other readers are urged to consult the wealth of information in the group literature (e.g., Yalom 2005; Shulman 2011). One norm worth explicating in more detail here is refraining from "rescuing" other group members (Walser and Pistorello, 2004). "No rescuing" means allowing fellow members to have their feelings without trying to solve them. A handout for group members, "Appendix 4B: Group Considerations," says the following about rescuing:

> As we get to know one another, group members will begin to share personal details about their lives, feelings, and thoughts. Our normal reaction when someone is suffering is to try to help them get away from their pain. We do this by urging them to look on the bright side, by offering them solutions, or by telling them it's going to be all right. In this group, we call these strategies "rescuing." We are going to try not to rescue each other in group—not because it's a bad thing to do, but because it's a strategy for controlling feelings. In this group, we will attempt to encounter pain without trying to change it. This might not completely make sense right now. But we will talk more about it as we proceed with the semester.

This passage, which can be discussed in the first group meeting along with other group considerations, sets the stage for conversations about each group member's reactions to the pain of others. The "no rescuing" norm is likely to be broken often, both by group members and leaders: it's a well-oiled part of most of our behavioral repertoires. However, everything is "grist for the mill," in that each attempt at rescuing provides an opportunity to discuss the interpersonal effects of trying to tamp down the feelings of others, as well as how this strategy, which is usually automatic, is both a manifestation of one's own discomfort with pain and also a potential barrier to interpersonal connection.

Group Format

ACT groups usually include some combination of education, mindfulness exercises, experiential exercises, group discussions, and homework exercises. A typical ACT group might start with a mindfulness exercise to lay the groundwork for a present-focused and self-aware discussion. Next, the group might discuss homework given during the previous session, whether a worksheet, a reading from an ACT self-help book, or a daily mindfulness exercise. The group leaders could then move on to a brief introduction of one of the six core processes of psychological flexibility, augmenting the instruction with interactive exercises to help students learn both intellectually and experientially. As the meeting progresses, group members could reflect on how the topic being discussed applies to their lives. These conversations provide a good opportunity for members to provide feedback to one another, as well as for group leaders to facilitate discussions about present-moment experiences. For example, group members might be encouraged to notice what their minds are saying about the discussion, observe what feelings are stirred up in response to their fellow group members, and consider what interpersonal behaviors might best serve their values. The facilitators might end the group by assigning a homework exercise based on the topic of the day.

INCORPORATING MINDFULNESS EXERCISES

Although mindfulness exercises are a good way to start (and sometimes end) group, mindfulness can be incorporated at any point during the meeting to assist students in witnessing what thoughts and feelings arise in response to others and observing where fusion and avoidance might be directing them away from values-driven actions. A brief process excerpt:

Counselor:	I notice we seem to have gotten away from today's topic: values. There is nothing wrong with that, but our distraction might tell us something about ourselves. Let's slow down for a minute and reconnect with the present. Start by noticing your breathing... Next, scan your body and notice any physical or emotional discomfort... Finally, take a second to watch your mind as your thoughts go by... What do you notice?... Let's talk about it.
Esteban:	I notice a heaviness in my chest. I think it's sadness.
Counselor:	Where do you think it comes from?
Esteban:	I'm so aware today that I've been ignoring what I care about in school. I've just been skating along in my classes, doing the minimum. That's not what I want to be about.
Counselor:	And although we might want to condemn sadness as "bad, " notice that it is telling you something important. It's like a little alarm letting you know you have drifted away from what you care about. Anybody else notice anything?

HOMEWORK

ACT comes from the behavioral and cognitive traditions in psychology and therefore emphasizes developing skills that can be generalized outside of counseling. To do this, some kind of homework is essential. Homework can be almost any activity which raises awareness or fosters skill building, from the simple act of stopping once a day to take an observer's perspective on one's thoughts and feelings to the more time intensive practices of completing worksheets, reading book chapters, and engaging in regular mindfulness. "Appendix 4C: Examples of Homework Assignments and/or Group Exercises," provides a number of possibilities; see also "Appendix 1A: Self-Help Books," for a list of self-help titles that can be used for between-session reading.

Group leaders should be mindful of the academic, vocational, and extracurricular demands on students' schedules and assign just enough homework to make a difference, but not so much that it feels overwhelming. Also, leaders must be sure to discuss the previous meeting's assignment in each meeting, lest members get the impression that homework is not important to complete. When group members do not complete homework, group leaders can facilitate a discussion about how experiential avoidance and fusion might have gotten in the way.

One useful assignment for college students is "Willingness with an Avatar," which entails carrying an avatar of a painful private experience between meetings and interacting with it as one would a welcome guest. Students are encouraged to pick any object that can usefully stand in for their private experiences: a rock, a 3x5 card with a word written on it, an action figure, a piece of string, etc. A facilitator can introduce the exercise by showing the group her own avatar (e.g., a small stuffed animal representing "fear of failure") and asking members to imagine the avatar sitting next to her computer monitor as she checks e-mail in the morning and, later, meets with clients. The facilitator could explain that she does not have to like the avatar to welcome it, but that treating it with kindness and compassion lessens its power. The exercise becomes a fun way to practice developing new relationships with painful thoughts and feelings by incorporating self as context (noting the difference between oneself and one's feelings), acceptance (welcoming painful feelings), defusion (letting go of the meanings usually associated with painful feelings), and values (moving forward in life despite the presence of pain). Detailed instructions for this exercise are included in Appendix 4C.

INTRODUCTORY EXERCISES

An exercise which can be used to experientially introduce acceptance is "The Butterfly," which is inspired by Harris's (2009) "clipboard" exercise and the ACT metaphor which encourages one to hold a private experience like a butterfly that has landed on one's hand (Hayes et al., 2011). In The Butterfly, multiple ways of responding to private experiences are acted out by group members. Students are divided into pairs, and one half of the pair volunteers to pick a difficult private experience with which she is willing to do something playful. The other half of the pair is called "Life" and assists the volunteer with the exercise. The volunteer is given a card (e.g., a 3x5 index card) on which to write the private experience, which can be represented by a symbol instead of a word if she does not want it to be known to her partner. The pairs are asked to find a place in the room where they can have a little bit of space to interact.

Counselor: Volunteers, please hand your card to Life. Face each other standing about 5 feet apart. Life, hold the card up with one hand so that it's facing your partner. Volunteers, take a good look at the card: this is your pain. Notice your immediate reactions to it. (Some of the students grimace and cringe.) I'm going to ask you to interact with it in a variety of ways. This exercise will be a little bit physical, so everyone should make sure to be careful. We don't want to add any new injuries to the pain you already have!

First, I would like you to gently press your hand against the hand of Life, holding the card between your hands... Now, add a little pressure. (The members of each pair begin pushing their hands against one another.)... Without getting too carried away, put a little bit more pressure on... Notice what happens in your body as you try to push the pain away. (The students begin visibly straining against one another.)... Notice all the effort this takes... Now back off the pressure... Go back to just holding the card between your hands... Tell me, has the card gone away?

Kelly: No. It's still here.

Counselor: Okay, notice that. Next, I would like volunteers to take the card from Life and hold it by its edges... Take a look at the card and let yourself become absorbed in it. This is your pain... Now squeeze the card as tightly as you can... Really put some effort into it. (The arms of some students are visibly shaking as they squeeze as hard as they can.)... Notice what that's like. Don't think about it too much. Just experience it... Now release the pressure and simply hold it in your hands... Someone tell me, has the card gone away?

Jackie: Nope, it's still here. But mine's pretty wrinkled!

Counselor: Wrinkled, but still there. Notice that... Now, we are going to do something a little bit more physical, so everyone be careful... Life, take the card back and hold it again so that it's facing your partner. When I give the cue, Life, start walking toward your partner. Volunteers, this is your pain. I want you to try to escape from it. Do whatever you can. Ready—go! (Group members begin moving around the room, some of them even running to get away from their pain. Members inevitably bump into one another. There is a lot of giggling and laughter. The counselor shouts over the din.) Notice what's going on right now... Notice the effort that you are putting into escaping... And when I give the cue, everyone stop where they are... Stop! (The students freeze in their tracks, many of them in comical positions.) Go ahead and relax. Someone tell me, is the pain gone?

Esteban: (Panting and laughing) No. It's right here with me. Just like in real life.

Counselor: Okay, notice *that*. Now we are going to do just one more thing. Everyone, face your partners again. Life, hold the card so that it's facing your partner. Volunteers, this is your pain. Life, slowly—very slowly—hand the card face up to your partner. Volunteers, hold out both hands and accept the card... Allow the card to land gently on your open hands as if it were a butterfly... Hold it gently like something precious, like something you would take care of... Now, while you're holding it, look around the room at the people around you... Look at the person in front of you and take in their humanity... And look down at the card again... Notice what this is like... Notice what it's like in your body... Now, someone tell me, is the card gone?

Robin: (Softly) Still here.

Counselor: What's different?

Robin: I'm different.

Counselor: How do you mean?

Robin: I'm more relaxed and open. I don't have so much energy devoted to the card. It's just a card.

Counselor: Nice. What else do people notice?

The counselor then facilitates further exploration of the exercise. Some students "get" this new relationship with their private experiences right away, but others have difficulty understanding how responding with acceptance is possible. Some worry that the feeling will never go away if they do not do something about it. As a response to this concern, the counselor could ask what might happen if a butterfly did indeed land on their hands. Would it stay? Maybe. Would it fly away? Eventually. Acceptance is like that: allowing your feelings to do what they will without trying to change them. At the same time, one can choose one's actions—e.g., looking around the room, taking in the humanity of one's partner. Some students say they understand the exercise, but wonder how they can actually make this new relationship happen in their lives. The counselor could respond that this is what the group is about: over the course of the semester, the group will practice, in a variety of ways, opening up like this to thoughts and feelings.

Although explaining the exercise in detail to group members would likely diminish its power and it's not recommended, some of its nuances are worth exploring here. The exercise is used to introduce acceptance, but elements of other processes are present as well. As noted in chapter 3, no ACT process is wholly distinct from the others. All are interrelated facets of psychological flexibility. Holding the private experience like a butterfly is an accepting posture, one that is open and gentle with a thought or feeling that otherwise might be suppressed, fought, or ignored. Writing the name of the private experience on a card and interacting with it metaphorically encourages a defusing posture, one in which the private experience is treated as merely an experience, rather than something "bad." Contact with the present moment is brought to bear in the counselor's direction to notice what's going on in one's body during the exercise and to notice that the card does not go away. It helps students observe the actual results of avoidance and control strategies rather than what the mind says "should" happen. Interacting with a private experience in this way can also facilitate self as context: a distinction is made between the self and the thoughts and feelings the self experiences, which opens up the possibility of responding flexibly (e.g., in more functional ways) when painful thoughts and feelings are present. Finally, "taking in the humanity of the person in front of you" is about values and committed action, if only briefly and subtly. It is rare to encounter a person who does not care about relationships in some way, regardless of how anxious, defensive, or angry she might be in the presence of others.

WORKING IN THE HERE AND NOW

In any counseling group, there is a dynamic tension between discussing events that happen outside the group and those that happen inside the group. A certain amount of talking about one's daily life, as well as one's life history, is necessary for group members to build relationships with one another. Without it, there is no frame of reference from which the group can discuss the impact of experiential avoidance, fusion, and disconnection from values on their lives. From an ACT perspective, however, narrating one's life can also be part of the problem. Excessive attachment to thoughts and beliefs about one's life (i.e., fusion), mentally inhabiting the past and the future (i.e., lack of present moment focus), and clinging to stories about who one *is* (i.e., failing to flexibly move between the self as context and the conceptualized self—see chapter 3) work in synchronicity with experiential avoidance and disconnection from values to create suffering. Therefore, it is necessary for counselors to encourage the group members to look beyond the content of what they are saying to discover what's happening within them and between them. Readers familiar with group counseling will recognize this as the "group process," and attending to it has been called "working in the here and now" (Yalom, 2005).

Working in the here and now helps the group members to make therapeutic use of the interpersonal patterns that manifest in the group. This is true in any counseling group. However, in an ACT group, in which students are learning to notice experiential avoidance and fusion as they show up, this process can be especially powerful. With the help of the acceptance and mindfulness skills they are learning, and the support of the group counselors, students can talk about and work through their reactions to one another as they happen. Furthermore, ACT gives students a vocabulary with which to talk about these experiences in a nonjudgmental way and a roadmap for responding differently to them. The following process excerpt gives an illustration. It occurs midway through the third group meeting, after mindfulness, acceptance, and defusion have been introduced.

Counselor 1: Thanks, everybody, for your comments on the Butterfly exercise. Robin, I notice as we've been talking you've been kind of silent. Can you share what's going on for you?

Robin: (Tears welling in her eyes) I haven't wanted to talk because I'm trying not to cry. I'm just realizing how much wasted effort I have put into struggling with my anxiety. When I could have been making friends and having fun these past couple of years, I've been living in fear, listening to my mind tell me that sharing anything about myself is too risky.

Kelly: But here you are in this group, working on it. That's good, right? You just have to keep trying.

Counselor 2: Kelly, it sounds like it's really hard for you to see Robin in pain.

Kelly: (Pauses) That was rescuing, wasn't it?

Counselor 2: (Smiles) I was wondering. You tell me.

Kelly: I think it was. It's really hard for me not to try to make things better.

Counselor 2: Tell me what's going on inside of you.

Kelly: I can't sit still. I feel like I want to jump out of my seat and give Robin a hug. I don't know the people in this group really well yet, but I care about what happens to her.

Counselor 1: I bet that we are all having some kind of strong reaction. And whatever you are feeling is probably kind of familiar. You have probably felt some version of it before. It really has nothing to do with Robin. We all enter this room with a whole history that has shaped how we are in relationships, including how we respond to the pain of others. Can other group members share their reactions?

Esteban: I'm embarrassed to say this, but I have an urge to leave the room. I'm just no good at dealing with other people's issues. I'm afraid I will make them worse.

Jackie: I get kind of sad, thinking of all the bad things that have happened in my life. I guess I kind of get "hooked" by all of my own negative thoughts and feelings. I'm off in my own head, barely listening to what's going on.

Counselor 1: If you were to allow those thoughts and feelings to be there, but act on something else—say, how you want to be in relationships—how would you respond to Robin?

Jackie: I guess I might just listen. I might ask some questions too—get to know what she's going through.

The counselors could take this interaction in many directions. They could encourage the group to continue talking about their responses to the pain of others and how those responses might help or hinder building relationships. They could explore with the other group members, as they have with Jackie, how they might respond in a values-driven way while mindfully welcoming their thoughts and feelings. Or they could return to Robin, exploring what it is like to be open about her pain, and encourage her, if she's willing, to continue trying on a new interpersonal behavior: openness. Notice, however, that none of these interventions focuses on the *content* of the conversation, but rather on the *process*. Furthermore, the process encompasses both what is going on in the here and now and also how what is going on in group mirrors what happens for the students in their relationships outside of the group.

ADVANCED EXERCISES

Once students have been introduced to the basics of ACT through didactics, metaphors, discussions, readings, and experiential exercises, the group counselors can incorporate more advanced exercises to enhance the participants' experiential learning. By "advanced" we mean exercises that are more likely to stir up discomfort and therefore require a greater deal of willingness on the part of group members. "Label Parade," which introduces this chapter, is one such exercise. Recall that it requires students to interview one another about painful private experiences and then stick name badge labels with the experiences written on them on their bodies. Asking students to be vulnerable with one another in this way requires a level of group development that is unlikely to be achieved in the first few sessions. Facilitators will need to pay attention to the degree of cohesion and trust present in the group before moving on to such exercises. That being said, under the right circumstances, a powerful exercise can help shepherd a group which is struggling to cohere into a more trusting and collaborative space.

Another such exercise is "Eyes On" (or "Eye Contact"; Hayes, Strosahl, & Wilson, 1999). Eyes On involves asking participants to split into pairs and sit facing one another with their knees touching. Over the course of 5-10 minutes the participants look into the eyes of their partners while willingly encountering whatever arises within themselves. Obviously, this is quite different from most social interactions; it is rare to engage another person without looking away periodically to modulate the intensity of connection. Maintaining eye contact requires the student to encounter a variety of experiences, from the relatively predictable and mundane, such as the urge to giggle, to the more unexpected and profound, such as judging oneself and one's partner while simultaneously feeling the vitality of greater intimacy. Depending on the student, Eyes On can simply offer practice at doing something uncomfortable or it can provide an enlightening tour of the variety of internal reactions one can encounter in close relationships. A process excerpt follows:

Counselor: Now let's bring the exercise to an end. Thank your partner in any way you see fit.

(Some smile. A few laugh. One pair bows.)

Counselor: Let's talk about the experience.

Johan: It was really hard at first. I really wanted to laugh. I kept worrying about what my face looked like, and then I was criticizing myself for not doing it right.

(Other group members chime in, noting similar feelings as well as less uncomfortable experiences, like feeling peaceful or connected.)

Counselor: How might your reactions tell you something about your relationships?

Esteban: I'm not sure doing this tells me anything about my relationships. I don't really ever sit like this with anyone. I just felt really wiggly and impatient.

Counselor: Perhaps it doesn't have anything to do with your relationships. But maybe "wiggly and impatient" mirrors something in your life. I'll give an example from my own life. The first time I did this exercise, at a training conference for counselors, I found myself thinking very critical thoughts about my partner—just judging like crazy. It reminded me of something I've learned before about relationships: when I get close to somebody, it's kind of scary, and I tend to get judgmental to protect myself. One of the things that the exercise really made clear was that my judgments are about me and my discomfort, not so much about the person I am with.

Esteban: I get it, I think. I guess I am prone to being impatient with people I care about. It never occurred to me it might be a reaction to being close to them.

Counselor: Maybe it is, and maybe it isn't. Perhaps this is something you could pay attention to over the next few weeks to see what you notice.

Obviously, a counselor's self-disclosure should always be carefully considered and accompanied by a clear clinical rationale. When thoughtfully executed, self-disclosure can be a powerful part of ACT and is consistent with ACT theory: fusion and avoidance are part of the human condition, and a counselor is no less susceptible to their power than a group member is. A counselor's self-disclosure, if done both delicately and with an eye toward moving the group process forward, can model acceptance, defusion, values, or any other dimension of psychological flexibility. In this example, the counselor is saying, in effect, "I struggle too. Pursuing a meaningful life does not mean avoiding pain. Just as I encourage you to be willing with yours, I try to be willing with mine."

Empirical Considerations

ACT has been conducted in group format with a variety of problems, including problems common to college students such as depression (e.g., Zettle and Rains, 1989). ACT has also been studied with college students as participants (e.g., Block & Wulfert, 2002). Chapter 3 offers a summary of the current state of evidence for ACT. To our knowledge, however, the effectiveness of a transdiagnostic ACT group has never been studied naturalistically in a CCC. To this end, the first author recently completed a pilot study (Boone & Manning, 2012) of a 10-session ACT group designed to fit within a single semester (from recruitment to termination) and accommodate any student who struggles with depression and/or anxiety.

To prevent disrupting the normal flow of clinical services in a busy CCC where research is rarely conducted, students were not required to be part of the study in order to join the group, and all participants had concurrent treatment at the center (i.e., some combination of individual therapy and/or psychiatric medication). Assessments of depression and anxiety, quality of life, and psychological flexibility were conducted before the group started, halfway through the group, when the group ended, and at three-month follow-up. There were a total of 18 student participants across two semesters, with two dropouts. The data showed statistically and clinically significant changes on all measures at termination, and gains were maintained at follow-up. Furthermore, students rated the group highly on satisfaction surveys, and all students who completed the group indicated that they would recommend the group to a friend. Although these data should be interpreted with caution given that there was no control group, the number of participants was small, and all students had concurrent treatment, they suggest that transdiagnostic ACT groups are acceptable to college students and may be a worthwhile intervention for CCCs, especially in light of the growing body of outcome data gathered in other settings (Ruiz, 2010).

Final Words

ACT is a good fit for colleges and universities: it is brief, interactive, and effective. However, implementing new services in a CCC can be challenging, especially in light of limited resources and heightened concern on campuses about violence. To address questions about whether offering ACT groups is a good use of resources, interested counselors can point to ACT's research base, short-term format, and broad applicability. Counselors can also note the wide availability of low-cost ACT resources (many of which are listed in the Appendix associated with this volume), which may cut down on planning time and therefore reduce the potential clinical hours lost to preparation.

To address concerns about students harming themselves or others, counselors can provide education about the ACT model and plan thoughtfully for managing risk. ACT-naïve clinicians and administrators sometimes express concern about "accepting thoughts and feelings." They understandably ask if this means *all* thoughts and feelings, including, for example, thoughts of suicide. Prospective group leaders can provide assurance that acceptance means letting go of struggle with private experiences, not necessarily buying into their content: holding a spontaneous suicidal thought compassionately in one's awareness while choosing to act in the service of one's values is very different from *giving in* to a suicidal thought. Furthermore, ACT groups, like other outpatient groups, should have exclusion criteria to rule out the participation of students who are at high risk to harm themselves or others. To this end, assessment by a professional prior to joining group is essential. To further ensure safety, group members can have a counselor assigned to them— one of the group counselors or the intake counselor—who can provide individual support should a crisis arise. Group leaders can also pull students aside after groups should especially painful feelings arise during the meeting and not be addressed.

References

Bach, P., & Hayes, S. C. (2002). The use of Acceptance and Commitment Therapy to prevent the rehospitalization of psychotic patients: A randomized controlled trial. *Journal of Consulting and Clinical Psychology, 70*(5), 1129-1139.

Block, J., & Wulfert, E. (2002, May). Acceptance or change of private experiences: A comparative analysis in college students with a fear of public speaking. In R. Zettle (Chair), *Acceptance and Commitment Therapy.* Symposium presented at the annual meeting of the Association for Behavior Analysis, Toronto, Ontario.

Boone, M. S., & Manning, J. (2012). *A pilot study of an Acceptance and Commitment Therapy group for anxiety and depression in a college counseling center*. Manuscript in preparation.

Eichler, R. J., & Schwartz, V. (2010). Essential services in college counseling. In J. Kay & V. Schwartz (Eds.) *Mental health care in the college community* (pp. 57-89). Chichester, UK: Wiley-Blackwell.

Eifert, G. H., & Forsyth, J. P. (2005). Acceptance and commitment therapy for anxiety disorders: a practitioner's treatment guide to using mindfulness, acceptance, and values-based behavior change strategies. Oakland, CA: New Harbinger.

Gallagher, R. (2011). *National survey of counseling center directors*. Alexandria, VA: International Association of Counseling Services.

Harris, R. (2009). *ACT made simple*. Oakland, CA: New Harbinger.

Hayes, S. C., Strosahl, K., & Wilson, K. G. (1999). *Acceptance and commitment therapy: an experiential approach to behavior change*. New York: Guilford Press.

Hayes, S. C., Strosahl, K., & Wilson, K. G. (2011). *Acceptance and commitment therapy: the process and practice of mindful change*. New York: Guilford Press.

Pearson, A. N., Heffner, M., & Follette, V. M. (2010). Acceptance and commitment therapy for body image dissatisfaction: a practitioner's guide to using mindfulness, acceptance, and values-based behavior change strategies. Oakland, CA: New Harbinger.

Ruiz, F. J. (2010). A review of acceptance and commitment therapy (ACT) empirical evidence: correlational, experimental psychopathology, component and outcome studies. *International Journal of Psychology and Psychological Therapy, 10*(1), 125-162.

Shulman, L. (2011). *Dynamics and skills of group counseling*. Belmont, CA: Brooks/Cole.

Walser, R. D., & Pistorello, J. (2004). ACT in group format. In S. C. Hayes & K. D. Strosahl (Eds.), *A practical guide to acceptance and commitment therapy* (pp. 347-372). New York: Springer.

Walser, R. D., & Westrup, D. (2007). *Acceptance and commitment therapy for the treatment of post-traumatic stress disorder: a practitioner's guide to using mindfulness and acceptance strategies*. Oakland, CA: New Harbinger.

Yalom, I. (2005). *The theory and practice of group psychotherapy* (5th ed.). New York: Basic Books.

Zettle, R. D., & Rains, J. C. (1989). Group cognitive and contextual therapies in treatment of depression. *Journal of Clinical Psychology, 45*, 438-445.

CHAPTER 5

Mindfulness-Based Cognitive Therapy (MBCT) and Acceptance and Commitment Therapy (ACT) at a College Counseling and Psychological Service

Philomena Renner

Elizabeth Foley

University of Sydney, Counseling and Psychological Services

Ann is a 26-year-old PhD student who reports benefiting from the MBCT group that she attended. She has a history of depression and generalized anxiety disorder, and several previous treatments with cognitive behavioral therapy. Ann's struggles with anxiety and perfectionism were causing both academic lack of progress and problems in her personal relationships. Ann found that the main benefit of the course was teaching her how to meditate. Mindfulness practice helped her to notice her inner monologue and to respond skillfully rather than getting stuck in reactive cycles of deterioration. When she now starts to stress and worry she takes a breathing space, sees the patterns objectively, and responds to the situation with conscious and kind choice. Ann's scenario is typical of older students with focused study requirements and academic anxiety. MBCT appears particularly effective in bringing about a proactive response versus reactivity, and instilling the capacity to switch attention from unhelpful to helpful modes of processing thoughts, bodily sensations, and emotions.

Vincent is a 19-year-old first year student who lives alone and avoids interaction with others. He was diagnosed with depression in high school but refused to cooperate with treatment. Recently he reports that he cries daily, feels numb and detached, and finds it hard to take in information and to produce work. When Vincent began the ACT course he was shocked by the level of interaction required but he found the directed and fun nature of group exercises less threatening than his previous exposure to mental health services. He was impressed by the willingness of other students to share, and he found that being taught how to describe and interact with his feelings gave him a way to work with, rather than hide from, what he was experiencing. He found that "letting go of the struggle" had simplified the way he was approaching his studies. He started to speak up more in the group and in his lectures. Vincent reports that the ACT course helped him "get out of his head." He was also surprised by how vital he felt when he interacted in the group exercises and this boosted his understanding of himself as someone who gets energy from connecting with other people and activities. Vincent's predicament is common for younger students who are depressed, have become socially withdrawn, and experience their life as lacking direction and enjoyment.

This chapter will consider the suitability for college students of two mindfulness and acceptance-based therapies, Mindfulness-Based Cognitive Therapy (MBCT; Segal, Williams & Teasdale, 2002) and Acceptance & Commitment Therapy (ACT; Hayes, Strosahl & Wilson, 2011). Clinical experiences, and some data, from a controlled trial of MBCT and ACT for students experiencing stress, anxiety, and depression will be presented. The challenges of delivering MBCT and ACT with this population will be addressed and recommendations will be made for the delivery of these interventions to college students.

A number of recent studies have reported concerning trends in relation to the psychological health and well-being of college students. For example, American data from the 2010 Cooperative Institutional Research Program (CIRP) Freshman survey indicated that first year college students' self-ratings of their emotional health had dropped to a record low level (Pryor, Hurtado, DeAngelo, Blake, & Tran, 2010). Only

51.9 percent of students reported that their emotional health was in the "above average" range. These results represented a drop of 3.4 percent from 2009 and a significant decline from the 63.6 percent who placed themselves in those categories in 1985.

Furthermore, while students' perceived emotional health fell, the CIRP survey also found that students' drive to achieve and their perception of their academic abilities trended upward. More students than ever before (71.2 percent) rated their academic abilities as "above average," and 75.8 percent rated their drive to achieve in the same terms. Twenge et al. (2010) also examined birth cohort increases in psychopathology among young Americans from 1938-2007 and demonstrated that American high school and college students reported significantly more symptoms of psychopathology over the generations. In Australia, recent college student surveys confirm both high levels of distress (Andrews & Chong, 2011) and self-reported mental health disorders such as depression, anxiety, and drug and alcohol problems (Vivekananda, Telley, & Trethowan, 2011).

Although these high levels of distress may indicate better detection of underlying mental health disorders in the community, Twenge et al. (2010) also suggest that the reported increases in the mental ill health of students result from a cultural shift toward extrinsic values and goals such as status and money and away from intrinsic goals such as community, meaning of life, and affiliation. This cultural shift may also compromise students' experience of learning and consequently their mental health and well-being. While positive interactions with faculty and other students (in addition to positive family relationships) may contribute to students' development of psychosocial resources and maturity (Adams, Berzonsky, & Keating, 2006), in our experience, academic learning can be frequently pressured, with little available time to experience engagement or opportunity to interact with peers or instructors. In Australia, and in many public universities within the U.S., this situation is exacerbated by the need for many students to work part-time to be financially viable. As a result, students' experience of learning can be one of isolation and striving to master content rather than cultivating intellectual curiosity, independence, and critical thinking.

Students stressed by the university context are likely to evaluate unwanted feelings as obstacles to academic success and may attempt to control unwanted subjective experience by using cognitive and emotional avoidance strategies such as rumination, worry, perfectionism, procrastination, eating dysregulation, drug and alcohol misuse, and self-harm. However, as noted in other chapters in this book (see chapter 3), experiential avoidance strategies are both ineffectual and have rebound effects: Attempts to inhibit unpleasant experiences both increase the frequency and distress of these experiences (Gross, 2002) and the sense of being disconnected from oneself (John & Gross, 2004). Students looking for assistance may often have expectations for "quick fixes" that will remove uncomfortable feelings and improve their academic functioning.

The Potential of Acceptance-Based Therapies on Campus

In contrast to the common assumption that internal discomfort has to be eliminated in order to improve functioning, mindfulness and acceptance-based therapies such as Mindfulness-Based Cognitive Therapy (MBCT; Segal et al., 2002) and Acceptance and Commitment Therapy (ACT; Hayes et al., 2011) suggest that functioning can be improved by changing the way people perceive and interact with their internal experiences rather than changing the experiences themselves. Acceptance-based interventions attempt to develop this perspective by providing "discovery" learning to students, in which they engage with experiential exercises and have the opportunity to reflect on what is meaningful for them. This explicit values dimension may be relevant for students who are developmentally at a stage of self-discovery and clarification about personal values. Students may be vulnerable to overidentification with extrinsic cultural values that may not deliver stable personal satisfaction. However, if students are aware of personal values and engage in balanced activities in areas covering love, work, play, and health, this expands opportunities for meaning and self-discovery. With a flexible and focused sense of awareness around personal meaning, the vicissitudes of academic stress and unpleasant experiences may be better managed.

Mindfulness-Based Cognitive Therapy (MBCT)

MBCT integrates the practice of mindfulness meditation, using the structure of insight-oriented meditation drawn from Mindfulness-Based Stress Reduction (Kabat-Zinn, 1990), with principles of cognitive therapy (Segal et al., 2002). It is a small-group program (up to 12 participants) across eight weeks. This program was initially developed for the treatment of recurrent depression, and it aims to interrupt the ruminative habits that fuel depressive relapse. The MBCT program uses intensive meditation practice to train the ability to "decenter" or "step back from" the content of current experience and to strengthen discernment regarding self-care.

Mindfulness is often described as paying attention on purpose, in the present moment, and nonjudgmentally (Kabat-Zinn, 1990). A key component of MBCT and MBSR (see chapter 6) is inquiry (Segal et al., 2002). Learning emerges from an investigative process that follows the practice, through a dialogue between the student and teacher, rather than being introduced in a didactic way. The intention of this investigative process is to "draw out whatever participants noticed during the practice and by doing this encourage them to reflect on and explore their experience, work together through dialogue about these observations to find out what is being discovered, and link these observations to the aims of the program" (Crane, 2009, p. 141).

MBCT draws a distinction between two modes of mind: "doing mode" and "being mode." The "doing mode" pertains to the goal-oriented actions where we are striving toward what we want or away from what we don't want (Crane, 2009). The "being mode" is characterized by an intentional placement of attention on the present moment and direct contact with the world through one's senses (Crane, 2009). The goal in MBCT is to increasingly cultivate the "being mode" through mindfulness meditation.

These and additional aspects of MBCT will be discussed below when addressing modifications made to adjust to a college student population.

Acceptance and Commitment Therapy (ACT)

The theory and practical application of ACT is described in detail in other chapters of this book (see chapters 3 and 4). Principles of behavior change are central to ACT, and this intervention accesses a wide range of techniques to further these aims. It uses metaphors, logical paradoxes, and experiential exercises to foster the six theoretical processes of defusion, acceptance, present moment awareness, self as context, values clarification, and committed action.

Some Similarities/Differences between MBCT and ACT

A thorough comparison of these two approaches is beyond the scope of this chapter, but we will outline a few similarities and differences between MBCT and ACT, particularly as pertaining to mindfulness. MBCT and ACT both utilize experiential exercises in order to help individuals become aware of automatic patterns of expectations and reactions and promote investigation of the "workability" of coping behaviors. They train acceptance of uncomfortable experiences, with an emphasis on moving forward *with* discomfort, by creating a different relationship with difficult experiences based on acceptance and equanimity (MBCT) or by maintaining a perspective on life's bigger meaning and purpose (ACT). Both therapies promote psychological flexibility and the viewing of thoughts as merely verbal events rather than actual events. An increased internal locus of control and sense of agency are common byproducts of acceptance-based learning (McCarthy, 2011).

Both therapies incorporate mindfulness. The elements of mindfulness (i.e., present awareness and nonjudgmental acceptance) that are a foundation of acceptance-based therapies are also antidotes against the habitual inflexible modes of functioning—hurry, worry, and evaluation. Mindfulness trains attention to be flexible and focuses on enabling adaptive working with thoughts, bodily sensations, and emotions (Denton & Sears, 2009). Mindfulness has consistently been associated with increased subjective well-being, reduced emotional reactivity, and improved behavioral regulation (see review by Keng, Smoski, & Robins, 2011).

The way mindfulness is presented in these two therapies, as well as other mindfulness approaches, varies greatly. MBCT, an intensive mindfulness program, utilizes systematic meditation practices to develop mindfulness skills experientially. Outside of meditation times, attention is drawn to mindless reactivity and to the generalization of formal practices to everyday activities of living. MBCT aims to cultivate decentered awareness, to disidentify from the contents of one's consciousness (i.e., one's thoughts, emotions) and to view moment-to-moment experience with greater clarity and objectivity (Shapiro, Carlson, Astin, & Freedman, 2006). Through daily meditation practice, the ability to "step back from" the content of current experience is developed, and discernment regarding self-care is a natural by-product of this awareness.

ACT mindfulness exercises combine aspects of acceptance, defusion, self as context (awareness that one is more than one's thoughts, feelings, and experiences), and contact with the present moment (Strosahl, Hayes, Wilson, & Gifford, 2004). Formal mindfulness meditation practice may or may not be included in ACT protocols, and the duration of in-session mindfulness practices tends to be shorter than in MBCT. Furthermore, aspects of guided visualization are often mixed with mindfulness instructions (e.g., the Leaves On a Stream exercise, Hayes, Smith, 2005). These differences in the dose and the type of mindfulness training across approaches may lead to different outcomes (Carmody & Baer, 2008).

MBCT and ACT for College Students at University of Sydney

We have recently conducted a study offering MBCT and ACT groups for college students at Sydney University Counseling and Psychological Services (Foley & Renner, 2012). Reflecting the constraints of the university timetable, protocols for six-week groups with weekly two-hour sessions were developed for both the MBCT and ACT conditions and included their central components. Protocols targeted stress, anxiety, and depression, and the group format aimed to increase a sense of connectedness and to emphasize common experience. There were two therapists and 8 to 16 student participants per group. A brief description of the empirical findings from this study will be presented later, after outlining the session content for each approach and describing some unique MBCT and ACT interventions used with college students.

EXAMPLES OF THE MODIFICATIONS OF MBCT AND ACT FOR COLLEGE STUDENTS

Protocols primarily relied on existing materials for both MBCT (Segal et al., 2002) and ACT (Harris, 2009; Hayes et al., 2011). However, several modifications were made to fit college students and/or the campus context. In-session and home meditations for the MBCT program were shortened and ranged from 3 minutes to 20 minutes. Sessions 2 & 3 and 4 & 7 of the traditional MBCT program were collapsed into one session each. MBCT sessions included meditation, inquiry, and some didactic material guided by the content of the original manual, with modifications to address the context (i.e., developmental stage of participants, university environment). See Table 1 for an outline of the session protocols. The MBCT intervention was more introverted in nature than the ACT program, with meditations and subsequent inquiry about student experience of these meditations being the central teaching tool. The importance of practicing meditation at home was particularly emphasized in the MBCT condition, although both conditions received the same CD with recordings of mindfulness meditations of 3 minutes to 30 minutes in duration. The sessions in the ACT condition had similar weekly themes as the MBCT condition; however, there was less emphasis on mindfulness practice. There was greater use of metaphors and interactive group experiences for those in the ACT group. The ACT condition also had explicit values work. Weekly handouts summarized the content of sessions and provided space to document details of home practice.

In the MBCT condition, the process of inquiry described above was facilitated by a diagram (see Figure 1 below) that was placed on the floor, in the center of the circle of students:

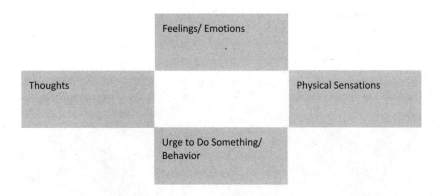

Figure 1. Floor Diagram to Facilitate Inquiry in MBCT

When students were describing their experience of home tasks, in-session exercises, or current experience, they would use this structure to do so. They would often literally walk around the diagram as they explained their experience: "When I first came in today, I was all in my head, worrying about all the things that I need to get done today" (standing on the "thoughts" card), "and then I started to notice just how tense I was in my body" (moving one foot to the "physical sensations" card), "and then, toward the end of the meditation, I could sometimes be still for a few moments" (the student stepped into the center of the diagram and moved her weight between this space and the "thoughts" card). Over time, we found that students used the diagram as a structure to notice their current mode, to direct their attention toward their physical sensations, and to achieve a "decentered" awareness. They became familiar with their automatic habits and could explain these using the diagram (e.g., "I am always in my head," "I don't tend to be aware of my body," or "I just take off and distract myself and then I start thinking about it and feel bad").

In the ACT condition, we also emphasized working externally with internal processes to combat the tendency toward intellectualization, to ease social anxiety, and to promote interaction. For example, in ACT students were asked to use play dough to create an external representation of the issue with which they struggled. After participants finished, they were required to describe, but not explain, their creation. For instance, one student described his "pain" as a ball with spikes all over it and another student described it as "a large flat object that is thin and stretched at some edges and curling over itself on others." Figure 2 below shows pictures of these two examples.

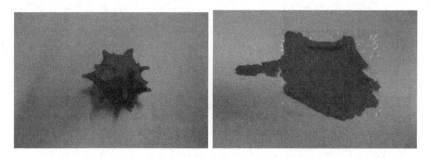

Figure 2. Play Dough Depiction of "Internal Pain" by Students in the ACT Condition

The students were then invited to stand with their creation. It was acknowledged that everyone differed and tended to interact with experience in different ways. Students were also invited to "strike a pose" that represented how they interacted with their struggle. Students engaged well with this task and "poses" included putting objects on heads, hiding them behind themselves, throwing them across the room, and curling up in a ball next to them. Rather than using such reactive experiential avoidance strategies of avoiding, altering, or controlling, the group then experimented with how to remain in contact with negative experiences and respond based on mindfulness, acceptance, and values.

Additional exercises, modified for college students, are included as "Appendix 5A: Modified MBCT Exercises," and "Appendix 5B: Modified ACT Exercises," at www.newharbinger.com/2225.

Table 1. An Overview of Protocols for MBCT and ACT Courses for Students

	MBCT	ACT
Session 1 Overview of the course; curiosity about how we are in the world	Arriving meditation Introducing the program & rationale Automatic pilot Defining mindfulness & raisin exercise (Segal, et al., 2002) Mindfulness of activity Body scan meditation to close *Home practice*: Mindfulness of activity, daily formal practice	Introducing the program & rationale for ACT Post-it exercise: Looking at "unwanted stuff" (See Appendix 5B) Increasing self-awareness: Rose exercise (See Appendix 5B), leaves on a stream mindfulness exercise *Home practice*: completing habits diagram, leaves on a stream

	MBCT	**ACT**
Session 2 Self-awareness	Arriving meditation & inquiry	Arriving mindfulness
	Reviewing rationale for program	Play dough exercise—an external representation of distress
	Discussion of challenges to practicing mindfulness	Self-awareness continued: the Sweet Spot (Wilson & DuFrene, 2008)
	Identifying patterns of reaction	Rationale for defusion: hand in front of face
	A modified version of the MBCT "Walking Down the Street" exercise to introduce mindfulness of thoughts/reactions (see Appendix 5A)	Developing the "Observer Self" in daily life: breathing space (Hayes, et al., 2011)
	Moving meditation	*Home practice*: daily mindfulness practice, self-awareness including taking inventory
	Home practice: Mindfulness of activity, daily formal practice	

Session 3 Dealing with stress	Arriving meditation & inquiry Application of mindfulness to patterns of reaction Introduce 3 minute breathing space Discussion about acceptance Mixed meditation including bringing in a difficulty Review of course themes *Home practice*: Daily formal practice and dealing with stress using mindfulness	Arriving mindfulness Auto-pilot and making wise choices in difficult situations Two little mice metaphor: amplifying pain Psychoeducation about stress: including ideas of perfectionism and the relationship between stress and performance. Discussion around "Safe Striving" (See Appendix 5B) Exercise: stress surfing—students to develop their own behavioural experiment (See Appendix 5B) *Home practice*: Mindfulness practice and stress surfing
Session 4 Mindfulness of thoughts	Arriving meditation & inquiry Discussion of automatic thoughts including common content Moods, thoughts, and alternative viewpoints exercise Breathing space as the first step toward a "wider view" Mindful walking *Home practice*: Daily formal and informal practice, breathing space	Mindfulness exercise Taking the mind for a walk Identifying frequent visitors/thought patterns Willingness: "Joe the Bum" (Hayes, et al., 2011) Why tolerate pain? Introduce idea of values T-shirt motto exercise (see Appendix 5B) *Home practice*: mindfulness, stepping back from frequent visitors and remembering life values at challenging times

	MBCT	ACT
Session 5 Integrating what is being learned in daily life	Arriving meditation & inquiry meditation: mindfulness of seeing, hearing, breath and body Explore link between activity and mood Personal signs of deterioration & how to deal with these (see Appendix 5A) Breathing space practice *Home Practice*: Formal practice, 3 minute breathing space	Arriving mindfulness Students "Mind Map" course (See Appendix 5B) Preventing Stress and using enhancing activities Passengers on the bus Mindfulness: Dealing with an uncomfortable feeling *Home Practice*: practice dealing with passengers on the bus and changing daily routine to be more nurturing
Session 6 Dealing with future challenges	Arriving meditation Meditation: Body scan practice Review whole course Discuss personal reflections and plans for future practice Closing meditation	Arriving Mindfulness Review course Barriers and Counter Actions Discuss personal reflections and plans for future practice

Empirical Considerations

A recent meta-analytic review of intensive mindfulness-based programs revealed medium to large effect sizes for improvements in anxiety and depression (Hofmann, Sawyer, Witt, & Oh, 2010). Both MBCT and ACT are evidence-based approaches. MBCT has received strong empirical support in the treatment of individuals with recurrent depression

(Ma & Teasdale, 2004; Teasdale et al., 2000) and has more recently been used for the treatment of a variety of psychological experiences including suicide ideation, anxiety, and health-related distress (e.g., Chiesa & Serretti, 2011; Foley, Baillie, Huxter, Price, & Sinclair, 2010). Similarly, ACT has obtained medium to large effect sizes across a variety of presentations (Ruiz, 2010; see chapter 3 for more detail).

As noted in chapter 1, this field is extending into college campuses: There is growing conceptual and empirical evidence for the inclusion of mindfulness in interventions promoting the well-being of college students. Frewen, Evans, Maraj, Dozois, & Partridge (2008) reported that among undergraduate students, higher mindfulness was related both to a lower frequency of negative automatic thoughts and to an enhanced ability to let go of those thoughts. In a randomized control trial, Oman, Shapiro, Thoresen, Plante, & Flinders (2008) found that participation in MBSR was associated with decreased stress and enhanced forgiveness among college students. Furthermore, in a recent study of MBCT for students, participation was associated with a reduction in negative affect and an increase in mindfulness, and these variables were significantly negatively correlated (Collard, Avny, & Boniwell, 2008). ACT has been used with college students as well with promising findings (see chapter 4).

As mindfulness-based approaches proliferate, the question of how they perform with different populations, such as college students, and relative to one another, becomes more salient—hence the authors' decision to conduct a study comparing MBCT and ACT with college students; 246 students had indicated an interest in the groups, but only 136 attended the first session and are thus considered to be study participants. MBCT and ACT packages were offered in randomized order, with students allocated to the next available group. The majority of participants were female (MBCT 67% and ACT 76%) and single (MBCT 83% and ACT 81%). The average participant was 26 years old and in his or her third year of study. Students were most commonly studying the arts, followed by science and business. There were no condition differences in these factors at baseline.

Levels of psychological distress, quality of life, mindfulness, and psychological flexibility were assessed before and after the treatment. There was a large attrition of students across the study (31%), a problem commonly reported by researchers working with this population (e.g., Forman et al., 2007 reported 43.5% attrition in a similar sample). Non-attendance tended to be common as finals approached. There was no significant difference between conditions in treatment dropout. However, dropouts across both conditions tended to have higher distress at initial assessment than completers.

College students completing either the MBCT or ACT course reported a significant decrease in psychological distress—a change of moderate to large magnitude (effect sizes 0.48-0.96)—and large increases in mindfulness and acceptance (effect sizes 0.71-1.49). There was no significant statistical difference between groups on these treatment gains. However, there was a non-significant trend for the MBCT condition being associated with greater reductions in anxiety. Results indicated that the only personality trait of students to interact with group allocation in contributing to treatment gains was openness, which was associated with greater gains in terms of anxiety reduction across groups. There was a trend for students who rated highly on both openness and anxiety to do better when allocated to the MBCT group. While there were no significant differences between MBCT and ACT, we made observations along the way that may be helpful to the field and guide future research.

Overall Facilitator Observations

A number of key observations across both conditions were made about the ways students engaged with the material. There was a strong tendency for intellectualizing in the early stage of the courses as students resisted the expectation for experiential learning (e.g., "I hoped someone would tell me what to do"). Students also tended to slip into a passive "lecture mode" at times, so the facilitators "knocked" the groups out of this "autopilot" repeatedly. We also found that concepts needed to be repeated several times and across sessions for students to integrate them. Finally, students tended to hear "distraction" when we were explaining mindfulness, and required a lot of support in understanding the distinction between mindfulness and distraction.

In the MBCT condition, students reported low levels of home practice and some struggled to connect with their current experience during in-session meditations. This meant that periods of inquiry were limited. The energy levels in MBCT groups were also lower than in the ACT groups. However, despite the low participation at times, MBCT students reported that they "were getting a lot out of it" and seemed to assimilate the ideas by the end of the course.

The ACT program seemed to be better received by less-motivated college students over the MBCT program, given the interactive nature of groups and the more relaxed requirements for meditation practice. However, the non-significant trend for MBCT in anxiety reduction may indicate that students with anxiety may have an enhanced response to the extended mindfulness practices. Encouraging "being" versus "doing mode" of mind seemed to provide an effective decentering perspective for anxious students.

Values Clarification

Although the impact of values was not assessed quantitatively, values work raises challenges for this age group and context. Students who overidentify with expectations of competitive academic achievement may readily understand values as goals to be attained rather than guiding principles for doing what matters in the present, so the nuances of how this is presented need to be carefully considered. Sheldon and Kasser (2001) suggest that as people grow older, they may be better able to orient toward issues that will satisfy their deeper psychological needs and less interested in short-term, superficial, or materialistic issues. Conversely, in line with the concept of "zone of proximal development" (Vygotsky, 1978), presenting the opportunity to interact with values thinking may itself prompt increased capacity for values exploration.

Our observation was that the MBCT group, which focused on shifts in modes of processing and reflections on lifestyle (e.g., noticing nourishing and depleting activities) rather than explicit reference to values, often resulted in students spontaneously bringing up personal life meanings. This is consistent with the finding that MBCT may assist participants in clarifying their important goals and increasing their confidence in their capacity to move in valued life directions (Crane, Winder, Hargus, Amarasinghe, & Barnhofer, 2011). For anxious and stressed students, values work may tip them into a "doing" mode of mind and they may get overwhelmed with the apparent discrepancy between living a valued life and their current status; conversely depressed students may have difficulty engaging values work due to mood, or the perceived pressure of purpose and motivation. In summary, it is our impression that the identification of life values is challenging with this population. In line with this hypothesis, Forman et al. (2007) did not identify values as a significant factor mediating clinical improvements in their ACT courses for students. This issue of the staging and impact of values work across various clinical issues and ages requires further investigation.

Mindfulness

The core process and discipline of regular mindful practice may at times be too abstract for students to integrate and apply, both in terms of their limited life experience and in terms of what fits their lifestyle choices. To enhance its workability, MBCT may benefit from being presented within a motivational frame (e.g., by exploring the costs and benefits of mindfulness practice) in order to promote engagement (Bricker & Tollison, 2011). These aspects, in addition to the intensive training in mindfulness required of trainers, may represent shortcomings in MBCT as a first-line approach with college students at counseling centers.

In ACT, mindfulness is only one element of the training, which also involves highly interactive exercises that seem to be energizing and promote connection with the self and with others. These briefer exercises may allow participants to be able to have "islands" of mindfulness within their college life, as research suggests that even brief doses of mindfulness result in improved functioning (Erisman & Roemer, 2010). In college contexts, the lighter dose of mindfulness offered in ACT may be suitable given student constraints in time and motivation.

Conversely, the potential of mindfulness may not be fully developed when it is used as a "means to an end" rather than using the practice in its more formal way to develop an awareness of impermanence, the patterns of human suffering, and the importance of nonjudgmental acceptance as a pathway out of suffering ("being mode"). Exposure to in-session doses of experiential acceptance may be particularly useful for students in enhancing friendly awareness linked to wise personal care (i.e., "being" before "doing"). The danger of the smaller dose mindfulness (especially when combined with visualization) is that it may be used simply as a distraction or an escape and may contribute to the creation of "successful (mind-less) strivers." For example, as a student becomes busy and fragmented he may use "mindfulness" to decrease his sense of fragmentation and with the intention of becoming better at being busy. There is some danger that such exercises can inadvertently function as avoidance. Regardless of the specific methods used, clinicians need to inquire how the students are using mindfulness techniques to ensure they are not absorbed into old patterns of avoidance.

Mindful approaches may be of most benefit in times of acute stress—when difficult things are happening emotionally or physically. A gentle, non-reactive awareness can enable stepping back from the eye of the storm, allowing a place to view experience from and prompting awareness that experience is not permanent or self-defining, that it will shift and change. This is different from mere distraction. While distraction techniques can be effective when intrusions are short lived, mindfulness is a more effective approach with more chronic issues (Kabat-Zinn, 2002). Similarly, while relaxation can reduce distress, mindfulness meditation does a better job of inducing positive states of mind and reducing ruminative thoughts and behaviors (Jain et al., 2007).

The more intensive mindfulness training included in programs such as MBCT is not goal directed, it is spacious and aims for a continuity of practice. The intention is to move toward living mindfully with occasional moments of non-mindful living/reactivity. The confusion about mindfulness training in the literature and in practice may be a consequence of fusion with the dialectic of Western society—the striving to improve functioning and the desire to feel whole and connected. For example, the mixing of mindfulness instructions with guided imagery may not be useful as the intention of mindfulness is to provide a space for participants to become connected with the current experience and to reduce clinging to their experience being a particular way. The trainer needs to be explicit about the intention of the exercise and the instructions provided to students to ensure that mindfulness is not confused with distraction and/or thought control (Fisher & Wells, 2009). We agree with the recommendation from Keng et al. (2011) that future work should examine who mindfulness training is most effective for and under what conditions, given that there is a suggestion that its effectiveness can vary according to individual differences (Cordon, Brown, & Gibson, 2009).

Final Words

Acceptance-based approaches seem fitting to the college context, given students' common overidentification with cultural expectations around success and distress, and their possible lack of capacity to decenter from the content of current experience. The college environment, which is often characterized by intellectualization and a pressure to perform, can further restrict the developmental process of exploration and self-discovery. Both the MBCT and ACT approaches facilitate self-awareness through direct contact with experience and encourage participants to step back from the "control and elimination agenda" of human suffering to promote the value of living an engaged and meaningful life. These therapies offer explicit experiential training in adaptive self-regulation facilitating psychosocial development and growth. Vygotsky (1978) wrote about "the zone of proximal development," which refers to the level of understanding that a student can reach with a teacher's help. Scaffolding instruction as a teaching strategy provides support to facilitate learner development. From this psychology of learning perspective, both approaches are engaging and effective.

Our research suggests that both MBCT and ACT work to reduce distress and promote important elements of psychological flexibility (mindfulness and acceptance). Although the measured outcomes were comparable across conditions in our study, the way students interacted with the programs seemed to differ. Our clinical experience suggests that ACT may be the more pragmatic intervention for traditional-age students, like Vincent at the beginning of the chapter, who are limited in time and motivation, given that ACT's range of behavior change techniques allows for more active engagement with self and others. Conversely, motivated older students struggling with more chronic problems, like Ann at the beginning of the chapter, may gain more from MBCT.

References

Adams, G. R., Berzonsky, M. D. & Keating, L. (2006). Psychosocial Resources in First-Year University Students: The role of identity processes and social relationships. *Journal of Youth and Adolescence, 35, 1,* 81-91.

Andrews, A., & Chong, J. L. Y. (2011). Exploring the wellbeing of students studying at an Australian University. *Journal of the Australian and New Zealand Student Services Association, 37,* 9-38.

Bricker, J., & Tollison, S. (2011). Comparison of Motivational Interviewing with Acceptance and Commitment Therapy: A Conceptual and Clinical Review. *Behavioural and Cognitive Psychotherapy, 39 (5),* 541-559.

Crane, R. (2009). *Mindfulness-Based Cognitive Therapy: Distinctive Features.* New York: Routledge.

Carmody, J. & Baer, R.A. (2008). Relationship between mindfulness practice and levels of mindfulness, medical and psychological symptoms and well-being in a mindfulness-based stress reduction program. *Journal of Behavioral Medicine, 31, 1,* 23-33.

Chiesa, A. & Serretti, A. (2011). Mindfulness-based cognitive therapy for psychiatric disorders: A systematic review and meta-analysis. *Psychiatry Research, 187 (3),* 441-453.

Collard, P., Avny, N. & Boniwell, I. (2008). Teaching Mindfulness-Based Cognitive Therapy (MBCT) to students: The effects of MBCT on the levels of Mindfulness and Subjective Well-Being. *Counselling Psychology Quarterly, 21 (4),* 323-336.

Cordon, S. L., Brown, K. W., Gibson, P. R. (2009). The role of mindfulness-based stress reduction on perceived stress: Preliminary evidence for the moderating role of attachment style. *Journal of Cognitive Psychotherapy. 23 (3),* 258-569.

Crane, C., Winder, R., Hargus, E., Amarasinghe, M. & Barnhofer, T. (2011). Effects of Mindfulness-Based Cognitive Therapy on Specificity of Life Goals. Cognitive Therapy & Research. Online publication accessed 21 Jan., 2011.

Crane, R. (2009). *Mindfulness-Based Cognitive Therapy: Distinctive Features.* New York: Routledge.

Denton, R. B., & Sears, R. (2009). The clinical uses of mindfulness. In J. B. Erikson, E. H. (1968). *Identity: Youth and Crisis.* New York: Norton.

Erisman, S. M., & Roemer, L. (2010). A preliminary investigation of the effects of experimentally-induced mindfulness on emotional responding to film clips. *Emotion, 10 (1),* 72-82.

Fisher, P. & Wells, A. (2009). *Metacognitive Therapy: The CBT Distinctive Features Series.* New York: Routledge.

Foley, E., Baillie, A., Huxter, M., Price, M. & Sinclair, E. (2010). Mindfulness-based cognitive therapy for individuals whose lives have been affected by cancer: A randomized controlled trial. *Journal of Consulting and Clinical Psychology, 78 (1),* 72-79.

Foley, E. & Renner, P. (2012). Acceptance based therapies for students: An exploration of MBCT and ACT for the treatment of distress. Manuscript in preparation.

Forman, E. M., Herbert, J. D., Moitra, E., Yeomans, P. D., & Geller, P. A. (2007). A randomized controlled effectiveness trial of acceptance and commitment therapy and cognitive therapy for anxiety and depression. *Behavior Modification, 31,* 772-799.

Frewen, P. A, Evans, E. M., Maraj, N., Dozois, D. J. A., & Partridge, K. (2008). Letting Go: Mindfulness and Negative Automatic Thinking. *Cognitive Therapy and Research. 32 (6)*, 758-774.

Gross, J. J. (2002). Emotion regulation: Affective, cognitive, and social consequences. *Psychophysiology, 39*, 281–291.

Harris, R. (2009). *ACT Made Simple: An Easy-to-Read Primer on Acceptance and Commitment Therapy.* Oakland, CA: New Harbinger Publications, Inc..

Hayes, S. C., & Smith, S. (2005). *Get out of your mind and into your life.* Oakland, CA: New Harbinger.

Hayes, S. C., Strosahl, K. D., & Wilson, K. G. (2011). *Acceptance and Commitment Therapy: The process and practice of mindful change.* New York: Guilford Press.

Hofmann, S. G., Sawyer, A. T., Witt, A. A., & Oh, D. (2010). The effect of mindfulness-based therapy on anxiety and depression: A meta-analytic review. *Journal of Consulting and Clinical Psychology, 78 (2)*, 169-183.

Jain, S., Shapiro, S. L., Swanick, S., Roesch, S. C., Mills, P. J., Bell, I., & Schwartz, G. (2007). Randomized controlled trial of mindfulness meditation versus relaxation training: Effects on distress, positive states of mind, rumination, and distraction, *Annals of Behavioral Medicine, 33 (1)*, 11-21.

John, O. P., & Gross, J. J. (2004). Healthy and unhealthy emotion regulation: Personality processes, individual differences, and life span development. *Journal of Personality, 72*, 1301–1333.

Kabat-Zinn, J. (1990). *Full catastrophe living: Using the wisdom of your body and mind to face stress, pain, and illness.* New York: Dell.

Kabat-Zinn, J. (2002 Winter). At home in our bodies. *Tricycle Magazine*, 34-36.

Keng, S. L., Smoski, M. J., & Robins, C. J. (2011). Effects of mindfulness on psychological health: A review of empirical studies. *Clinical Psychology Review, 31*, 1041–1056.

Ma, S. H., & Teasdale, J. D. (2004). Mindfulness-based cognitive therapy for depression: Replication and exploration of differential relapse prevention effects. *Journal of Consulting and Clinical Psychology, 72*, 31–40.

McCarthy, J. J. (2011). Exploring the relationship between goal achievement orientation and mindfulness in collegiate athletics. *Journal of Clinical Sport Psychology, 5 (1)*, 44-57.

Oman, D., Shapiro, S. L., Thoresen, C. E., Plante, T. G. & Flinders, T. (2008). Meditation Lowers Stress and Supports Forgiveness among College Students: A Randomized Controlled Trial. *Journal of American College Health, 56 (5)*, 569-578.

Pryor, J., Hurtado, S., DeAngelo, L., Palucki-Blake, L., & Tran, S. (2010). *The American freshman: National norms fall 2010.* Los Angeles: Higher Education Research Institute, UCLA.

Ruiz, F. J. (2010). A review of Acceptance and Commitment Therapy (ACT) empirical evidence: Correlational, experimental psychopathology, component and outcome studies. *International Journal of Psychology and Psychological Therapy, 10*, 125-162.

Segal, Z. V., Williams, J. M. G., & Teasdale, J. D. (2002). *Mindfulness-based cognitive therapy for depression: A new approach to preventing relapse.* New York: Guilford Press.

Shapiro, S. L., Carlson, L. E., Astin, J. A., & Freedman, B. (2006). Mechanisms of mindfulness. *Journal of Clinical Psychology, 62,* 373-386.

Sheldon, K. M., & Kasser, T. (2001). Goals, congruence, and positive well-being: New empirical validation for humanistic ideas. *Journal of Humanistic Psychology, 41,* 30-50.

Strosahl, K. D., Hayes, S. C., Wilson, K. G., & Gifford, E. V. (2004). An ACT primer: Core therapy processes, intervention strategies, and therapist competencies. In S. C. Hayes & K. D. Strosahl (Eds). *A practical guide to acceptance and commitment therapy* (pp. 21-58). New York: Springer.

Teasdale, J. D., Segal, Z. V., Williams, J. M. G., Ridgeway, V. A., Soulsby, J. M., & Lau, M. A. (2000). Prevention of relapse/recurrence in major depression by mindfulness-based cognitive therapy. *Journal of Consulting and Clinical Psychology, 68,* 615–623.

Twenge, J. M., Gentile, B., DeWall, C. N., Ma, D., Lacefield, K., & Schurtz, D. R. (2010). Birth cohort increases in psychopathology among young Americans, 1938-2007: A cross-temporal meta-analysis of the MMPI. *Clinical Psychology Review, 30,* 145-154.

Vivekananda, K., Telley, A., & Trethowan, S. (2011). A five-year study on psychological distress within a university counselling population. *Journal of the Australian and New Zealand Student Services Association, 37,* 39-57.

Vygotsky, L. (1978). *Mind in society: The development of higher psychological processes.* Cambridge, MA: Harvard University Press.

Wilson, K. G. & DuFrene, T. (2008). *Mindfulness for Two: An Acceptance and Commitment Therapy Approach to Mindfulness in Psychotherapy.* Oakland, CA: New Harbinger.

CHAPTER 6

Mindfulness-Based Stress Reduction (MBSR) with College Students

Michael C. Murphy, PhD

University of Florida Counseling and Wellness Center

David walked into the college counseling center (CCC) complaining that he can't sleep and that this is leading to considerable anxiety regarding his ability to do his academic work. He claims to be exhausted most of the time, has little motivation to study, and when he does study, he reports an inability to concentrate. He says he is spending a great deal of time on the web, e-mailing, and texting. Additionally, he told the counselor that he feels anxious for no reason most of the time and "sort of" depressed.

Liza was referred to the CCC by Tutoring. She says that recently her test anxiety has gotten so bad that she either "blanks out" when she is taking a test or is so anxious that she is unable to study.

Both of these students were referred to the center's Mindfulness-Based Stress Reduction group and illustrate some presenting issues that can be addressed in this type of group.

Mindfulness Meditation as a Treatment Modality: Background

Over the past thirty years, there has been a rapidly increasing body of literature demonstrating the effectiveness of meditation on physical and psychological health (e.g., Hoffman, Sawyer, Witt, and Oh, 2010). Mindfulness meditation, a specific form of meditation, has been shown to be particularly promising (e.g., Kabat-Zinn, 1984, 1990, 2003; Kabat-Zinn, Lipworth, Burney, & Sellers, 1987; Khalsa and Stauth, 2002).

Mindfulness meditation is a simple yet profound practice. Although there are many different schools of thought and practice in terms of mindfulness, Kabat-Zinn has defined mindfulness as "the awareness that emerges through paying attention on purpose, in the present moment, and nonjudgmentally to the unfolding of experience moment-to-moment" (Kabat-Zinn, 2003, p. 145). It is based on the premise of cultivating a mind-state that is focused in the present moment in a nonjudgmental way (Kabat-Zinn, 1990). In the beginning of mindfulness meditation, people are taught to focus on the rising and falling of their breath, and to bring their attention back to the breath anytime they notice that their mind has wandered. After some time with this practice, the focus of meditation widens to include awareness of sound, smell, touch, and movement. Later the focus expands to include awareness of all that is happening in the present moment. In this way, people learn to focus on what is happening now rather than worrying about what happened in the past or what will/might happen in the future. Being fully present in each moment in a nonjudgmental way, accepting what is, is the focus of the practice. Ultimately, the practice of mindfulness allows us to interact with the world in a more balanced, efficient and aware manner.

8-Week MBSR Group at a CCC

This chapter describes a mindfulness meditation group program at the University of Florida Counseling Center that treats students dealing primarily with anxiety-related, but also other, issues. The group, described below in detail, is based on the MBSR program developed by Dr. Jon Kabat-Zinn (1990). The group, advertised to college students as "Taming Your Anxious Mind," was initiated twelve years ago and has run every semester since it was first offered (Murphy, 2006). Its popularity has soared. Whereas in the beginning we had to vigorously advertise and recruit group members, now we have to offer multiple groups per semester and they fill quickly and easily via within-center clinician referrals. The group meets for 1.5 hours every week for eight consecutive weeks. Students are referred to the group by CCC clinicians or self-referred from group advertisements on the CCC's website or in the university newspaper. Group size hovers around 10-12 students per group.

Pre-Group Considerations

The group is run in a group therapy room at our CCC. There are no special needs facility-wise for this group: The space does not need to be especially quiet or soundproof; nor does it need to be away from center traffic. Learning to meditate amidst the "distractions" of life is essential to the effectiveness of this training, and therefore, welcomed rather than avoided.

SCREENING INTERVIEW

Each student who is referred to the group goes through an individual pre-group screening interview with one of the group leaders. In the early years of the group, this pre-group screening session was not always conducted, but after analyzing group dropout patterns we decided to *require* the screening in order to select more appropriate members, screen out inappropriate members, and prepare the student for the group. This practice has resulted in dramatically decreased dropout rates and improved treatment outcomes. We now strongly recommend this facet of the program.

Each screening interview lasts thirty minutes. In the interview, we assess whether the client's psychological issue is appropriate for this treatment modality and make referrals if that is not the case. We often have clients who are in both individual counseling and the group (e.g., eating disorder, sexual abuse, panic disorders, and so on). We also assess for degree of disturbance in order to avoid enrolling students who might require more time than the group can provide (e.g., students who are in crisis or suicidal). The mindfulness group is not a "counseling" group, but rather a "skills" group; hence we do not spend time in the group talking about individual psychological issues. If a client needs that individual time, we use individual counseling to complement the group treatment. We also carefully assess for any contraindications for meditation practice—e.g., someone who tends to dissociate—and we refer this student to a more appropriate treatment modality. Most importantly, we assess potential group members' motivation for the group: their openness to the idea of mindfulness meditation, their willingness to attend *each and every* group session, and their willingness to practice the meditation techniques daily. If a student cannot commit to attending each and every session *and* to practicing the meditation techniques every day, we screen that person out of the group, telling her that she can be in the group in a later semester when she can commit to these two requirements. Though it is tempting for group leaders to not have such stringent screening requirements, we have found that enforcing these requirements has dramatically reduced dropout rates and increased the chances that members will experience positive gains from the group. In the pre-group screening interview, we also educate clients about the format and content of the group and how it can be appropriate for their psychological issues. In essence, once we determine that the person is appropriate for the group, we begin "treatment" even during the screening process. This prepares them for the group meetings. We have found that most any psychological issue can be treated effectively in this group, either by group treatment alone or by the combination of group and individual treatment. Communication between individual and group counselors is important to enhance treatment outcomes.

If, during the course of the group, we find that a client is not appropriate (e.g., a trauma survivor who experiences intense flashbacks during meditation), we will meet with this member and make the appropriate referral to individual counseling. With careful screening, the occurrence of such an event is rare. However, it does occur occasionally, and group leaders should be prepared to recognize the problem and deal with it immediately.

GROUP FACILITATORS

Who can lead a mindfulness meditation group? In our experience we have found that unless the leader (1) has been trained in mindfulness meditation, and (2) is actively practicing mindfulness meditation in her own life, she *will not* be an effective leader for this group. Hence at our center we require leaders to meet these two requirements. With center clinicians or trainees at our center (practicum students or interns) who want to learn how to lead this type of group, we use an apprenticeship model. We ask that they first experience the group as a member (for one semester), and then move into a "junior co-leader" role the second semester. We also require that they develop their own daily meditation practice. After they have satisfied these three requirements, they are then "qualified" to lead a mindfulness-based group. Though this training is rather extensive, we have found that it leads to more effective leaders.

Session Content

The following is a description of the content of the weekly sessions.

Session 1

In session 1, the leader introduces herself and then asks members to introduce themselves. In introducing themselves, group members are asked to say their name, what they are studying, and a few words about the psychological issue that has caused them to join the group. We do not encourage them to go into detail about their reason for joining, but we do comment on how the members can benefit from the group in relation to their presenting issues. We also "build bridges" between students by commenting on how different members have similar presenting issues and how mindfulness meditation can be effective in addressing these particular issues. We discuss with the group that this is not a "counseling" group but rather a skill-based group and that we will not use group time to delve into their specific personal/life issues, explaining that delving into these issues reduces needed time to learn the mindfulness skills. We have also found that the skills themselves often address

123

psychological issues, without having to ever get into the actual content. This, in fact, is a hallmark of mindfulness training—that it focuses on *how* the mind works rather than on *what* we think about. We remind students that we will refer them to individual counseling (in addition to the group) if that seems to be appropriate.

The format of the group is then discussed, with the leader reinforcing that this is an 8-week commitment and that members must (1) attend each and every session, and (2) practice the meditation techniques every day. We have found that this commitment is perhaps the most important factor in determining success for group members; hence we stress it at the pre-group screening interview, as discussed above, and in each and every group meeting.

All members are given a workbook which includes (1) home practice assignments for the week related to what was taught in that week's meeting, (2) a short (1-2 page) informative/inspirational reading which they are to read prior to meditating each day—taken from various meditation books, (3) an overview of the 8-session group, (4) a log form to record the time and place of their home meditation practice, (5) a form to record their reactions to each home practice session, and (6) a journal entry form where they are to reflect on how their meditation practice went each week.

Members are then led in the traditional "Eating a Raisin" exercise, in which the principles of mindfulness meditation (e.g., paying attention to small details of taste, smell, texture) are experienced in the eating of a raisin. This is followed by a ten-minute mindfulness meditation exercise where members focus on the rising and falling of their breath, and are instructed to bring their attention back to the breath each time they notice that their minds have wandered off of the breath. We then process their reactions to these exercises and give an explanation of what mindfulness meditation is and is not. For example, when doing mindfulness meditation, we tell them that in mindfulness meditation it is common and normal for the mind to wander and be distracted. Members often see this wandering as proof that they are doing it "wrong." We remind them that with mindfulness meditation the purpose is not to have a mind that never wanders, but rather to be able to recognize when the mind wanders and then bring it back to the present moment. We also emphasize that we initially focus on bringing our attention back to the breath because the breath is a tether line to the present moment. We also emphasize that mindfulness meditation is not about "blissing out" and "feeling good"; rather, it is about living in the present moment and experiencing the present moment with increasing clarity and vividness.

The first session ends with (1) a description of the 8-week program, (2) a discussion of the format of the group, and (3) handing out and explaining the "home practice" for the week. The home practice for the first week includes: (1) doing a 5-minute sitting meditation practice session each and every day, (2) recording time, place and reaction to each session, (3) eating one "mindful meal" where the focus of the meal is on the present moment of each bite—and noticing when their mind has wandered and bringing the attention back to the eating, and (4) stopping and doing a 30-second "mindfulness break" once or twice each day— where the student stops whatever she is doing, closes her eyes, and focuses on her breathing for 30 seconds.

Sessions 2 through 8, described below, have basically the same general format: (1) each session begins with a practice of the meditation technique assigned as homework the previous week, (2) a processing of the home practice—which includes the leaders using members' experiences and reactions as a way to teach the principles of what mindfulness meditation is and how it works, (3) an exercise to teach a mindfulness principle (e.g., why we focus on the breath when we meditate) or mindfulness technique (e.g., walking meditation), (4) another period of mindfulness meditation practice, and (5) going over the home practice for that week.

What follows are some specific topics and exercises/practices that are incorporated into sessions 2 through 8:

Session Two

1. Conduct opening exercise: Conduct body scan meditation (15-30 minutes) focusing on sensations in the body rather than bringing the attention back to the breath. In this exercise, students close their eyes and then focus on different parts of the body (e.g., stomach, jaw, foot). While focusing on the body part, they are asked to pay very close attention to any sensations that they feel in that body part (e.g., hot/cold, tingling, tightness). They are instructed to *not* try to change the sensation, but simply

to "accept" it and to observe it with curiosity and close attention. The emphasis on the body gives members another concrete element to focus on that will bring them back to the present moment. It also serves to emphasize "acceptance"—accepting whatever sensation you are having in that part of your body without trying to change it. This acceptance is a core principle of mindfulness meditation.

2. Review and process homework: Time is taken in this session to reiterate that there are no "failures" in meditation (e.g., your mind wandering) and that "success" comes from simply performing the meditation each day.

3. Teach a principle of the day: the importance of the breath in meditation (as previously described).

4. Conduct a mid-session exercise: e.g., a 5 to 10 minute period of sitting/breath meditation.

5. Answer questions about meditation, home practice, and so on.

6. Assign home practice for the week: (1) Do the body scan meditation every other day, alternating with sitting/breath meditation; (2) do sitting meditation every other day, alternating with body scan meditation; (3) do a 30-second "mindfulness break" two times each day; (4) be mindful when doing one "routine" activity (e.g., brushing teeth); and (5) record the time and place of each daily meditation session, reactions to each session, and reflections on this week's meditation practice. During this first discussion of home practice, we emphasize that finding a *place* to meditate often presents some obstacles for college students given that some roommates may be noisy and/or intrusive. We suggest finding a comfortable place to meditate and going to that same place each time they meditate. We also emphasize trying to develop a regular *time* to meditate. Both of these patterns reinforce the practice and make it more likely that students will actually do the meditation. Likewise, we emphasize that it is *not* necessary to have a completely quiet place in order to meditate. We discuss how to deal with distractions (e.g., phone ringing, roommate playing music, sounds down the hall) by making

these distractions part of the meditation practice (e.g., "notice the phone ringing and then come back to your breath"). This approach begins to teach the concept that *anywhere or anytime* can be an opportunity to practice meditation and that one doesn't need "special circumstances" to do mindfulness meditation.

Session 3

1. Review/process home practice: Discuss challenges with meditation practice (e.g., where to practice, noise) and reinforce "just doing it" (rather than requiring it to be a "good/successful" meditation).

2. Conduct opening exercise: Lead group in body scan meditation (20-30 minutes), emphasizing attention to body awareness and using the body (instead the breath) as the "tether line to the present moment."

3. Introduce new mindfulness concepts (during processing/reviewing of home practice): "being" vs. "doing"; the need to "be productive" and do multiple tasks, and how these are obstacles to being in the present moment. David, the student we introduced at the beginning of the chapter, for example, struggled with this issue, feeling pulled to multi-tasking instead of focusing on just one thing. The following is an excerpt from a group interaction between the facilitator and David:

Counselor: David, what is it like to focus on just one thing, for example the breath, and to not let your mind just wander all over the place?

David: It's hard. My mind seems to just wander all the time, like I'm in class and I start thinking about what I'm going to post on Facebook, and it seems impossible to keep it focused on one thing, like what the teacher is saying.

Counselor: I know it's hard...very hard. This is not a skill that you will learn overnight. It's a skill that you need to practice daily, like lifting weights or working out. Or like learning to play the piano. The more you practice or "work out," the better you get. But it doesn't happen all at once. The learning is incremental, almost not noticeable at first. But, in fact, you are developing the skill to focus each and every time you notice that your mind has wandered and you bring it back to the breath, the present moment. Noticing the breath is a way to practice the skill, but you can use that same skill to be present in your classes, when listening to your girlfriend, or when studying for a test.

4. Lead exercise: sitting meditation (10 minutes).

5. Assign and discuss home practice: (1) Meditate daily for 5-10 minutes alternating focus on breath and focus on body; (2) experiment with "mindful driving" (of car or bike); (3) experiment with walking from one class to another while practicing mindfulness and being in the present moment.

Session 4

1. Lead sitting meditation exercise (10 minutes)

2. Review and process home practice while emphasizing and reinforcing mindfulness concepts.

3. Introduce new mindfulness concept (during home practice discussion): the importance of "not judging" in cultivating mindfulness, happiness, and contentment. Liza, the student we introduced at the beginning of the chapter, for example, struggled with judgments in the context of her test anxiety. The following excerpt is from a group interaction between the facilitator and Liza:

Counselor: Liza, what's it like to try and not judge yourself when your mind wanders or you get distracted when you meditate?

Liza: Well, I find that I am *constantly* judging myself. My mind is always saying things like "you should be better at this,"or "what's wrong with you, your mind shouldn't wander like this." I feel like a failure when I meditate.

Counselor: I want you to know that these thoughts and feelings are very common when we first start to meditate, especially for people who are very hard on themselves. Many of us find that we have a "little voice in our head" that is very self-critical. In mindfulness practice I want you to try to just notice this "voice" every time it comes up. Don't try to change it. Just notice it (e.g., "Oh, there is that voice again") and then return your attention to your breath. Try to not judge when this voice pops up. Just notice it without judgment and then come back to your breath.

Liza: ·   But that's so hard! The voice is constant.

Counselor: I know it's hard. I really do. But what you will find is that with practice that voice will lose its power over you. You will begin to notice that it is "only a thought." You will learn to not judge yourself so harshly. And this self-judgment is at the root of most anxiety—especially test anxiety.

4. Lead exercise in walking meditation (20-30 minutes): Introduce walking meditation and then have group members go outside and practice. Discuss reactions to the exercise. In walking meditation members are instructed to walk very slowly, in silence, and notice the movements of the body (e.g., the lifting and placing of the foot) in a very precise way. In walking meditation you are not "going" anywhere; you are simply noticing what it is like to move. This focus on body movement now becomes your "tether line to the present moment"—instead of the breath or the body. And whenever your mind wanders off of the walking, you simply notice that it's wandered and bring your attention back to your walking. Walking meditation is a very powerful technique and one that college students really enjoy. The pace of the walking should be very slow and deliberate so that each movement can be noticed and examined.

5. Lead exercise in sitting meditation (focus on breath or sounds or body)—10 minutes.

6. Assign home practice for the week: (1) Do sitting or walking meditation (breath or body) for 10 minutes each day; (2) practice "non-judgment" once each day when in public arena (e.g., on the bus, walking across campus); (3) do one act of "generosity" this week.

Session 5

1. Lead sitting meditation exercise (10-15 minutes).

2. Discuss home practice. In addition to doing sitting and/or walking meditation, the homework for the past week included doing "one act of generosity." This exercise is usually very powerful for group members. The intention of the exercise is to "get outside of oneself—one's "little ego"—and to practice "giving" rather than "taking." Students report various interesting acts that they have done (e.g., taking a gift to a friend, helping someone who is struggling with groceries) and they often report that this act of generosity is very powerful for them—that "giving" instead of "taking" is more satisfying than they ever imagined. This act of "getting outside of oneself" is at the core of mindfulness meditation. Doing this allows us to develop a larger perspective—a perspective that is beyond our focusing on what *we* want or think *we* deserve. It encourages people to see how focusing on something other than "what I want" makes them feel more content.

3. Introduce new mindfulness concepts during meditation exercise and home practice discussion: Emphasize that meditation is like "training a puppy"—be gentle but firm, be consistent in bringing the mind back to the present moment, over and over and over again. Also we emphasize how mindfulness meditation develops the power of attention and a grateful heart.

4. Lead sitting meditation exercise (10-15 minutes) with focus on body awareness or awareness of sounds.

5. Conduct exercise (20-30 minutes): Have students go outside, find a busy place on campus to sit, and just "observe without judgment." This exercise emphasizes the use of mindfulness meditation in daily life—of being curious about what is happening in the world, and bringing your mind back to "just observing" anytime the mind wanders. This exercise is very powerful in demonstrating to students the practical application of mindfulness meditation to daily life.

6. Assign homework: (1) Do sitting meditation for 20 minutes each day; (2) do one small act of generosity each day; (3) have one period of "no judgment" this week; (4) do one meditation period outside this week.

Session 6

1. Lead exercise in sitting meditation (10-15 minutes) with focus on breath, body, sounds.

2. Process home practice and introduce new mindfulness concept: the physical/medical and psychological benefits of mindfulness. In this session we present research evidence regarding the positive impact of meditation on various psychological (e.g., anxiety, panic, eating disorders, trauma, and so on) and medical conditions (e.g., headaches, irritable bowel syndrome, high blood pressure, and so on). This evidence always seems to impress the group members. At this point they often comment on how the mindfulness meditation has changed their lives either psychologically or medically.

3. Lead exercise in walking meditation (20-30 minutes).

4. Assign and discuss home practice: (1) Do sitting meditation each day (10-15 minutes); (2) this week see if you can be aware of "your first thought upon waking up."

Session 7

1. Lead exercise in sitting meditation (20 minutes).

2. Process home practice and introduce new concept: how mindfulness meditation naturally cultivates the "arising of wisdom and compassion." This concept introduces another core concept of mindfulness meditation; that is, that when you do regular practice you *naturally*, without effort, develop compassion and wisdom. Members often report that they have indeed noticed this in their lives; for example, feeling less judgmental of their partner or their parents. They also report that they seem to have a larger perspective on life—an example of a kind of wisdom. Liza, for example, reported more compassion for herself, which resulted in less perfectionism and self-criticism—and ultimately, less anxiety. She also reported that she can now see that her exams are not as important as she had always thought they were—that there is more to life than getting As (an example of "wisdom").

3. Exercise: Go outside and practice sitting meditation in a public place.

4. Assign home practice: (1) Do sitting meditation every day (15-20 minutes), (2) see if you can be aware of when something happens that you "don't like" (e.g., a comment from a roommate or a poor grade), watch your attachment to "getting what you want," and see if you can let go of that need.

Session 8

1. Lead exercise in sitting meditation (20 minutes).

2. Process home practice and introduce new concept: how to continue your mindfulness practice once group is over. Member feedback (and research) supports the notion that continuing the daily meditation practice is very difficult once the group is over. In this last session we discuss ways to increase the chances that

members will continue to practice mindfulness meditation and mindful living. Some of the suggestions for continuing the practice are: finding a meditation group in the community and attending regularly, or finding a meditation "buddy"—someone who will hold you accountable and encourage you to meditate, read books and articles on mindfulness meditation, and attend meditation retreats. Facilitators also offer to meet with group members individually if they need help continuing, or re-starting, their practice.

3. Review what was covered in the group.

4. Ask students about changes they have experienced as a result of their practicing mindfulness and mindfulness meditation.

5. Conduct a closing meditation exercise emphasizing what they have learned in the group and the need to continue practicing mindfulness. Facilitators do a meditation/guided imagery exercise where, once students have closed their eyes and gotten into a meditative state, facilitators review what they have learned in the group, affirm all the positive changes they have made, affirm their commitment to continuing to practice mindfulness meditation and mindful living, and encourage them to continue their commitment to being more compassionate with themselves and with others.

6. Have members fill out a group feedback form asking about the strengths and weaknesses of the group.

Empirical Considerations

MBSR has been applied with a range of issues, including chronic physical pain, illnesses such as cancer, mental illnesses, including anxiety and depression, and non-clinical issues, such as stress and burnout (cf. de Vibe, Bjørndal, Tipton, Hammerstrøm, & Kowalski, 2012). There have been a number of recent meta-analyses of studies on MBSR and other mindfulness-based interventions A recent meta-analysis of 31 randomized controlled trials of MBSR (exclusively) showed medium effect sizes for anxiety, depression, stress, mindfulness, quality of life, and personal development, and a small effect size for somatic health (de Vibe et al., 2012). Other reviews showed that mindfulness-based approaches such as MBSR and Mindfulness-Based Cognitive Therapy (MBCT) were effective in reducing anxiety and depression (Fjorback, Arendt, Ørnbøl, Fink, & Walach, 2011; Hofmann, Sawyer, Witt, & Oh, 2010), that integrating MBSR in behavior therapy may enhance the efficacy of mindfulness-based interventions (Bohlmeijer, Prenger, Taal, & Cuijpers, 2010), and that MBSR is effective with non-clinical populations as well, in terms of showing a non-specific effect in reduction in stress, ruminative thinking, and trait anxiety, as well as an increase in empathy and self-compassion (Chiesa & Serretti, 2009). Another meta-analysis found that MBSR may indeed be helpful for the mental health of cancer patients; however, more research is needed to show convincing evidence for an effect on physical health per se (Ledesma & Kumano, 2009).

Although many MBSR trials have included college students as participants, we are only aware of one study that tested the application of MBSR in a randomized control trial specifically with a college student sample. In that study (Oman, Shapiro, Thoresen, Plante, & Flinders, 2008), college undergraduates were randomly assigned to an 8-week, 90 minute/week training in MBSR, to another type of meditation program, or to a no-treatment waitlist. Data were collected at posttest and at 8-week follow-up. Results showed that relative to those on the waitlist, students who received training in MBSR or the other meditation program experienced significant benefits for stress and forgiveness, with marginal benefits for rumination.

MBSR appears to be acceptable and effective with college students. The program described in this chapter resembles the one evaluated in the randomized controlled trial described above that showed positive findings (Oman et. al., 2008). Additionally, our experience conducting MBSR groups at a CCC for a number of years is that student members' reactions to the group have been very positive. Members' subjective reports suggest that the experiential exercises and home practice are helpful in getting the concepts of mindfulness meditation across. Anecdotal reports from members suggest changes in their lives, including: (1) decreased levels of general anxiety, performance anxiety, test anxiety, social anxiety, (2) improvements in relationship, both romantic ones and friendships, (3) an increase in feelings of contentment and happiness with life, (4) decreased need for control in daily life (e.g., over a boyfriend's behavior), (5) improved sleep, (6) decreases in headaches and/or muscle pain, (7) enhanced ability to study and do academic tasks (e.g., study, write papers).

In the future, it would be helpful to conduct research related to the success of MBSR groups with college students, particularly studying the impact of such a group on college student-specific presentations, such as test anxiety. Likewise, research examining what mindfulness techniques are most effective with this population would provide valuable information.

Final Words

There are a few issues to consider before running an MBSR group with college students. Not all college students can successfully learn, let alone benefit from, mindfulness meditation. Two of the biggest obstacles to group members learning mindfulness are (1) members failing to do the home practice, and (2) members missing group sessions. We believe that the key to learning mindfulness is the consistent, daily practice, and the attending of every group session. Indeed, a recent study found that between-session practice over the course of eight weeks of mindfulness-based relapse prevention was predictive of mindfulness at post-treatment (although not at follow-up) (Bowen & Kurtz, 2012). The need for students to engage in group and regular mindfulness practice has led us to do a much more careful screening with students who want to be in the group. As noted above, we now meet with students interested in being in the group and screen for their level of motivation and commitment to attending all eight group sessions and to practicing daily. Any potential member who has any doubt about whether or not she can commit at this level is screened out of the group. This policy has led to a much lower dropout rate, thus increasing group cohesion and motivation. This screening approach has decreased the dropout rate from 30-40% to less than 10%.

Group facilitators' training and experience with mindfulness meditation matter. It is essential that therapists running MBSR groups be well-trained and have their own daily meditation practice. Our experience is that clinicians may become excited by the potential benefits of

MBSR and decide to offer this type of group without adequate training and/or without their own daily practice. With mindfulness meditation it is not just about the technique—it is also about the lived experience of the leader. Recent findings lend preliminary support to this position that therapists's training in mindfulness might enhance client outcomes (e.g., Grepmair et al., 2007).

Finally, although there is strong empirical support for MBSR in general (Kabat-Zinn, 2003) and some support for using it with college students specifically (Oman et al., 2008), there is still a great deal we don't know about the application of MBSR groups with college students. For example, we don't know which college students are more likely to benefit from an MBSR group, or if there are ways to increase students' motivation to engage in daily practice. We also don't know what impact participation in an MBSR group might have on academic performance per se. Therefore, future studies could investigate potential moderators of treatment effects in this population, as well as the potential impact on academic performance.

References

Bohlmeijer, E., Prenger, R., Taal, E., & Cuijpers, P. (2010) The effects of mindful-ness-based stress reduction therapy on mental health of adults with a chronic medical disease: A meta-analysis. *Journal of Psychosomatic Research*. 68(6), 539-544.

Bowen, S., & Kurtz, A. S. (2012). Between-session practice and therapeutic alliance as predictors of mindfulness after Mindfulness-Based Relapse Prevention, *Journal of Clinical Psychology*, 68(3), 236-245.

Chiesa, A., & Serretti, A., (2009). Mindfulness-based stress reduction for stress management in healthy people: A review and meta-analysis. The Journal of Alternative and Complementary Medicine, 15(5), 593-600.

de Vibe, M., Bjørndal, A., Tipton, E., Hammerstrøm, K.T., Kowalski, K. (2012). *Mindfulness-based stress reduction (MBSR) for improving health, quality of life and social functioning in adults*. Campbell Systematic Reviews: Oslo, Norway.

Fjorback, L. O., Arendt, M., Ørnbøl, E., Fink, P., & Walach, H. (2011). Mindfulness-Based Stress Reduction and Mindfulness-Based Cognitive Therapy—a sys-tematic review of randomized controlled trials. *Acta Psychiatrica Scandinavica*, 124, 102–119.

Grepmair, L., Mitterlehner, F., Loew, T., Bachler, E., Rother, W., & Nickel, M. (2007). Promoting mindfulness in psychotherapists in training influences the treatment results of their patients: A randomized, double-blind, controlled study. *Psychotherapy and Psychosomatics, 76*, 332, 338.

Hofmann, S., Sawyer, A., Witt, A., & Oh, D. (2010). The effect of mindfulness based therapy on anxiety and depression: A meta-analytic review. *Journal of Consulting and Clinical Psychology, 78(2)*, 169-183.

Kabat-Zinn, J. (1984). An outpatient program in behavioral medicine for chronic pain patients based on the practice of mindfulness meditation: Theoretical considerations and preliminary results. *General Hospital Psychiatry, 4*, 33-47.

Kabat-Zinn, J. (1990). *Full Catastrophe Living.* New York: Delta.

Kabat-Zinn, J. (2003). Mindfulness-Based Interventions in Context: Past, Present and Future. *Clinical Psychology: Science and Practice, 10(2)*.

Kabat-Zinn, J., Lipworth, L., Burney, R., & Sellers, W. (1987). Four-year follow-up of a meditation-based program for the self-regulation of chronic pain: Treatment, outcome and compliance. *Clinical Journal of Pain, 2*, 159-173.

Khalsa, D. S., & Stauth, C. (2002). *Meditation as Medicine.* New York: Fireside.

Ledesma, D., & Kumano, H., (2009) Mindfulness-based stress reduction and cancer: A meta-analysis. *Psycho-Oncology, 18(6)*, 571-579.

Murphy, M. (2006). Taming the Anxious Mind, *Journal of College Student Psychotherapy, 21(2)*, 5-13.

Oman, D., Shapiro, S. L., Thoresen, C. E., Plante, T. G., & Flinders. T. (2008). Meditation lowers stress and supports forgiveness among college students: A randomized controlled trial. *Journal of American College Health. 56(5)*. 569-578.

CHAPTER 7

Using Acceptance and Commitment Therapy (ACT) to Treat Perfectionism in College Students

Jesse M. Crosby

Utah State University, Department of Psychology

McLean Hospital/Harvard Medical School

Andrew B. Armstrong

Utah State University, Department of Psychology

University of Missouri-Columbia, Counseling Center

Mark A. Nafziger

Utah State University, Department of Psychology

Utah State University, Counseling and Psychological Services

Michael P. Twohig

Utah State University, Department of Psychology

J ohn is in his junior year of an engineering program. He is in the top of his class with a high grade point average, but he repeatedly complains of intense anxiety, stress, fatigue, and low self-esteem. Sarah is in her sophomore year in a graphic design program. Sarah is intelligent and motivated, but she is on academic probation for low grades and has lost an academic scholarship. She reports difficulties with late assignments, missed assignments, poor class attendance, and several failed classes. Surprisingly enough, both of these students are struggling with the same thing: perfectionism.

Perfectionism is a common problem among college student populations and is often part of treatment in college counseling centers (CCCs) as either a presenting problem or an underlying feature of a variety of other psychological problems. This chapter will review the nature of perfectionism with a focus on clinical presentations in college student populations, followed by a discussion of how to conceptualize perfectionism from an Acceptance and Commitment Therapy (ACT) perspective and a "how to" section with a session by session outline of how ACT can be applied to perfectionism. Empirical considerations for the application of ACT for perfectionism will be reviewed, followed by a few concluding comments on potential issues in applying ACT with perfectionism with college students. The information in this chapter comes from a review of the current empirical literature on both perfectionism and ACT, but also relies heavily on our clinical experience working with perfectionism and related issues in college student populations.

Defining Perfectionism

Perfectionism is generally defined by two criteria: 1) unreasonably high standards or expectations, and 2) excessive self-criticism when one fails to meet those standards (Burns, 1980). Perfectionistic thinking can be irrational and dysfunctional as evidenced by the perception of catastrophic outcomes when standards are not achieved. Performance is often evaluated by all-or-nothing criteria in which anything less than perfection is interpreted as failure, and there is persistent emotional and cognitive distress, best described as the "tyranny of the should" (Horney, 1950, p. 197).

Current research suggests perfectionism can be multidimensional. This includes excessively high standards; heightened levels of concern over mistakes; a sense of doubt about the quality of one's performance; concern over parents' expectations and evaluations; and an overemphasis on precision, order, and organization (Frost, Marten, Lahart, & Rosenblate, 1990). Perfectionism can be experienced as self-oriented (i.e., exacting standards and excessive critical evaluation of one's performance), other-oriented (i.e., exacting standards and excessive critical evaluation of others), and socially prescribed (i.e., the perception or experience of exacting standards and excessive criticism from others; Hewitt & Flett, 1991b).

Adaptive and maladaptive dimensions of perfectionism have also been identified (Stoeber & Otto, 2006). Adaptive perfectionism has been characterized as a healthy pursuit of excellence, quality work, accomplishment, and high standards that can be adjusted according to the circumstances; whereas maladaptive perfectionism has been defined as inflexible high standards, impossible expectations, persistent dissatisfaction with performance, and performance motivated by a fear of failure. This chapter will focus on the maladaptive presentation of perfectionism, although the adaptive dimension highlights the insidious nature of perfectionism where good intentions (e.g., a desire to achieve high academic standards) can take a pathological turn.

Perfectionism has been linked to a host of negative outcomes, including depression (Hewitt & Flett, 1991a), anxiety (Alden, Ryder, & Mellings, 2002), eating disorders (Goldner, Cockell, & Srikameswaran, 2002), obsessive-compulsive disorder (Frost & Steketee, 1997), and suicidal ideation (Hewitt, Flett, & Weber, 1994). In student populations, perfectionism has been linked to poor overall adjustment to college life (Rice & Dellwo, 2002), procrastination (Flett, Blankstein, Hewitt, & Koledin, 1992), low self-esteem and interpersonal difficulties among gifted students (Parker, 2002), greater psychological distress in medical, dental, pharmacy, and nursing students (Henning, Ey, & Shaw, 1998), depression and hopelessness in medical students (Enns, Cox, Sareen, & Freeman, 2001), and even suicide, particularly among minority students (Chang, 1998). In a diathesis stress model, socially prescribed perfectionism has been shown to interact with stress to influence overall psychological adjustment in college students (Chang & Rand, 2000).

Clinical Presentations of Perfectionism in College Students

Typical clinical presentations of perfectionism occur either as a primary presenting problem or as an underlying issue of another psychopathology. As a primary issue, individuals may present with perfectionistic cognitive/emotional distress, and/or perfectionistic problematic behaviors that may lead to poor performance. The distress may include feelings of anxiety, anger, or sadness associated with the irrational all-or-nothing cognitions. It is common to see symptoms of both anxiety and depression as a manifestation of the fear of failure coupled with the sense of hopelessness and low self-worth from the perception of poor performance. It is also common to see a presentation of the cognitive/emotional distress without any problematic behaviors. For example, as in the case of John from the introduction, a student may seek help because he feels "overwhelmed" or "stressed," stating that he feels that he is not doing well in school. Further assessment reveals that his grades are near perfect and he is managing his current course load, but he has been "pushing through" in an attempt to satisfy the high standards. The distress is typically a result of the immense amount of effort required to consistently meet these standards and/or the intense self-criticism because the performance is never "good enough."

When perfectionistic behaviors are present, it is also common to see a student who is performing well below her academic potential, as exemplified in the case of Sarah discussed at the beginning of the chapter. The poor performance may manifest in three different ways. First, a student may avoid class or assignments because of the pressure to be perfect or because she would rather receive no credit for an assignment than achieve something less than perfection. Second, a student may perform poorly because of procrastination. Because of the desire to perform perfectly (create the perfect set of flash cards, have perfect focus on reading a chapter), she may put the task off until she has time to really do it well only to end up cramming for an exam or rushing to complete an assignment, turning it in late, or not finishing it at all. Third, a student may "push through" trying to meet the high standards and tolerating the self-criticism, but eventually burn out because of intense cognitive, emotional, and physical distress. She may stop attending classes altogether or fall far behind on coursework resulting in low grades for the semester. In these cases, the student typically will regroup for the next semester and begin again with the perfect performance, only to burn out again as the semester progresses, and may present for services in a CCC after the first semester of burnout or after several semesters when her academic standing is in jeopardy. The great irony is that all of the attempts to achieve perfection typically result in performance that falls much further below the standards of perfection.

When perfectionism is an underlying issue of other psychopathology, it may be a central problem behind the symptoms, or it may be an auxiliary feature that makes addressing the primary symptoms difficult. In the case of the former, a student may present with clear symptoms of depression, but one of the central underlying issues is perfectionism. As an auxiliary feature, it may impede efforts to deal with adjustment issues from the transition to college life, or it may be a component of an eating disorder or obsessive compulsive disorder.

In all of these cases, whether as a presenting problem or an underlying issue, perfectionism may also be present in the treatment process. The unrealistic expectations and self-criticism may be manifest in how the student interacts with treatment goals, homework assignments, expectations of the therapist, and overall expectations for the therapy process. These problems can sometimes be interpreted as a lack of motivation or interest, or taking comments too literally, so it is important to watch for the presence of perfectionism and make it a target of treatment when merited.

Conceptualizing Perfectionism from an ACT Perspective

To understand perfectionism from an ACT perspective, it is important to first clarify the difference between internal experiences and behaviors. Internal experiences include thoughts, feelings, and physical sensations, all of which are manifest in the experience of perfectionism (e.g., all-or-nothing thinking accompanied by a fear of failure and the physical symptoms of anxiety such as muscle tension and a nervous stomach). These internal experiences are only experienced by the individual and are difficult, if not impossible, to control, and stand in contrast to overt behaviors that are generally observable and possible to control. Typical perfectionistic behaviors include excessive effort or time spent on a task, or the behavioral avoidance of working on tasks.

Psychological Inflexibility

The ACT construct of psychological inflexibility provides a clear conceptualization of perfectionism that addresses both internal experiences and behaviors. Psychological inflexibility refers to a rigid, literal, and inflexible style of responding to internal experiences (thoughts, feelings, and physical sensations) resulting in psychological distress and is often accompanied by problematic or avoidant behaviors (Hayes, Luoma, Bond, Masuda, & Lillis, 2006). The characteristics of inflexibility and rigidity are common in perfectionism. Perfectionistic standards are inflexible by definition, and perfectionists rigidly hold to those standards.

The idea of psychological inflexibility is central to a relatively new conceptual model of perfectionism that differentiates positive (adaptive) and negative (maladaptive) perfectionism based on how an individual interacts with high standards (Stoeber & Otto, 2006). Perfectionism is characterized by the presence of perfectionistic strivings (high standards) and positive and negative perfectionists are distinguished by their type and level of perfectionistic actions. Perfectionistic concerns are characterized by rigid and inflexible concern over mistakes, doubts about actions, evaluation of the discrepancy between achievement and standards, self-criticism, and a fear of failure. In this functional model, the flexible relationship between perfectionistic concerns and action exemplifies the idea of psychological inflexibility—that literal and rigid interaction with internal experience can, but does not have to, occur.

A functional approach to perfectionism differentiates adaptive and maladaptive perfectionism, suggesting that high standards are not inherently problematic (to be clear, there are some times when standards are clearly unreasonable); instead, it is the inflexible interaction with the high standards that is the problem. This is an important consideration for work with college students because of the nature of the academic environment in which the standards are high and competition can be fierce. Sometimes, the standards may be high but appropriate for the situation and the nature of the intervention is developing a flexible set of responses to the high standards and internal experiences that arise from falling short. In contrast to basic cognitive interventions in which the rationality of the standards is challenged, an ACT intervention would target the rigid response to the standards and the way the individual interacts with internal experiences. The student does not have to be asked to lower or change his standards, but instead, to evaluate his response to the standards.

The basic science behind ACT provides an explanation for how and why individuals can develop these patterns of inflexible interaction with internal experiences. Relational Frame Theory (RFT) forms the underlying basic science that leads to ACT as a therapeutic intervention (Hayes, Strosahl, & Wilson, 2011). RFT is a broad research program on human language and cognition, and the research suggests that because of the relational way in which learning language occurs, internal experiences, along with their verbal labels, can form complex relational networks that can assume meaning beyond the actual literal content of the thought or experience. To clarify this in the context of perfectionism, consider how irrational it is for a perfectionistic individual to take zero credit for an assignment as an alternative to a less than perfect performance. In this case, the thought, "anything less than perfect is a failure," is taken literally and thus makes no credit (failure) effectively equivalent to "anything less than perfect." If the thought, "anything less than perfect is a failure," is taken literally, then it makes sense that he would engage in such apparently irrational behavior, because in the literal world of internal experience, he is acting rationally. RFT explains how a thought can assume so much literal influence over behavior. Imagine the personal history of experiences, particularly emotional experiences, connected or related to this thought, "anything less than perfect is a failure." This thought, which may seem ridiculous to the clinician, may carry years of relational meaning that makes the content of the thought something that has to be addressed, so that in responding to this thought the student may be figuratively cowering in fear before a demanding parent. This literal interaction with internal experiences is referred to as cognitive fusion, in which an individual treats a stimulus (e.g., a thought) as though it is literal and true and must be followed, rather than treating the thought as just a thought (an example of defusion). Thus, certain private experiences have significantly more influence over behavior. The nature of this relational learning can then lead to rigid patterns of interaction with internal experiences that may result in psychopathology and maladaptive behaviors (Hayes et al., 2006).

Experiential Avoidance

The construct of psychological inflexibility provides a theoretical explanation for the role of internal experiences (thoughts, feelings, physical sensations) in perfectionism. To understand perfectionistic behaviors, another central idea from ACT, experiential avoidance provides important insight. In an ACT conceptualization, maladaptive perfectionistic behaviors function to control or avoid perfectionistic thoughts, feelings, and/or physical sensations. Experiential avoidance is apparent in the three types of perfectionistic behaviors discussed in the clinical presentations. In the case of avoiding academic tasks, the student may skip an assignment to avoid experiencing the thoughts, "I'm a failure," feelings of fear and sadness, and the physical manifestations of anxiety. When procrastination occurs, the student may put off an assignment to avoid the thought, "it isn't good enough," along with the accompanying anxiety and frustration. When a student "pushes through" and burns out trying to produce perfect work, he may be avoiding the fear of failure. In all of these situations, unwanted immediate internal experiences are exchanged for long-term consequences.

Experiential avoidance has an insidious nature, as it works well in the short term, but can ultimately make the struggle with these internal experiences worse. According to RFT, attempts to control internal experience will only create additional complex relationships, and the individual will become increasingly entangled in the content. For example, if an individual tries not to think about something, he will likely think of it more often as proposed in RFT and supported in the thought-control literature (Wenzlaff & Wegner, 2000). RFT also suggests that whatever the individual does to avoid or change the distressing thoughts will now be associated with the distressing thoughts (Hayes et al., 2011). Thus, in an attempt to control internal experiences, he may become more entangled with the content of his thoughts, resulting in maladaptive behaviors and neglecting important activities in his life.

The target of ACT for perfectionism is increasing psychological flexibility (Hayes et al., 2006). The intended outcome is to decrease problematic behaviors (maladaptive experiential avoidance) and increase adaptive behaviors more consistent with the values of the student such as engaging and successfully completing academic tasks. The focus of the intervention is on the willingness to experience whatever internal experiences may occur and shift the focus to behavior guided by values. As discussed in chapter 3, this is achieved by fostering six core processes: 1) *acceptance*, the active and willing experience of the problematic internal experiences that have been previously avoided, 2) *defusion*, the process of recognizing the literal function of cognitions instead of their derived cognitive relational functions, 3) *contact with the present moment*, the awareness of all of the internal experiences that are occurring without judgment, 4) *viewing the self as context*, the process of seeing the self as the arena in which internal experiences occur and not as defining qualities, 5) *values*, the direction in life that an individual chooses to follow that motivates and guides the choices he makes, and 6) *committed action*, an increase in patterns of behavior that are consistent with what the individual values in life.

ACT Treatment for Perfectionism

Using the conceptual foundation from this chapter, any ACT exercise, metaphor, or technique (see Hayes et al., 2011) can be adapted to treat perfectionism in a college student population. This section will provide an outline of ACT for perfectionism. Where standard ACT material is appropriate, only general references will be made, whereas material that has been specifically adapted or created for work with perfectionism will be presented in more detail. The order of presentation is generally appropriate and a 12-session outline is provided, but because ACT is a principle-based intervention, the order or number of sessions can easily be adjusted as needed.

Session 1: Establish Treatment Goals

Discussion about the pros and cons of perfectionism can introduce the need for treatment goals. As perfectionistic behaviors can be adaptive, the targets for treatment are not always immediately clear to the therapist or the client. This is a collaborative process and the therapist assumes a supportive posture to help the client identify personal treatment goals. Expect the goals to change as treatment progresses, but try to identify some concrete behavioral goals from the outset of treatment so that there is a clear goal, such as increasing the percentage of assignment completion or class attendance for someone struggling academically, or increasing the number of outside pleasurable activities for someone who is headed toward burnout. Additional treatment goals can be added as treatment progresses.

As discussed in the conceptual section in this chapter, make a clear distinction between internal experiences (i.e., thoughts, feelings, physical sensations) and overt behaviors. This can be done experientially by having the client describe an experience with perfectionism that was particularly difficult. Guide the discussion and point out the internal experiences. It can be helpful to choose a label that will generically refer to the variety of perfectionistic internal experiences that the client experiences (e.g., "shoulds"). The question of control can also be introduced here using the following exercise:

Therapist (T): Let's say that I will give you $100,000 if you are able to complete all of your assignments in the next week. Could you do it?

Client (C): I think so. I would definitely try.

T: Sounds good. Now, what if I told you that I would double your money if you could also make it through that week without experiencing any of the "shoulds" we talked about?

C: I think that's impossible.

This exercise reinforces the difference between internal experiences and overt behaviors, and also introduces the idea that one key distinction is control. Sometimes, instead of immediately recognizing that control of internal experience is impossible, a perfectionistic student may respond, "I know that other people can do that, and I should be able to, but I haven't figured it out yet." The counselor can respond to this by pointing out that he responded to a question about controlling the "shoulds" with one more "should," and point out how perfectionism can be part of the treatment process. Encourage the student to trust his experience (i.e.,

"Have you ever been able to totally control the 'shoulds?'"), and be skeptical of the "shoulds." For homework, ask the client to pay close attention to this process in his experiences between sessions.

Session 2: Creative Hopelessness

Ask the client to identify all of the strategies he has used to control or avoid the "shoulds." Write them down and once a good list has been created, ask the client to rate the short-term effectiveness of each strategy. Then, ask for a rating of the long-term effectiveness of each strategy. Ask if he would even be in therapy if the long-term strategies had been effective. Suggest that the perfectionistic behaviors should be on the list as well, as they are probably one of the primary strategies to control or avoid. Ask the client to identify the negative outcomes associated with perfectionistic actions, and then ask him to identify the negative outcomes associated with the "battle" with the "shoulds." Help the client see that this has been an ineffective battle, and that it may have resulted in negative outcomes in quality of life. Compare this struggle to trying to use a shovel to dig his way out of a hole ("Man in the Hole" metaphor, Hayes et al., 2011). It is helpful here to point out the persistent effort: that the client has continued to try despite repeated struggles, and the failures may not be because of a lack of effort or intellect, but simply due to using the wrong tool for the job. Ask the client if he is willing to "put down the shovel." Ask the client to think about and practice this idea between sessions.

Session 3: Control Is the Problem

The goal of this session is to help the client understand and experience the paradox of control over internal experiences, that the effort to control or avoid internal content is not only ineffective but typically results in an increase in the frequency and intensity of the internal experiences and greater difficulty in life in general. This can be accomplished using standard ACT interventions such as the "Chocolate Cake" exercise or "Polygraph" metaphor (see Hayes et al., 2011), while also reminding the student of his inability to stop "shoulds" from occurring in his head even if guaranteed $100,000. Encourage the client to identify and describe personal experiences in which this paradox occurred. This can all be tied together using the following discussion, which often resonates with perfectionistic thinking:

T: Do you participate in sports, art, music, or anything like that?

C: I play the piano.

T: How do you become a good piano player?

C: Practice. A lot of practice.

T: Right, the more effort you put into it, the better you become. You would expect then, that all your effort, or practice, to control the "shoulds" would get you somewhere. Are things getting easier?

C: No, much harder.

T: And it seems you try harder each year. It seems to be working the other way—the more you fight, the worse your problem becomes.

After the client feels the nature of the paradox of attempted internal control, introduce the idea of acceptance as an alternative: that it may work better to acknowledge the internal experiences and focus on behaviors that can occur independently of internal experience (e.g., turn in an assignment while experiencing the feeling of dread and the thought, "it isn't good enough"). This can be illustrated using the "Two Scales" metaphor (Hayes et al., 2011). Ask the client to practice this by identifying two or three concrete behavioral goals where he can practice accepting the inner experiences that show up (e.g., read a chapter in a limited amount of time, turn in an assignment, or prepare flash cards for a test). One can expect mixed success with this homework, as it can be difficult to behave independently of internal experiences. Difficulties with the idea of acceptance can be used to create a need for further material and introduce the importance of cognitive defusion.

Sessions 4-6: Cognitive Defusion

The "Tug-of-War with a Monster" metaphor (Hayes et al., 2011) provides a nice review of acceptance and introduces the idea of defusion. In the metaphor, letting go of the rope is compared to letting go of ineffective strategies to control one's inner experiences. This metaphor can resonate with clients with perfectionism because they often hold fast to the idea that if they just keep trying, they will eventually succeed and there is evidence for this because they have done it in other areas of life. This can be compared to the metaphor, where they do gain ground in the tug-of-war and there is hope that they may eventually win if they can just put together a consistent pattern of perfect "tugging." A client may say, "I struggle, but I just need to be more disciplined and then things will be okay," or, "I really want to live my life like this, I just need to be more consistent." A student may be reluctant to let go of the attempted internal control strategy for several reasons: 1) it may help him be productive, 2) his efforts are often reinforced by teachers, peers, and parents, and 3) it can be frightening to let go of something that provides a sense of structure (e.g., the metaphorical rope) because at least he has something to hold on to. Be sensitive to these fears, but point out the cost of the perfectionism and encourage him to take the risk of trying something new. As the client metaphorically tries to "let go of the rope," the idea of defusion can be introduced by asking him:

T: What have you been battling against in this tug-of-war anyway?

C: A monster. The "shoulds."

T: I wonder if you have been so busy fighting to hold your ground that you don't know much about what you are fighting against. I mean, what are the "shoulds," anyway? Maybe we can take a look at what they are.

Here, traditional defusion exercises (Hayes et al., 2011; see chapters 3 and 4 in this book for additional ideas) can be used to target cognitive fusion, including the limits of language, undermining verbal rules, and teaching nonjudgmental awareness. Verbal rules can be particularly strong with perfectionism and can provide good material for defusion work. Several verbal rules may be observed as concepts are introduced (e.g., "Oh, so if I do this acceptance thing, then I will finally be okay"). This can be undermined by being intentionally vague, ambiguous, or funny when the client is forming a rule, such as "Yes, I can 100% guarantee that anxiety may go down… (pause), or it may go up, or stay the same."

Sessions 7-8: Self as Context and Contact with the Present Moment

The "Passengers on the Bus" metaphor (Hayes et al., 2011), where internal experiences are related to passengers on a bus that influence the behavior of the driver (i.e., the student), can be both a defusion and a self-as-context intervention and provides a nice transition between the two processes. The idea that the student can define who he is by where he decides to drive the bus (i.e., what he does), independent of the passengers, is poignant for a perfectionistic student. Being in control is the primary objective of perfectionism. Many of the passengers on the student's bus have to do with the need to be perfect: "This is not A work;" "You need to work harder;" "It's better to not do the assignment than to turn in something mediocre;" anxiety when doing something fun or facing an assignment, and so on. To quiet these passengers down, the student may simply "comply" with the passengers and do as they say (i.e., work harder or stop working, going out or not going out with a friend, depending on the student). At other times, he may argue back with the passengers or try to get rid of them. The irony is that in his efforts to argue back ("But I always get As") or try to get the passengers (e.g., anxiety) off the bus, he has often stopped driving altogether and totally lost sight of who he wants to be. This can be an important moment in treatment as he can decide who he is, independent of the internal content, and he can define who he is by what he does instead. Standard self-as-context exercises (Hayes et al., 2011; see chapters 3 and 4 in this book) can be used to reinforce the process as needed.

Contact with the present moment work can occur in two ways. First, because the perfectionistic "shoulds" can become direct stumbling blocks in the treatment process, there are many opportunities to identify struggles with perfectionism in session, in the present moment. The therapist can point out experiential avoidance or cognitive defusion as they happen in the moment and guide the client through application of the acceptance and defusion interventions. This helps undermine a common occurrence with perfectionism, wherein a client will intellectually understand an idea and then think that he will have to practice it "when I get a chance" outside of the session, or "when I have time to really focus on it and maybe do some extra reading to make sure I really understand this." The "shoulds" are influencing the student in this scenario and the therapist can help him engage the present moment, just as it is, with what skills he has, as understood at that moment. Second, a perfectionistic client will often be preoccupied by thoughts about the future. Every experience is evaluated against a future-oriented perfectionistic ideal, not for what it is in the present moment. There is a sense of "waiting." You may notice language such as, "As soon as," or "If only I had." The client is so focused on what he wants to become that he loses sight of the only thing that can help achieve those goals—what he chooses to do in the present moment. Present-moment interventions will call attention to what the student's mind is doing at that very moment, such as "What is your mind saying or trying to do right now?" "Which passengers are showing up now as I say this?" "Where can you feel it in your body?" The purpose of these interventions is to help the student catch these unhelpful processes as they occur in the moment.

Sessions 9-10: Focus on Client Values

Values work with a perfectionistic client can proceed as in standard ACT interventions (Hayes et al., 2011). Values are defined as the overall direction(s) an individual would like to take in life. Reinforce the idea with the student that values are a choice, independent of internal experiences, and can serve to guide life goals as well as everyday decisions. A values clarification exercise can be used to identify personal values to provide direction now that the student is more in control of her life. This is a place for caution, as it is rare to find a perfectionistic student who has not spent time developing goals, personal mission statements, or any other similar personal organization tasks. Thus, the values work is fertile ground for application of all of the ACT skills as he has to practice acceptance of, and defusion from, the "shoulds" as he considers what he wants his life to be all about. With some clients, less structure is better when it comes to values work.

Sessions 11-12: Committed Action and Ending Treatment

Committed action can be addressed throughout treatment as you encourage the client to engage academic or personal tasks as part of homework to practice the other ACT skills. Try to develop a theme of "doing," "engaging," or "completing" throughout treatment, in contrast to the trap of experiential avoidance or excessive perfectionistic behaviors. A good metaphor to illustrate this theme is a comparison of engaging in perfectionist behaviors with a sports team that focuses all its efforts on playing defense and never takes the risks necessary to score points. Encourage the client to focus more on offense and taking risks in order to be more engaged in life.

At this point in treatment, the idea of acceptance can bring together all the ACT processes. The goal is for the client to recognize that if he can be accepting about who he is, what he experiences (internal experiences, in particular), and what he is capable of, then he can be free to become who he wants to be. He can live a life independent of internal experience. This can be presented using a metaphor that arose from our work with perfectionism.

T: Can you describe one of your favorite places in nature?

C: I like to hike in the mountains near where I grew up. When I am there, I feel a sense of peace and I am in awe of the beauty of nature.

T: How much order, straight lines, or symmetry is there in nature?

C: Not much, there seems to be a randomness to it all, but it is beautiful.

T: So it may not meet traditional standards of perfection, at least as you've been describing, but it is still beautiful. I would even go so far as to say that the "random" beauty of nature is more beautiful than the meticulously manicured, symmetrical gardens of any country estate.

C: Yeah, I would choose the mountains anytime.

T: When you are being perfectionistic in school, in your life, I have this image in my mind of you in the mountains trying to rearrange the rocks and replant the flowers to bring more organization and more symmetry to the landscape. I wonder if that is what you have been doing with school, with your family, with your life.

C: (Laughs.) Yeah.

T: Can you see how this is a choice? What if you chose to appreciate the world around you, and the world inside you, for what it is, and focus on living the best you can?

This metaphor can be used as a reminder when the client is getting stuck. For example, if he is focusing on the need to be perfect, you can ask, "What are you doing now…replanting the wildflowers?"

Empirical Considerations

Because perfectionism is often an underlying feature of a specific disorder or an overt behavioral problem (e.g., poor academic performance), it has received relatively little attention in the treatment literature compared to common Axis I disorders like major depressive disorder or generalized anxiety. However, the widespread impact of the problem (i.e., the association with negative outcomes and severe psychopathology) would suggest the need for a treatment that directly targets perfectionism. There are a handful of treatment studies looking at cognitive behavioral therapy for perfectionism (Kearns, Forbes, & Gardiner, 2007; Riley, Lee, & Cooper, 2007), but there is a clear need for treatment research that directly addresses perfectionism. It is hoped this chapter will contribute by providing a theoretical framework based on the current literature to initiate outcome work with ACT for perfectionism.

ACT has been shown to be an effective treatment for numerous functionally similar psychological problems in which experiential avoidance is an issue, including depression, substance abuse, and chronic pain (Hayes et al., 2006). Cognitive theory suggests that experiential avoidance is a common causal factor across the anxiety disorders (Olatunji, Forsyth, & Feldner, 2007), and this would support the use of a treatment that targets experiential avoidance. There is also an evidence base that ACT is effective with disorders often associated with perfectionism, such as depression (Zettle & Rains, 1989), generalized anxiety (Roemer, Orsillo, & Salters-Pedneault, 2008), and obsessive compulsive disorder (Twohig et al., 2010). There is evidence that the individual ACT processes are effective individually in producing the intended change, including acceptance (Eifert & Forsyth, 2003), defusion (Masuda, Hayes, Sackett, & Twohig, 2004), and values work (Dahl, Wilson, & Nilsson, 2004). Preliminary research has been conducted in a case study using the ACT approach described in this chapter and the initial findings show an increase in productivity, assignment completion, and class attendance, as well as decreased distress and improved overall quality of life (Crosby & Twohig, 2009).

Final Words

The intervention, as presented here, is adapted to traditional individual therapy, but the approach is also appropriate for other venues. For official clients of a CCC, the material can be presented in a traditional therapy group or even in a group that has a psychoeducational focus. Because many individuals struggling with this problem fall in the nonclinical range and may not see themselves as candidates for formal psychotherapy, we have had a lot of success (i.e., high attendance) presenting the material in an educational workshop format. We have found advertising for a "Perfectionism Workshop" generates a lot of interest, and many individuals have expressed appreciation for the resource. We believe presenting it as an educational workshop eliminated some of the barriers of seeking help, especially the stigma of being in therapy. We also cooperated with the university academic resource center, and this relationship was a helpful source of referrals and workshop coordination. We have experimented with presenting the material in a single session as part of a series of workshops and as a four-part workshop spread over four weeks. A link to a series of workshop videos created by the authors demonstrating an ACT intervention for academic issues, including perfectionism found in Appendix 7A at www.newharbinger.com/22225.

References

Alden, L. E., Ryder, A. G., & Mellings, T. M. B. (2002). Perfectionism in the context of social fears: Toward a two-component model. In G. L. Flett & P. L. Hewitt (Eds.), *Perfectionism: Theory, research, and treatment* (pp. 373-391). Washington, DC: American Psychological Association.

Burns, D. D. (1980). *Feeling good: The new mood therapy.* New York: New American Library.

Chang, E. C. (1998). Cultural differences, perfectionism, and suicidal risk in a college population: Does social problem solving still matter? *Cognitive Therapy and Research, 22(3),* 237-254.

Chang, E. C., & Rand, K. L. (2000). Perfectionism as a predictor of subsequent adjustment: Evidence for a specific diathesis–stress mechanism among college students. *Journal of Counseling Psychology, 47(1),* 129-137.

Crosby, J. M. & Twohig, M. P. (2009). Acceptance and Commitment Therapy for the Treatment of Perfectionism Associated with Generalized Anxiety Disorder. Unpublished manuscript.

Dahl, J., Wilson, K. G., & Nilsson, A. (2004). Acceptance and Commitment Therapy and the treatment of persons at risk for long-term disability resulting from stress and pain symptoms: A preliminary randomized trial. Behavior Therapy, 35, 785-801.

Eifert, G. H., & Forsyth, J. P. (2003). The effects of acceptance versus control contexts on avoidance of panic-related symptoms. *Journal of Consulting and Clinical Psychology, 57,* 414-419.

Enns, M. W., Cox, B. J., Sareen, J., & Freeman, P. (2001). Adaptive and maladaptive perfectionism in medical students: A longitudinal investigation. *Medical Education, 35,* 1034-1042.

Flett, G. L., Blankstein, K. R., Hewitt, P. L., & Koledin, S. (1992). Components of perfectionism and procrastination in college students. *Social Behavior and Personality, 20(2),* 85-94.

Frost, R. O., Marten, P., Lahart, C., & Rosenblate, R. (1990). The dimensions of perfectionism. *Cognitive Therapy and Research, 14,* 449-468.

Frost, R. O., & Steketee, G. (1997). Perfectionism in obsessive-compulsive disorder patients. *Behaviour Research and Therapy, 35,* 291-296.

Goldner, E. M., Cockell, S. J., & Srikameswaran, S. (2002). Perfectionism and eating disorders. In G. L. Flett & P. L. Hewitt (Eds.), *Perfectionism: Theory, research, and treatment* (pp. 319-340). Washington, DC: American Psychological Association.

Hayes, S. C., Luoma, J. B., Bond, F. W., Masuda, A., & Lillis, J. (2006). Acceptance and Commitment Therapy: Model processes and outcomes. *Behaviour Research and Therapy, 44,* 1-25.

Hayes, S. C., Strosahl, K. D., & Wilson, K. G. (2011). *Acceptance and Commitment Therapy: The process and practice of mindful change.* New York: Guilford.

Henning, K., Ey, S., & Shaw, D. (1998). Perfectionism, the imposter phenomenon and psychological adjustment in medical, dental, nursing and pharmacy students. *Medical Education, 32*, 456-464.

Hewitt, P. L., & Flett, G. L. (1991a). Dimensions of perfectionism in unipolar depression. *Journal of Abnormal Psychology, 100*, 98-101.

Hewitt, P. L., & Flett, G. L. (1991b). Perfectionism in the self and social contexts: Conceptualization, assessment, and association with psychopathology. *Journal of Personality and Social Psychology, 60*, 456-470.

Hewitt, P. L., Flett, G. L., & Weber, C. (1994). Dimensions of perfectionism and suicide ideation. *Cognitive Therapy and Research, 18*, 439-460.

Horney, K. (1950). *Neurosis and human growth*. New York: Norton.

Kearns, H., Forbes, A., & Gardiner, M. (2007). A cognitive behavioural coaching intervention for the treatment of perfectionism and self-handicapping in a nonclinical population. *Behaviour Change, 24*, 157-172.

Masuda, A., Hayes, S. C., Sackett, C. F., & Twohig, M. P. (2004). Cognitive defusion and self-relevant negative thoughts: Examining the impact of a ninety-year-old technique. *Behaviour Research and Therapy, 42,* 477-485.

Olatunji, B. O., Forsyth, J. P., & Feldner, M. T. (2007). Implications of emotion regulation for the shift from normative fear-relevant learning to anxiety-related psychopathology. *American Psychologist, 62(3)*, 257-259.

Parker, W. D. (2002). Perfectionism and adjustment in gifted children. In G. L. Flett & P. L. Hewitt (Eds.), *Perfectionism: Theory, research, and treatment* (pp. 133-148). Washington, DC: American Psychological Association.

Rice, K. G., & Dellwo, J. P. (2002). Perfectionism and self-development: Implications for college adjustment. *Journal of Counseling and Development, 80*, 188-196.

Riley, C., Lee, M., & Cooper, Z. (2007). A randomised controlled trial of cognitive-behaviour therapy for clinical perfectionism: A preliminary study. *Behaviour Research and Therapy, 45*, 2221-2231.

Roemer, L., Orsillo, S. M., & Salters-Pedneault, K. (2008). Efficacy of an acceptance-based behavior therapy for generalized anxiety disorder: Evaluation in a randomized controlled trial. *Journal of Consulting and Clinical Psychology, 76*, 1083-1089.

Stoeber, J., & Otto, K. (2006). Positive conceptions of perfectionism: Approaches, evidence, challenges. *Personality and Social Psychology Review, 10*, 295-319.

Twohig, M. P., Hayes, S. C., Plumb, J. C., Pruitt, L. D., Collins, A. B., Hazlett-Stevens, H., & Woidneck, M. R. (2010). A randomized controlled trial of Acceptance and Commitment Therapy vs. Progressive Relaxation Training for obsessive-compulsive disorder. *Journal of Consulting & Clinical Psychology, 78*, 705-716.

Wenzlaff, R. M., & Wegner, D. M. (2000). Thought suppression. *Annual Review of Psychology, 51*, 59-91.

Zettle, R. D., & Rains, J. C. (1989). Group cognitive and contextual therapies in treatment of depression. *Journal of Clinical Psychology, 45(3)*, 436–445.

CHAPTER 8

Podcasts to Help Students Overcome Academic Barriers in Australia and Italy

Giovanni Miselli

Anna B. Prevedini

Francesco Pozzi

IULM University Milan, IESCUM Italy

Julian McNally

*M.Psych, Counseling Psychologist,
Melbourne, Australia*

Giulia is a 20-year-old student in her second year of a three-year undergraduate course in Interpreting, Translation, Linguistic and Cultural Studies at IULM University in Milan. She recently lost several university credits during her first year due to a misunderstanding. She believes that she had talked to the professor's assistant and received permission to skip a seminar included as part of the class. The assistant reportedly gave her the permission, but at the end of the year Giulia learned that she had not received credits for the class. She talked about the problem with the professor and his assistant but they attributed it to a misunderstanding and noted that the situation could not be remedied. They found a compromise, where Giulia was allowed to attend the seminar and take the final exam during her second year. This meant that Giulia had to take extra hours of classes during the second year and that she would not receive the credits for a long period of time.

This event resulted in Giulia feeling very upset, desperate, and victimized. Giulia is a very enthusiastic and effective student when she feels comfortable with the subject matter and the professor. However, when she doesn't, she tends to withdraw from the situation and lose interest. Her grades were quite good during the first year, despite her varying motivation. After losing those credits, she felt so overwhelmed by the idea of retaking part of the course and the exam that she started losing interest in both classes and studying. She started missing some of the exams and thought about giving up studying. She reported feeling helpless and resentful that this had happened to her due to someone else's fault, and seemed to be losing confidence in both herself and the university's professionals.

This case illustrates a frequent problem on campuses: When students become distraught, they are more likely to stop their studies. One of the main objectives of college counseling centers (CCCs) is to help students cope with their difficulties during the process of adaptation to the university life and context. University administrators generally share this goal, particularly given that emotional difficulties encountered by students in the first year of college are frequently associated with dropout (Rickinson & Rutherford, 1995).

Persistence and Retention Problems in Higher Education Are Pervasive and Costly across the World

High dropout rates among college students are not a situation unique to the U.S.A. Other countries, such as Australia and Italy, suffer from similar issues regarding the need to improve retention on college campuses (Maslen, 2004; ISTAT, 2009). In 2004, the Australian federal education minister, Dr. Brendan Nelson, expressed concern that 40,000 Australian students would drop out of degree courses that year (Maslen,

2004). The Australian Commonwealth government's "Review of Australian Higher Education" determined that Australian universities had an average dropout rate of 28% (Bradley, Noonan, Nugent, & Scales, 2008). Similarly, as outlined in the latest data made available by the Organization for Economic Co-operation and Development (OECD) and the Italian National Institute for Statistics (ISTAT), high dropout rates from college plague the Italian university system as well (ISTAT, 2009; OECD, 2010). The OECD data on the number of students enrolled in a tertiary education program who graduate ("completion rate") in Italy, as well as Germany, Greece, and Switzerland, are missing. Among the 18 OECD countries for which this data is available, the percentage of students who begin higher education but are unable to obtain a degree (e.g. Bachelor's or Master's degree) is 31% (OECD, 2010). This percentage rises to 54% in the U.S., while it is lower for several other European countries: 35% in the United Kingdom, 21% in France, 24% in Spain, 28% in Portugal, 24% in Belgium, 16% in Denmark, and 28% in Finland.

In Italy, the latest available data (ISTAT, 2009) reveals that within the cohort of university students who enrolled in 2001-2002, 62% had not obtained a terminal university degree by 2007. These data, although not directly comparable with those collected by the OECD, seem to indicate a higher dropout rate, or at least a slower completion rate, in Italy than in other OECD countries.

In addition to dropping out of college, Italian students are taking longer to graduate: In 2007, according to ISTAT data (2009), almost 63% of the 249,593 graduates took longer to graduate than expected. As many as 76.5% of students who obtain a Master's degree take longer than expected (ISTAT, 2009)—a fact that has led to a saying in Italian Universities that "3+2 (years of education) usually is equal to 7 or more."[2]

---

2   Since 1999 the Italian system for degree fits the framework of the so-called 3+2 system, developed in the contest of the Bologna Process (see http://en.wikipedia.org/wiki/Bologna_Process for more details). Degree studies start immediately after high school and involve the students full-time. The first degree is the *Laurea triennale* that can be achieved after three years of studies and corresponds to a Bachelor's Degree. Two additional years of specialization lead to the Laurea Magistrale, which corresponds to a Master's Degree. Only the Laurea Magistrale grants access to third cycle programs (Post-MA degrees, Doctorates, or Specializing schools). There is also a five-year degree, "Laurea Magistrale Quinquennale" (Five Years Master of Arts), for programs such as Law and Medicine.

Although one may argue that delayed graduation can also be attributed to an ineffective curriculum that needs reprogramming, from the point of view of CCCs, this is recognized as a potential indicator of student distress. Delayed graduation and dropout from universities may impact students in terms of less motivation to study, a reduction in self-efficacy, guilt over the protracted cost of studies to the family, and, finally, a delay in gaining economic autonomy.

Giulia, the student described at the beginning of the chapter, never thought to seek help at the CCC, because she felt very deeply that she was a victim of unfair circumstances and had become increasingly distrustful of university faculty and staff. Throughout the chapter we will use Giulia's story to illustrate the potential utility of the mindfulness-based podcasts to be described later in the chapter. Giulia's story conveys the difficulty in reaching students who may not be willing to come into treatment.

We Need More Accessible Ways to Reach Psychologically Distressed College Students

Although CCCs, across the world, are the first resource available to students, these services are almost always available through face-to-face contact. However, the counselor-student ratio may sometimes be as high as 1:5,500 (Gallagher, 2011). Thus, if the prevalence of mental health problems in the student population reflects that of the population at large, it would be impossible for CCCs to address these problems through in-person counseling. Additionally, students who work may not be able to access counseling services, which typically operate during business hours. There is also a large proportion of college students who might never consult with counseling services because of the stigma associated with "seeing a shrink" (Eisenberg, Downs, Golberstein, & Zivin, 2009).

In addition to diagnosable mental health problems that can impact students' achievement (Andrews & Wilding, 2004), incoming college students face a number of developmental challenges: moving to a different context both in terms of social and family relationships, facing higher study demands, and experiencing increased personal and social expectations about grades and performances, to name just a few. Thus, the average student, who may not be suffering from a clinically diagnosable problem or feel stressed enough to seek services at a CCC, might nonetheless benefit in some way by learning coping skills. Two factors could guide the selection of a medium for delivery of psychological interventions to college students: a) finding a training format fitting to young adults' habits and language and b) being able to reach the largest number of students in order to contain costs. Both of these factors point to online resources to provide college students with life skills.

Targeting Common Psychological Processes among Disorders Is Ideal

Although online resources seem to allow for the most scope in reaching students, the type of intervention also matters. Given the diversity of student mental health concerns on college campuses (Gallagher, 2011), the approach selected for these online interventions would ideally help students struggling with a variety of disorders and developmental problems, by targeting core processes (Biglan, Hayes, & Pistorello, 2008). From a Functional Contextual view (Hayes, 1988), although analyzing socio-economic variables (e.g., parents' level of education) could help identify students who may be more vulnerable to dropout (e.g., Bui, 2002), these are not student characteristics that can be readily changed, particularly not through psychological means. Instead, it seems useful to identify processes that can be impacted through counseling, and that can help students better adjust to the university setting (Ramos-Sanchez & Nichols, 2007)—psychological flexibility, as addressed through Acceptance and Commitment Therapy (ACT; Hayes, Strosahl, & Wilson, 2011), appears to be one such target.

The purpose of this chapter is two-fold: 1) to describe the development and use of podcasts, based on ACT, with college students in Australia and 2) to present some preliminary data, along with lessons learned, on the impact of these podcasts (after translation) in Italy.

Six Acceptance and Commitment Therapy (ACT) Conversations: Teaching Psychological Flexibility through Podcasts

In 2005, the Aeronautical and Mechanical Engineering School at RMIT University,[3] Australia, invited the university's CCC to provide freshman students with a series of four two-hour tutorials to enhance their emotional intelligence skills. The teaching faculty considered that enhancing these skills would further two important objectives: 1) increasing students' engagement with the academic programs in the short term, and 2) building their long-term capability to work in teams, which is a crucial context for the work of engineers.

The tutorial sessions covered conventional social and emotional skill development topics such as stress management, time management, and interpersonal communication skills. Two of these sessions incorporated standard ACT (Hayes, Strosahl, & Wilson, 2011) interventions. To support these ACT tutorials, a set of six podcasts and associated downloadable worksheets entitled "6 ACT Conversations" were developed. Students in the Aeronautical and Mechanical Engineering first-year classes were encouraged, but not obliged, to visit the "6 ACT Conversations" web pages (See Figures 1 and 2 for the screenshots).

Dissemination Strategy

The six ACT Conversation podcasts (see "Appendix 8A: Links to 6 ACT Conversation Podcasts, RMIT University, Australia," at www .newharbinger.com/22225 for links) were initially offered as supplementary support for learning the ACT skills demonstrated in the tutorials.

---

3 RMIT University is Australia's largest tertiary institution by student enrollment, with a total student population of over 70,000 students including 17,000 studying offshore either by distance education or at one of the university's two Vietnam campuses. There are three campuses in Melbourne. The university has a substantial enrollment of international students and focuses on technology, design, health sciences, and business studies.

However the RMIT University Counseling Service also conceived of this project as an experimental foray into offering a service via a new technology that would increase students' access to the psychological expertise of the CCC. The dissemination strategy also demanded that the program be easily "digested" by the students. This was effected by keeping the program in a modular format with an average session duration of 26 minutes (maximum 40 minutes) and by explaining on the front page of the site and at the start of each session that the student could start and end anywhere in the program.

Unfortunately, but typical of the financial situation in many CCCs, no funding was available to research program utilization or effectiveness, and the development of the modules spread across many months. Some indication, though, of the need for such a site world-wide was that in the first twelve months after completion, the 6 ACT Conversations site was accessed more frequently by users outside than inside the university (Samulenok, 2008).

Podcast Development

The order of the sessions in 6 ACT Conversations is similar to the order of ACT treatment protocols available at the time (e.g., Eifert & Forsyth, 2005). A set of six audio e-learning lessons (podcasts), each one accompanied by a variable number of worksheets, were then designed, recorded, and uploaded on a specific and dedicated website where they can either be listened to online or downloaded to personal and portable devices (i.e., laptop, mobile phone, MP3 player). As seen in the figure 1 screenshot, when the student clicks on any one of these lessons, two tabs appear: an Introduction tab that explains the concept, and an Audio/ Worksheets tab where the student can listen to/download a particular lesson and print handouts to complete. Figure 2 below shows an example of what the student will see after she clicks on the Audio/Worksheet tab. Students are then guided to listen to an Introduction and subsequent segments, numbered (e.g., Part 1, Part 2) so that students know which order to follow.

The content of the examples was specifically directed to college students, and particularly to address barriers and obstacles they were likely to encounter in their studies. For example, right from the introduction to the audio program, the student is asked to identify a specific barrier she has encountered.

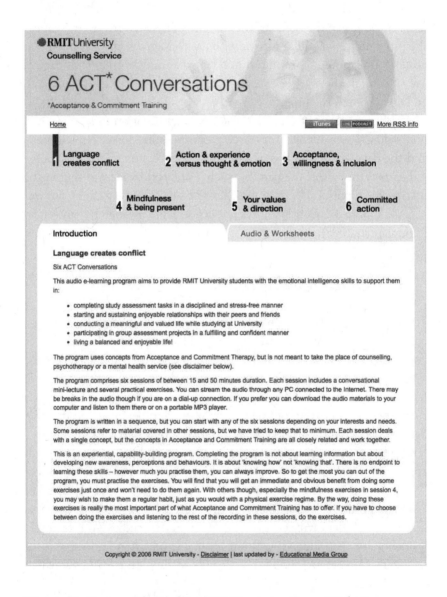

Figure 1. Screen Shot of 6 ACT Conversations Website

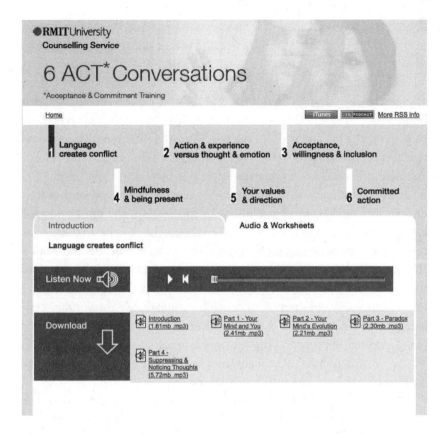

Figure 2. Screen Shot of Audio/Worksheets

LANGUAGE CREATES CONFLICT

The first session, "Language Creates Conflict," is the most didactic and demonstrates how language and the cognitive processes it relies on are often the source of "barriers" or problems. This is paradoxical and counterintuitive for many educated people, such as college students, as it is their facility with these processes that has often brought them success. Without the safety and predictability of the conventional counseling environment, exposing individuals to these paradoxes has the potential to alienate or disengage them. To counter this risk, the session uses humor and a lighter touch with the questions it asks the listener to face: "Has it been the case with this barrier, or others like it, that the more thoughts you had, the further it seemed you got from a solution? That doesn't make sense, does it?" This session also orients the listener to workability and values, in preference to logic or conventional thinking, as a criterion for relating to one's own thoughts.

While the session is largely provided as an explanatory piece, it does engage the listener in a simplified and generic version of the "creative hopelessness" process (Hayes, Strosahl, & Wilson, 2011). This process is used to lay the groundwork for the processes of defusion and acceptance that follow (see chapter 3 for a detailed description of ACT processes). As these processes are counterintuitive, it is helpful to motivate the listener to at least consider an alternative to conventional approaches that depend on "figuring out" a solution. In this session, the creative hopelessness process is initiated by way of two exercises. The first exercise requires the listener to simply observe the mind in silence and notice that thoughts are constantly present. For the second part of this exercise, the listener is instructed to try not to have thoughts. This emphasizes the impossibility, or hopelessness, of controlling apparently involuntary cognitive behavior. From that point the listener may be open to or curious about another approach. This learning is reinforced at the end of the session by instructing a thought suppression exercise from Hayes & Smith (2005).

Going back to Giulia, the student we met at the beginning of the chapter, this first audio lesson could be helpful to her in a number of ways. It could: 1) pique her curiosity and prompt her to listen to the rest of the program; 2) help her identify as a barrier the thought "I won't waste my efforts anymore in classes. It was unfair that I lost my credits" as a precursor for doing something different in her life; 3) lead her to notice how many stories her mind is telling her about this event and its consequences; and 4) help her find some self-compassion, given the podcast's explanation about how this "mind-y" process is human beings' natural proclivity, deep-rooted in the history of our evolution.

ACTION AND EXPERIENCE VERSUS THOUGHT AND EMOTION

The second session, "Action and Experience Versus Thought and Emotion," introduces the listener to the primacy of experience and to the possibility of relating to thoughts in a way that may facilitate more direct contact with experience. In this session, defusion exercises such as "Thoughts on the Highway" and "Thank Your Mind" are introduced (e.g., Hayes & Smith, 2005). It is also the first session to provide a worksheet, in this case, one offering several defusion exercises. The "Thoughts on the Highway" exercise is a variant of the "Leaves in a Stream" exercise (Hayes & Smith, 2005) and it involves asking students to imagine standing safely on the side of a highway, and putting each rising thought, image, emotion, or action urge on one of the vehicles going by.

In response to this podcast, Giulia might deepen her experience of how her thoughts and emotions catch her off guard all the time, profoundly influencing her actions. She might start noticing that her involvement in university courses was almost completely based on her pleasant or unpleasant emotions about the subject matter and the professors. She might have an "aha" moment when conducting defusion exercises, such as the one that asked her to put all the stories about the credits she lost on the screen and then make up many different scenarios, like a musical with dances and songs about the stories.

EXPANSION, WILLINGNESS, AND INCLUSION

Following the second session, the stage is set for introducing the idea that if logic and clever thinking cannot be relied on to enhance life, an alternative—acceptance and willingness—is needed.

The third session asks the listener to complete a potentially uncomfortable physical exercise as a way of contacting the emotions and thoughts commonly arising with the experience of unwillingness. The exercise requires the listener to stand upright, but with her legs bent, for about sixty seconds. For most people this becomes uncomfortable after thirty seconds or so. The podcast then trains the listener in the practice of Russ Harris's (2008) "Expansion" exercise as an alternative to struggling with the discomfort normally associated with unwillingness.

The sitting-standing exercise tends to elicit positive responses from students, and in Giulia's case it could strengthen her understanding of the last session, about how thoughts and emotions can impact actions, by having her practice noticing the physical sensations, thoughts, and feelings coming and going during the exercise while trying to expand her breath to make room for them.

MINDFULNESS AND BEING PRESENT

The fourth ACT Conversations session, "Mindfulness and Being Present," includes five distinct and fairly conventional mindfulness exercises: "Awareness of Breathing," "Mindfulness of Thoughts," "Eating a Raisin," "Walking," and "Just Sitting." The slow eating of a raisin is a commonly practiced mindfulness exercise. It is generally used, like all ACT exercises from the "Contact with the Present" point on the ACT Hexaflex (see chapter 3), to give the student the opportunity to contact the direct stimulus properties of the experience. ACT practitioners frequently "borrow" mindfulness exercises from spiritual traditions such as Buddhism and Hinduism, and this is the case with these five exercises.

Defusion and acceptance are very much ACT processes for dealing with struggles as they arise. Therefore exposure to one or two samples of these behaviors is often all that is needed for a client to generalize the skill to common in vivo experiences.

In Giulia's situation, the raisin exercise might give her an opportunity to start practicing mindfulness with something tangible. If she was having difficulty noticing private events such as thoughts and feelings, the raisin exercise might make the concept of mindfulness a little easier to understand, given that physical experiences, such as taste and texture, may be easier to notice. In the podcast, she would be instructed in this session to engage in routine practice of at least one of the other four exercises as well. This is intended to enhance the attentional skill of mindfulness (Siegel, 2007).

VALUES AND DIRECTION

The fifth session expands this focus on initiating action by asking the listener to identify values in several areas of life. This session introduces the notion that "motivation" stems from clarity about values and the taking of even very small steps in support of them. The work the listener is called on to complete is supported by three worksheets, "Values Inquiry," "Achievements, Actions and Values," and an ACT "classic" exercise in which the individual is invited to imagine her funeral.

What could happen to Giulia in this session? Through various values training exercises, Giulia might be able to start discriminating the difference between "going through the motions" of getting a degree versus being engaged and full of vitality in the process. Sometimes, a student is not aware of how "stale" life gets when a valued direction is not being followed, until she is able to notice the difference, based on actual experience. While working on the first part of the "Achievements, Actions and Values" worksheet, she might remember how involved and enthusiastic she had felt at the beginning of her first year while writing a paper on a topic of great interest to her. She might have a glimpse of how scary it is to acknowledge, even to herself, that she cares about her studies, lest she be disappointed again. This could open the door toward re-engagement in school for Giulia.

COMMITTED ACTION

The final session, "Committed Action," shifts the listener's focus from internal cognitive and emotional processes to contacting the challenges and joys of planning and initiating actions based on values. This session and the accompanying worksheets are perhaps most like those one might find in a non-ACT program (e.g., Nelson & Low, 2003; Covey, 1998). It is important to acknowledge here that there is no specific podcast addressing the fourth point on the Hexaflex, Self as Context (see chapter 3). Nonetheless, it is addressed in some of the exercises, especially "Sit or Stand" (session 3) and "Thoughts on the Highway" (session 2), and, at least tangentially, in all of the session 4 exercises. For example, the "Sit or Stand" exercise in the third session draws the listener's attention simultaneously to the content of her thoughts and to her act of choice in the moment of either sitting or standing. By implication, there is a self who chooses and a self who is aware of the thoughts passing by.

For Giulia, this stage could mark a shift toward behaving differently. Completing the worksheet would require her to write her purposes in the academic values area (see worksheet in Figure 3). She would have the opportunity to notice what shows up for her while setting her goals for her lifetime, next year, next month, next week, and today. In the worksheet, "Barriers and Counter-Strategies," she would have an opportunity to write down scary feelings and thoughts as possible barriers and the defusion and acceptance strategies to use in this case (see worksheet in Figure 4).

Giulia is a prototype of the kind of student we wanted to reach with the ACT podcast training. She was experiencing external and internal barriers to her course of study, and because in that moment she was blaming others and generalizing the lack of trust to all university services, she was unlikely to seek help at the CCC. Giulia's story is similar to that of many students we interviewed after the podcasts's deployment, who found it a useful resource when facing distressing internal and external experiences that made them think of dropping out of college. In the next section, we will review the results of a study utilizing this set of podcasts, after a brief discussion about the challenges of translating this type of material.

The Process of Translating the ACT Podcasts from English to Italian

Although ACT is an empirically supported treatment, "no one has yet developed an adequate model of how to modify empirically supported treatments to deal with the vast differences between human beings in areas of culture…religion, class, age, personality, and so on" (Hayes, Muto, & Masuda, 2011, p. 236). In non-technical terms, we approached translation knowing that preserving the function of different exercises, as we migrated from English/Australia to Italian/Italy, was crucial. Thus, the question leading the translation process was: "How do we talk about this model and influence the behavior of the Italian students listening to these podcasts, in a way functionally equivalent to the original version?" This was accomplished by selecting functionally equivalent words that were easily understandable and did not elicit aversive reactions in the target population.

For example, in the Italian verbal community, the word "values" has unwanted religious connotations, while for other verbal communities it works perfectly. Moreover, in some contexts the word "acceptance" in Italian would be functionally equivalent to "giving up" or "being passive or oppressed." In the case of Giulia, a student listening to a podcast at home by herself, the nuance of even a single word might make a difference between continuing to listen to the podcast or turning it off. Therefore, we opted to translate "acceptance" as "expansion" or "willingness." Furthermore, since in Italian there is not a specific word for mindfulness (*consapevolezza* = "awareness"), the English word was used, with a brief introduction on the meaning and function of the word in this context. Finally, special attention was given to the verb "to feel," which in Italian (*sentire*) also means "to hear." This double meaning could interfere with the function of a mindfulness exercise (e.g., driving the attention to the speaker's voice and not to the stimuli of interest).

Fortunately, the translation of the first two ACT books in Italian (Harris, 2008; Hayes & Smith, 2005) co-occurred with the translation of these podcasts, and this helped establish guidelines for the use of a functional language for mindfulness-based materials within the Italian community. Readers who are considering translating materials, particularly mindfulness ones based on audio such as those discussed here, are encouraged to proceed with caution.

◉RMIT University
Counselling Service

6 ACT*Conversations

*Acceptance & Commitment Training

Session 6: **Committed Action**

Value and Goals Sheet

1. Identify a value (quality of lived action) that is important to you.

2. Choose a domain of life from the list below in which you plan to honour or express that value. Set goals for each of the time frames in the list.

3. Goals at different timeframes do not have to be logically connected although you will find they often are.

Life Domains

Family	Work / career	Study / learning
Health / fitness / wellbeing	Religion / spirituality	Partner / spouse / marriage
Community / society / politics	Recreation / leisure	Travel
Arts / creativity / play	Parenting / children	Finances / wealth
Mental / emotional wellness	Other: _____	Other: _____

Value

_____

Domain

_____

Lifetime goal (mission)

_____

_____

_____

_____

_____

10 year goal

_____

_____

_____

_____

5 year goal

_____

Figure 3. Screen Shot of the "Values and Goals" Worksheet

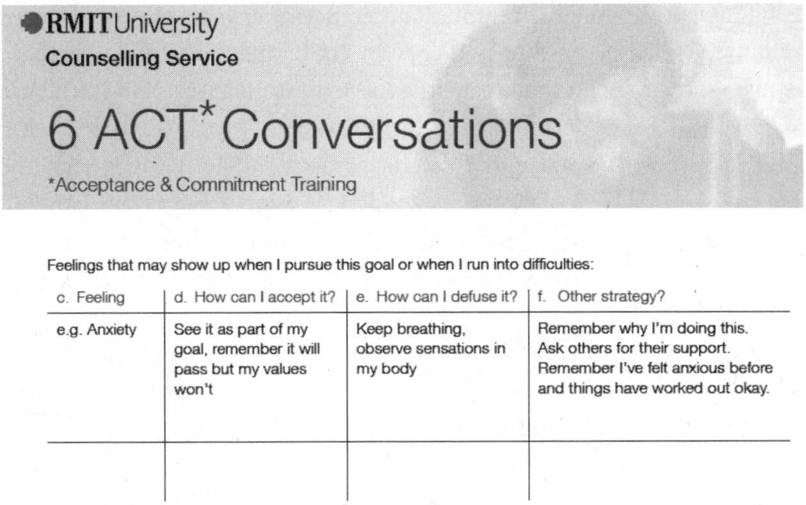

RMITUniversity
Counselling Service

6 ACT* Conversations

*Acceptance & Commitment Training

Feelings that may show up when I pursue this goal or when I run into difficulties:

c. Feeling	d. How can I accept it?	e. How can I defuse it?	f. Other strategy?
e.g. Anxiety	See it as part of my goal, remember it will pass but my values won't	Keep breathing, observe sensations in my body	Remember why I'm doing this. Ask others for their support. Remember I've felt anxious before and things have worked out okay.

Figure 4. Screen Shot of Page 2 of the "Barriers and Counter-Strategies" Worksheet

Empirical Considerations: Preliminary Data of the ACT Web-Based Podcast Program Applied with Italian Students

After the six podcasts based on ACT developed by RMIT University in Australia were translated into Italian and adapted for delivery at the IULM University in Milan, Italy, they were systematically evaluated in a controlled study (Prevedini, Pozzi, Miselli, Rabitti, & Moderato 2012). A second set of six audio e-learning lessons and worksheets was also developed, based on popular Cognitive Behavior Therapy self-help books on different topics (e.g., Rovetto, 1990; Ellis, 1990; Anchisi & Gambotto Dessy, 1995; Ramirez Basco, 2010); the relevance and quality of fit for the target population was supervised by an expert CBT-trained psychotherapist.

There were some substantial differences between the ACT-based and the CBT-based set of podcasts in the content included (both in terms of processes and reliance on experiential exercises) and in the use of language. An in-depth analysis of the different processes in ACT and CBT is beyond the scope of this chapter, but suffice it to say that the emphasis in ACT experiential exercises was on helping the student regain contact with the direct contingencies and shaping new functions of behaviors, while the CBT-based one was focused on fostering more rule and verbally directed behavior. The ACT podcasts walk through the six processes (see chapter 3) and try to lead the listener to recognize the side effects of language and to gain some detachment and relief from the power of language, basing actions on values-based choices instead, while the CBT-based podcasts offer psychoeducational strategies and reinforce the process of rule-governed behavior, aiming at establishing a new and more functional set of verbal rules (Törneke, 2010).

Between October 2010 and May 2011, 207 students of three different courses at IULM University of Milan completed the pre- and post-intervention assessments. The classes of students were randomly assigned to the three conditions (ACT, CBT, and no intervention). In order to ensure a good rate of participation, students in the experimental groups were offered the equivalent of extra credit for participation.

Participants completed questionnaires on psychological distress, anxiety, psychological flexibility, values success, mindfulness, and academic and study behaviors at pre- and post-training.

Acceptability Ratings

As illustrated in Table 1 below, students in the ACT condition ($n = 56$) indicated moderately satisfactory ratings with the ACT audio e-learning program. On a 5-point Likert-like scale (0-Not at all, 5-very much), most students gave a rating to the ACT podcasts of 3 or above in terms of having learned something useful (86%), thinking the content was relevant to college students (88%), and believing the podcast format was practical (91%). Similar percentages were reported by students assigned to the CBT condition. Finally, more than 80% of the students in both groups reported that they would recommend the program to a friend.

Table 1. Acceptability of the Podcast Programs in the ACT and CBT Conditions

	ACT-based podcast (n = 56)		CBT-based podcast (n = 110)	
	% for the 5-point Likert-like scale			
	4-"a lot"/ 5-"very much"	3-"quite enough"	4-"a lot"/ 5 -"very much"	3-"quite enough"
I learned something useful from listening to the podcast program.	30.9%	55.2%	37.6%	49.5%
I believe the content of the podcasts was relevant for a college student.	34.5%	53.4%	51.4%	41.3%
I believe the podcast format is practical for this kind of lessons.	75.4%	15.8%	62.4%	31.2%
	% of yes/no answers			
	Yes	No	Yes	No
I would suggest this podcast program to a friend.	87.7%	12.3%	83.5%	16.5%

Outcome Findings

To assess the outcomes in the self-reported standardized measures, generalized linear models for repeated measures were performed, using the group variable as the between-subjects variable. No statistically significant condition differences emerged in terms of changes in psychological flexibility and mindfulness.

The results showed a significant main effect from pre- to post-training in worry and values consistency scores, but no interaction (condition) effect emerged. Both the ACT-based and the CBT-based groups reported having less pathological worry and acting more consistently with their values at the end of the term. The no-intervention control group always changed in the opposite direction from the two intervention groups, making it more likely that positive effects could be attributed to the ACT- and the CBT-based podcast interventions. There was no significant effect on psychological distress, except for an interaction effect on a phobic anxiety subscale, which typically assesses fear and avoidance responses and escape behaviors, with scale scores increasing from pre- to post-training assessment in the CBT-based and control groups, and decreasing in the ACT-based podcast group.

Importantly, analyses of the academic and study behaviors questionnaire showed that the CBT-based podcast group mostly did not change and the control group showed significant changes in the undesired direction from pre- to post-training, whereas the ACT group reported greater academic engagement (e.g., less reading/texting during classes). See Table 2 below.

Table 2. Academic and Study Behaviors Questionnaire in the ACT Condition

	ACT-based podcast ($n = 56$)		
Questionnaire items M (SD)			
	Pre	**Post**	**Wilcoxon,** p
Reading something not concerning the subject matter while attending classes	1.20 (0.90)	0.80 (0.86)	Z= -3.016, p=.003

Making telephone calls while studying	1.25 (0.98)	1.02 (0.92)	Z= -2.166, p=.030
Reading something not concerning the subject matter while studying	0.75 (0.83)	0.50 (0.69)	Z= -2.086, p=.037
Texting while studying	2.11 (0.99)	1.85 (0.93)	Z= -2.887, p=.004
Rehearsing material out loud, while studying	2.46 (1.36)	2.84 (1.13)	Z= -3.006, p=.003
Studying with other students	2.07 (0.98)	2.30 (0.93)	Z= -2.313, p= .021

Note: The last two items are considered positive academic behavior, with higher means being indicative of higher engagement.

There were several limitations to the study and to the study design, such as assigning classrooms (and not students) to condition, not having follow-up data, and collecting data via both paper-and-pencil and computer-based venues.

Final Words

Podcasts may be an option for delivering mindfulness and acceptance-based content to a wide number of college students with relatively low costs. The majority of students reported finding the themes relevant to college students and claimed that they were helped by listening to the podcasts. The percentage of students listening to the ACT-based podcast who found it relevant and useful was comparable to those exposed to more traditional CBT-based podcasts. The great majority of students in both intervention groups also reported that they would suggest it to a friend.

However, CCCs considering adding podcasts to their resource list may do well to consider the quality of the product they may be able to develop, as this will be the primary cost of having such a resource, and how much they care about tracking usage by students. We found that the quality of the product, not just in terms of content but also production, is important. At post-training assessments, many Italian students involved in the research in both groups pointed out that the intonation of the narrating voice was perceived as boring and monotonous. For economic reasons, the Italian podcasts were not recorded by a professional speaker or recorded with high quality equipment.

In our study, both groups completed a brief evaluation of the podcasts' content (10 true or false questions) as a check on whether students actually completed the audio and worksheet material. Only students who correctly answered 70% of the questions were included in the experimental groups and had their data analyzed. However, we were not able to monitor specific program usage; we were only able to determine that all the students included in the study did register on the podcast platform and either played or downloaded all the materials. Unfortunately, the advantage of the podcast format in being downloaded to any personal portable device also carries the disadvantage of making it difficult to monitor actual usage. Unless a system similar to the one set up during our study is implemented (e.g., sign-in required, post-training quiz), most schools might be restricted to gauging podcast use by tracking hits on their website and/or knowing how many students have downloaded their podcasts. Although requiring a sign-in might help with tracking usage, it would also introduce a step that might deter students from actually utilizing these resources.

The most compelling data from this study, and one likely to be useful in illustrating the relevance of acceptance and mindfulness to possibly increasing student retention, is that students reported significantly higher engagement in their academic activities in the ACT condition. This matches recent findings from two ACT online programs. One highly interactive multimedia online program, targeting values training and acceptance, showed significant between-group differences in terms of an increase in both intrinsic/positive motivation toward education and success in living out education-related values (Levin, Pistorello, Seeley, & Hayes, 2012). The other study, described in detail in chapter 9, found that a brief online values training was associated with same-semester increases in academic performance (Chase, 2010).

References

Anchisi, R., & Gambotto Dessy, M. (1995). *Non solo comunicare*. Torino: Libreria Cortina.

Andrews, B., & Wilding, J. M. (2004). The relation of depression and anxiety to life-stress and achievement in students. *British Journal of Psychology 95*, 509–521.

Biglan, A., Hayes, S. C., & Pistorello, J. (2008). Acceptance and commitment: Implications for prevention science. *Prevention Science, 9*, 139-152.

Bradley, D., Noonan, P., Nugent, H., & Scales, B. (2008). *Review of Australian Higher Education: Final Report*. Canberra: Australian Government.

Bui, K. V. T. (2002). First-generation college students at a four-year university: Background characteristics, reasons for pursuing higher education, and first-year experiences. *College Student Journal, 5 (1)*, 3-11.

Chase, J. A. (2010). The additive effects of values clarification training to an online goal-setting procedure on measures of student retention and performance. *Dissertation Abstracts International: Section B: The Sciences and Engineering, 71(6-B)*, 3921.

Covey, S. (1998). *The 7 Habits of Highly Effective Teens*. New York: Simon & Schuster.

Eifert, G. & Forsyth, J. (2005). *Acceptance and Commitment Therapy for anxiety disorders*. Oakland, CA: New Harbinger.

Eisenberg, D., Downs, M., Golberstein, E., & Zivin, K. (2009) Stigma and help-seeking for mental health among college students. *Medical Care Research & Review, 66(5)*, 522-541.

Ellis, A. (1990). *How to stubbornly refuse to make yourself miserable about anything – yes anything!* New York: Carol Publishing (Italian translation, *L'autoterapia razionale emotiva*. Trento: Edzioni Erickson, 1993).

Gallagher, R. (2011). *National Survey of Counseling Center Directors*. Pittsburgh, PA: University of Pittsburgh.

Harris, R. (2008). *The Happiness Trap: How to stop struggling and start living*. Boston, MA: Trumpeter (Italian translation, *La trappola della felicità*, Trento: Edzioni Erickson, Trento, 2010).

Hayes, S. C. (1988). Contextualism and the next wave of behavioral psychology. *Behavior Analysis, 23*, 7-23.

Hayes, S. C., Muto, T., & Masuda, A. (2011). Seeking cultural competence from the ground up. *Clinical Psychology: Science and Practice, 18*, 232-237.

Hayes, S.C., & Smith, S. (2005). *Get out of your mind and into your life*. Oakland, CA: New Harbinger (Italian translation, *Smetti di soffrire, inizia a vivere*, Milano: Franco Angeli, 2010).

Hayes, S. C., Strosahl, K., & Wilson, K. G. (2011). *Acceptance and Commitment Therapy: The process and practice of mindful change*. New York: Guilford Press.

ISTAT (2009). *Università e lavoro: orientarsi con la statistica.* Retrieved September 7, 2011, from http://www.istat.it/it/supporto/per-gli-studenti/universit%C3%A0-e -lavoro.

Levin, M. E., Pistorello, J., Seeley, J., & Hayes, S. C. (2012). Transdiagnostic web-based prevention for mental health problems among college students: Results from a pilot trial. Manuscript submitted for publication.

Maslen, G. (2004). Australian dropout rates undermine enrolment rise. *Times Higher Education Supplement (Online).* Retrieved April 11, 2012 from http://www.timeshighereducation.co.uk/story.asp?storyCode=183553&sectioncode=26

Organization for Economic Co-operation and Development. (2010). "How many students finish tertiary education?" in OECD, *Education at a Glance, 2010: OECD Indicators,* OECD Publishing.

Nelson, D.B. & Low, G.R. (2003). *Emotional Intelligence: Achieving Academic and Career Excellence.* Upper Saddler River, NJ: Prentice Hall.

Prevedini, AB; Pozzi, F. ; Miselli G.; Rabitti, E. Moderato P., (2012). Effects of ACT-based and CBT-based podcasts on students' academic behavior: The experience of a university counseling project in Italy. Manuscript in preparation.

Ramirez Basco, M. (2010). *The procrastinator's guide to getting things done.* New York: The Guilford Press (Italian translation, *Prima o poi lo faccio! Come modificare la cattiva abitudine di rimandare sempre,* Firenze: Eclipsi, 2011).

Ramos-Sánchez, L., & Nichols, L. (2007). Self-efficacy of first-generation and non-first-generation college students: The relationship with academic performance and college adjustment. *Journal of College Counseling, 10* (1), 6-18.

Rickinson, B. & Rutherford, D. (1995). Increasing undergraduate student retention rates. *British Journal of Guidance & Counselling,* 23, 161-172.

Rovetto, F. (1990). *Il piacere di apprendere.* Milano: Arnoldo Mondadori Editore.

Samulenok, D. (2008). Personal communication from the Senior Coordinator, Multimedia Production, RMIT University to the fourth author.

Siegel, D. (2007). *The mindful brain: Reflection and attunement in the cultivation of well-being.* New York: Norton.

Törneke, N. (2010). *Learning RFT: An introduction to relational frame theory and its clinical applications.* Oakland, CA: New Harbinger.

CHAPTER 9

Web-Based Values
Training and Goal Setting

Todd A. Ward

Ramona Houmanfar

University of Nevada-Reno, Department of Psychology

Jared Chase

Chrysalis, Inc.

S andra has just started her first semester in college. Her parents
have long stressed the importance of her attending college. Since
most of her friends also attend college, it seems like "the thing to
do." However, she feels like she lacks direction. She has not declared a
major and doesn't seem to be passionate about any particular career path.

Sandra is not alone. Most academic advisors have interacted with
students just like Sandra. What is one to do in such a situation? The
current chapter is designed to offer potential solutions for these types of
students. The values exploration and goal-setting procedures discussed
herein are based on a recent study that demonstrated a significant
increase in cumulative GPAs as well as student retention among undergraduate psychology majors at a medium-size public institution (Chase,
2010). The system consisted of a series of text- and audio-based modules
designed to encourage students to think about why they are pursuing a
college education, what they value in an education, and how to set goals

that will facilitate their progression toward graduation. The brief, web-based nature of the system offers many practical advantages in terms of dissemination and cost-benefit analyses and will be discussed in more detail in the following pages.

The Problem of Student Retention

College student retention is a critical issue in higher education that is practically, institutionally, and socially important. The following section explores the multitude of factors that contribute to the problem of student retention in the student's social and academic life.

The Advantages of a College Education

When compared to those without college degrees, college graduates typically enjoy more employment opportunities, including more chances for advancement and higher salaries (Dohm & Wyatt, 2002). For example, in the last quarter of 2009, college graduates with full-time jobs earned a median weekly salary of $1,121 compared to $638 for high school graduates and $449 for those who did not graduate from high school (U.S. Bureau of Labor Statistics News Release, 2010). In addition, college graduates can expect to earn an average of $2.1 million over their lifetime, compared with $1.2 million for high school graduates. Furthermore, those with Master's degrees can expect to earn approximately $2.5 million over their lifetime compared to $3.4 million for those with Doctoral degrees (U.S. Census Bureau, 2002). Although the educational process is time consuming, these statistics indicate a substantial return on the investment in terms of earnings, not to mention the social and cultural accolades generally given to those with college degrees.

Student Retention as a University Problem

Given the documented benefits of a college degree, one would expect high retention rates in our universities, but this doesn't seem to be the case. According to the U.S. Department of Education (2007), approximately 35% of students coming into public four-year institutions do not obtain a degree. In addition, only 47% of students entering four-year institutions complete their degree within six years. For public institutions, this rate drops to a mere 41% of students, and only 34% complete their degrees in four years (Astin, Tsui, & Avalos, 1996).

Insufficient University Resources Devoted to Student Retention

It is surprising to find that many colleges and universities lack sufficient resources directed toward student retention (e.g., Hood, 1999; McLaughlin, Brozovsky, & McLaughlin, 1998). According to a recent survey of administrators at more than 1,000 colleges and universities, retention policies have not universally been a top priority for administrators (American College Testing, 2008). Less than half (47%) of the administrators in the survey reported any organizational goals related to retention efforts of first-year students and even less (33%) reported any goals related to increasing degree completion rates. Lastly, only 52% reported having staff members who are specifically responsible for coordinating retention efforts.

Setting Factors Involved in Retention

Considerable resources have been devoted to researching college student retention. Vincent Tinto (1993), a prominent retention researcher, developed a popular model of retention that conceptualizes institutes of higher education as comprised of an academic system and a social system. According to the model, an imbalance in either of these two systems is positively correlated with student attrition. More specifically, the less a student is integrated into the social system (e.g., extracurricular interactions with peers) or the academic system (e.g., attending classes, studying, and faculty interactions), retention becomes less likely. According to Tinto, greater goal commitment (e.g., commitment to obtaining a degree) and value assessments, along with other contextual factors, impact social, academic, and institutional integration and academic performance

(1993). When students' campus experiences conflict with previously established values, integration may be more challenging (Tinto, 1993).

A good deal of research has also investigated the specific factors at the institutional, social, and individual levels that are responsible for university student retention (e.g., Berger & Braxton, 1998; Pascarella & Terenzini, 2005; Richardson, Abraham, & Bond, 2012; Tinto, 1993). As a whole, this research attributes retention to a set of historical and situational factors involving high school performance, socio-economic status, family support, personality traits, the size of the institution, the quality and quantity of faculty interactions, and peer relationships (e.g., Pascarella & Terenzini, 2005; Richardson, Abraham, & Bond, 2012).

From the student's perspective, however, arriving at college may bring with it an amalgam of new responsibilities brought about by the increased independence of living away from home. Behaviorally speaking, this new life experience is characterized by a multitude of competing contingencies related to peer groups, finances, and extracurricular activities that may lessen one's contact with academic contingencies related to class attendance, the completion of assignments, and, ultimately, satisfactory academic performance.

It is important that colleges and universities develop effective retention programs because retention affects the future opportunities of students themselves, the financial viability of educational institutions, and the competitiveness of the nation as a participant in the global economy. The majority of the literature on student retention focuses on student finances, advising, student-faculty interactions, classroom environments, stress reduction, and minority status (e.g., Kerkvliet & Nowell, 2005; Seidman, 2005; Stover, 2005). Surprisingly, only a few researchers use academic performance as an outcome measure in their research (e.g., Bowen, Price, Lloyd, & Thomas, 2005; Thomas, 2002).

In addition, research suggests that the students most in need of academic assistance are the least likely to seek it out. Karabenick and Knapp (1988) found that seeking out assistance increased as students' needs went from low to moderate, but dropped substantially as the need grew and grades dropped below a C- range. One possibility is that increasingly more difficult thoughts and feelings, including some self-stigma perhaps, may be associated with seeking out academic assistance when it is truly needed.

Gaining Personal Control over Learning

Research suggests that the more students have access to strategies that enable them to exert personal control over their learning, the more likely they are to be successful in college (Zimmerman & Risemberg, 1997). However, given the before-mentioned retention statistics, it is likely that many students lack appropriate self-management skills that would enable them to exert control over their own academic success.

Self-management training has been used in organizational and educational settings for decades (Luthans & Davis, 1979). Self-management involves recognizing, setting, and monitoring progress toward the completion of goals, and utilizing reinforcement and punishment to promote goal attainment (Frayne, 1991). Though the literature suggests that self-management programs directed at academic behavior may have an encouraging impact, recent research in the area is lacking (Gerhardt, 2007). Most research efforts investigate goal setting as part of an intervention package rather than in isolation, leading to mixed conclusions on the effectiveness of goal setting separate from other interventions.

Even when the effects of goal setting are specifically studied, the findings are mixed. For example, Loewy and Bailey (2007) found no effect of goals when added to an already-existing system of performance feedback for customer service employees in a retail setting. However, Amigo, Smith, & Ludwig (2008) found that goal setting increased busing times at a restaurant only when coupled with task-clarification and feedback. In addition, Goomas, Smith, & Ludwig (2011) found that a combination of goals and feedback significantly increased the performance of employees in a distribution center. The current chapter describes a method of utilizing goal-setting in the context of values training exercises delivered online to promote effective self-management skills and, subsequently, improved student academic performance and retention in a university setting.

Goal Setting for Students

Among the simplest types of performance-improvement interventions is goal setting, which is due, in large part, to the work of Edwin Locke and Gary Latham. Below we will discuss the specific features that can improve the effectiveness of goal setting.

Seven Characteristics of Effective Goal Setting

Most goal-setting research focuses on the relationship between an individual's goals and performance. According to Locke, Shaw, Saari, and Latham (1981), an effective goal-setting program includes seven characteristics: (a) challenging goals, (b) specific goals, (c) the ability to change one's own performance, (d) feedback on goal progress, (e) monetary reinforcement for goal attainment, (f) a supportive supervisor (e.g., an academic mentor), and (g) goal acceptance.

Locke and Latham (1990) suggest that challenging and specific goals motivate individuals to achieve goals based on *choice, effort,* and *persistence.* The more specific a goal can be, the easier it is for an individual to choose appropriate actions to take toward goal attainment and exclude those actions that may interfere with the goal. When specific goals are made to be somewhat challenging, this motivates the individual to exert effort and adjust that effort appropriately on the way to meeting the goal. Finally, specific goals tend to promote persistence through the steps needed in obtaining the goal.

Locke and Latham (2002) also suggest that performance toward goals is influenced by *personal commitment, feedback on goal attainment,* and *task complexity.* The importance that an individual gives a goal, as well as an individual's self-efficacy, affects one's personal commitment to a goal (see also Bandura, 1997). Feedback is useful because it facilitates an individual's ability to track his progress toward goal completion and adjust his behavior accordingly. Lastly, task complexity relates directly to the complexity of repertoire needed to achieve a particular goal in terms of skill sets.

Unfortunately, students sometimes have a problem using goal setting, precisely for some of the reasons Locke and Latham mention: they are not clear that this is a choice and they are not truly committed to the outcomes. Role expectations may have brought the student into higher education and he has not thought sufficiently about what his education is really about. For that reason, we began to explore whether goal setting could be augmented by work on values.

Values Training for Students

Values training has a long and complicated history in education and has been defined in a multitude of ways. Modern work from a behavioral perspective in the form of Acceptance and Commitment Therapy (ACT; Hayes, Strosahl, & Wilson, 2011) makes it easier to conduct values work and to combine it with goal setting.

Values Education: Empirical Research

Values training procedures gained popularity in the late 1960s fueled by a seminal text by Simon, Howe, and Kirschenbaum (1972) on the subject, and have typically emerged in the areas of moral and character education which focus on teaching basic values that are seen as "good" by society (Easterbrooks & Scheetz, 2004). This type of values training generally follows the same procedure, wherein a group discussion format is used to encourage people to discuss moral issues and their underlying values. For example, Mosconi and Emmett (2003) implemented a four-part values training curriculum with 54 high school students, where students were asked to contemplate their own values, defend their values in a dialogue with their peers, and engage in discussion, group work, and journaling. This procedure tended to modify students' perceptions of success from an initial society-based materialistic definition to definitions more in line with the activities themselves. Recent laboratory studies with 7th graders showed that African-American students who were instructed to write about a high-ranked value, as opposed to a low-ranked value, reported a lessened experience of feeling stereotyped and significantly improved their grades—reducing the racial achievement gap by 40% (Cohen, Garcia, Apfel, & Master, 2006).

Values training appears to have a salutary impact on college students as well. Ohlde and Vinitsky (1976) examined the effects of a 7-hour values training procedure in undecided college undergraduates. Their method involved small-group activities where students expressed their values to one another, outlined action plans, and identified barriers to action; this intervention produced significantly greater value awareness than a control condition. In a recent laboratory study, undergraduate students were randomly assigned to give a speech about either a top-ranked or lowest-ranked valued outcome. Results showed that participants who gave a speech on a more valued outcome had lower salivary cortisol responses to stress tasks, relative to control participants (Creswell, Welch, Taylor, Sherman, Gruenewald, & Mann, 2005). Salivary cortisol is considered a measure of stress, and when consistently high for extended periods of time, may result in decreased resilience and higher vulnerability to chronic mental and physical problems (McEwen, 1998).

In order to mix values work with goal setting as part of a behavioral intervention, a clear understanding of the principles involved is necessary. We have found it helpful to consider these topics from the point of view of Relational Frame Theory (RFT; Hayes, Barnes-Holmes, & Roche, 2001).

Goal Setting, Values, and Relational Frame Theory (RFT)

RFT is an empirically validated theory of language and cognition developed from a behavior analytic perspective, which offers a novel account of goal setting and values (Hayes et al., 2001; O'Hora & Maglieri, 2006). RFT is based on the idea that humans learn to derive relations among stimuli and to bring that ability under the control of arbitrary cues. A simple example is the relationship between a dime and a nickel. Young children prefer the nickel because it is larger, but when their verbal abilities improve, they prefer a dime because it is said to be "more than" a nickel.

A goal statement functions as a rule that establishes a set of verbal relations between behavior and specified consequences (Hayes & Hayes, 1989; O'Hora & Maglieri, 2006). The ability to derive relations between performance and the goal (e.g., "I am not going to reach the goal") allows the individual to adjust behavior accordingly and to contact reinforcement ("I'm going to make it") in the absence of tangible consequences (O'Hora & Maglieri, 2006). In RFT terms, goal setting is a kind of "track."

From an ACT perspective, values are not just a matter of classical values clarification: rather they are a combination of the choice of qualities of action and an orientation toward the present. Values in ACT are "freely chosen, verbally constructed consequences of ongoing, dynamic, evolving patterns of activity, which establish predominant reinforcers for that activity that are intrinsic in engagement in the valued behavioral pattern itself" (Wilson & DuFrene, 2009, p. 66). Goals are tangible consequences that can be achieved and finished. Conversely, values establish qualities of ongoing patterns of action as reinforcers – they can be instantiated but not obtained like an object. In other words, values are a verbal establishing stimulus, or in RFT terms, an "augmental," and the qualities that they establish as reinforcers can fit with concrete goals, but cannot be reduced to them because they are ongoing.

For example, suppose a student values learning. Studying for a test could have a goal of getting a good grade and passing a course, in which case the goal is reached and finished, but if it also has the value of learning, learning can continue. Even if nobody knew what the student was doing, actions such as reading or paying attention might now have properties that are intrinsically reinforcing.

Values work appears to be a crucial component in ACT. For example, a recent pain study showed that adding values training increased the effectiveness of an acceptance component for pain tolerance when compared to acceptance alone or control conditions (Branstetter-Rost, Cushing, & Douleh, 2009). A review of ACT components confirmed the utility of values interventions on their own or added as a component (Levin, Hildebrandt, Lillis, & Hayes, 2012).

Goal-Directed Behavior in the Service of Values

The addition of values to goal-setting may help address a gap in the goal-setting literature. Successful goals are more likely to be obtained when those goals are tied to something an individual values (Sheldon & Elliot, 1999; Sheldon & Houser-Marko, 2001; Sheldon, Ryan, Deci, & Kasser, 2004). Values may help overcome the known failure of goal setting to ensure that progress will be maintained in the face of obstacles (Gollwitzer & Brandstatter, 1997).

No study has yet explored the impact of adding an ACT values intervention to goal-setting training in increasing student retention in college. In order to do this, ACT values work needs to be delivered en masse in a cost effective way, such as through an online venue. The aim of this chapter is to provide an overview of ways in which this might be accomplished.

Building Online Modules

Below, we will describe a set of online modules that incorporate an ACT-based values training for college students, as well as best practices in terms of goal setting. These modules are designed to prompt students to think about what they value in their college education and to create academic goals that are in line with their stated values.

The Academic Values Module

Several factors need to be considered when designing an online values program.

HOW TO GET STUDENTS TO REFLECT ON AND WRITE ABOUT THEIR LIFE VALUES

When designing a values module, one is initially struck with the problem of how to get a student to clarify "freely chosen" values while at the same time not imposing particular values on the student. After all, from an ACT perspective, values work is meant to function as an augmental (establishing reinforcers) in order to promote "tracking" on the part of the student (i.e., sensitizing the student to how behavior is values-based). This is explicitly opposed to "pliance" (i.e., behavior governed by a socially-mediated rule imposed by others; Hayes et al., 2011).

Let's think back on Sandra, the undecided student described at the beginning of this chapter. It is important that the academic values module not imply that she *should* value education. Rather, the module would instead discuss what values are and are not, interspersed with examples tied to an academic setting, thus empowering Sandra to *choose* her values (See the "Thinking and writing about values" screenshot in Appendix 9A [www.newharbinger.com/22225]).

The module incorporated a "Tending the Garden" metaphor in an effort to have the student experientially understand the process of valuing by having the student imagine he is a gardener who values his task even though droughts, floods, pests, and other obstacles may interfere with the quality of the crops. Even so, the gardener can find something in the act itself that he values. Values are about the process rather than the concrete outcomes (See the "Tending the Garden" metaphor screenshot in Appendix 9B.) The module concludes with open-ended questions in which the student can freely state his values. However, this component is worded in such a way that the student is asked to think about his values as they relate to education. In other words, the student is asked to find a way to link education to life values that he freely chooses.

COMMUNICATING WHAT VALUES ARE AND ARE NOT

The academic values module starts by discussing what values are and what they are not, without using overly technical terms. For example, we discuss values as "areas of life that have meaning to you" and emphasize that, unlike achieving a goal, valuing choices are ongoing. We found it useful to discuss values as a direction in life. Values are like a direction on a roadmap, with particular stops along the way (e.g., college, visiting family, a particular job), but the trip never ends (See the "What are values?" screenshot in Appendix 9C.)

Four other points about values are emphasized. *First, values are choices.* Values are not right or wrong. If the student were alone on an island and nobody would know what he valued, what would he choose? *Second, values help a person be present in what he is doing*: walking to campus, having a conversation with a roommate, or studying for an exam. Once someone has stated his own values, it becomes easier to monitor the correspondence between the value and one's own behavior. *Third, values help orient a person to a life direction yet allow for flexibility* in how one travels along the direction. This means that "valuing" can take a variety of forms. For example, "learning" is not restricted to a school setting – one can "learn" from any life situation. *Fourth, one does not have to have experience with a particular situation in order for it to be values-based.* Future goals such as "graduation" can still be linked to chosen qualities of action.

Next, the module describes what values are *not* through four additional points. *First, values are not outcomes or achievements.* These refer to goals, not values. Values refer to a life direction and can be demonstrated but not fully achieved or finished. However, clarifying one's own values may reveal particular goals that are aligned with one's values. *Second, values are not feelings.* Many times, engaging in activities aligned with particular values bring happiness. However, many times these activities bring about discomfort and pain (e.g., a long-term relationship is oftentimes accompanied by discomfort and conflict). The third and fourth points relate to other people. Specifically, *the third point emphasizes that values are not just about pleasing others;* although pleasing others may arise from living in a valued direction, it is also important that a student is valuing a direction because it matters to him to do so. Engaging in behaviors out of guilt or to please others results in less desirable psychological outcomes (e.g., Sheldon et al., 2004). This point helps distinguish values as augmentals from pliance. *The fourth point is that values are not assertions about what others must do.* Emphasized here is the fact that we are discussing *personal* values, which pertain to one's own behavior, not the behavior of other people.

The Academic Goal-Setting Module

The academic goal-setting module consists of text and audio that discuss what goals are, how they might relate to education, and how to set them, and concludes with several open-ended questions designed to prompt the student to think about and state goals related to his educational career at the university. Most importantly, the goal-setting module comes after the values training module, thus goals are set to be aligned with the education-related values the student set previously.

HOW TO SET SMART GOALS

The module focuses on setting SMART *(Specific, Measureable, Attainable, Realistic, and Time-oriented)* goals (Nelson & Quick, 2006). During the open-ended section of the module, the student is prompted to set academic goals and state how each element of SMART relates to his goal. *Specific* means the goal is a clear and specific statement of what the student wants. It is emphasized here that when a target goal is vague, one can confuse oneself, give up, or go after the wrong goal. *Measurable* refers to setting goals in a way that the student can easily track his own progress toward completion. The more measureable a goal is, the more readily a student can recognize if he is moving in the right direction, gauge how far he needs to go to meet the goal, and adjust his behavior accordingly. It is also emphasized that a measureable goal is typically also a specific goal that articulates actions that the student can take to achieve the overall objective. *Attainable* means the goal should be achievable, but not easy. We recommend using an 80% probability of goal achievement for short-term goals, while long-term goals can be more difficult. *Realistic* is closely related to *Attainable* but also means that the actions associated with goal obtainment are behaviors that the student can actually do given his life situation. For example, it may not be realistic for the student to read 200 pages every day given that the student may also work, have four other classes to attend, and so on. Lastly, the term *Time-oriented* refers to setting clear deadlines for goals. It also emphasizes that setting goals that have natural endings (e.g., the end of the day, week, month, or semester) can be particularly useful in maintaining focus and motivation toward goal obtainment (see the "SMART Goals" and "Writing SMART Goals" screenshots in Appendix D).

SETTING PROXIMAL, INTERMEDIATE, AND DISTAL GOALS

SMART goal setting comes with one caveat, however. SMART goals are generally meant to apply only to short-term (e.g., end of the week) and intermediate goals (e.g., end of the semester). Long-term or distal goals (e.g., 2-3 years) help students not lose sight of "the big picture." In this case, the big picture could be "graduation." At this point, it is OK for the student to set long-term goals even if he has no idea how to get there. As the student progresses toward achieving the long-term goal, it becomes easier for him to determine how to achieve it with short-term and intermediate SMART goals.

After the student indicates his goals in the module, he is then prompted to write out the potential obstacles to achieving the goals as well as possible solutions for each obstacle. Then, the student indicates why the goal(s) is/are important to him, which serves to further link the goal(s) to his previously stated values. Lastly, the student provides specific action steps on the way to achieving his ultimate goal, and when these steps should be completed.

SELF-MONITORING WITH THE GOAL-SETTING CALENDAR

When implementing a goal-setting training for students, it may be useful to have students generate a goal-setting calendar. The calendar serves as a self-monitoring tool for the student in which he sets deadlines for each of his goals, listing specific actions and potential obstacles to meeting his goals. The student may also be encouraged to write important academic deadlines on the calendar (e.g., due dates for class assignments and exams) that may help him gauge the *Time-oriented* aspect of his SMART goals.

Empirical Considerations

The current chapter is based on a recent dissertation by Chase (2010). The purpose of this study was to assess the additive effects of values training to an online goal-setting training procedure on academic performance and student retention. Psychology majors in their second year or beyond were recruited and randomly assigned to one of three groups: a goal-setting training only group (n = 48), a goal-setting plus values training group (n = 51), and a waitlist control group (n = 33). The modules were constructed using an online survey management system and consisted of text with an audio component consisting of a voice speaking the words on the page. Each part of the module ended with multiple-choice questions to ensure that students were retaining the information in the module. Goal setting alone was not effective, but when the values module was added to goal setting there were statistically significant improvements in cumulative grade point average (GPA) as well as in student retention (i.e., students in the goal-setting plus values condition were significantly more likely to continue their enrollment in the university the next semester). In the subsequent semester, the impact of goal setting plus values on GPA was not maintained; however, when values work was added to the waitlist condition, GPA again increased, thus replicating the positive impact of values training. This indicates that these short modules had medium-term effects over a semester, but not long-term effects. Thus, future research should investigate ways to maintain the effects.

Final Words

There are a few issues to consider when implementing values training with college students. In creating the current set of values modules, the challenge of not "telling students what to value" quickly became apparent, and a good deal of effort went into preventing this from happening. With any values procedure based on an ACT conceptualization, it is important to prevent subtle communications that could control the student's behavior via pliance. The aim of values training is to have the student generate his own value statements, which will lead to him tracking the correspondence between his behavior in relation to his previously stated values. The crucial feature of tracking is that it sensitizes the individual's behavior to the environment such that he may self-regulate his behavior in the service of his own values. If such values are imposed on the student by another person, then the student may focus his efforts on avoiding aversive consequences from another person or authority figure rather than tracking the correspondence between his or her behavior and the valued direction. Tracking places the individual's behavior under the influence of the natural consequences of the behavior. In this context, behavior is in the service of values. Values choices cannot be turned over to other people.

The challenge, then, was to create a situation in which students could freely state their values while at the same time guiding the students' values statements to focus on their college career. As mentioned previously, the modules guided the student's focus by interspersing examples of values and behavior related to academic settings while not imposing judgments on any particular value or behavior. At the end of the values module, the student was asked to think about his current college situation and everything it entails, both pleasant and unpleasant. Then, the student was asked to try and find something in that situation that mattered to him and to try to link that to larger life values. Thus, instead of telling the student to value "education" or "learning," the student was asked to try and link his college experience to larger life values. The student is the one who chooses his own values, not the administrator conducting the training.

Since students are free to decide for themselves what they value, they are also free to decide what they do not value. As briefly mentioned by Herbst and Houmanfar (2009, p. 65), one should be prepared for the possibility that some individuals may come to realize that their values do not align with a particular domain—in this case, a college education. While at first glance this may be seen as troublesome, values in-and-of themselves are neither "good" nor "bad" in any absolute sense. Although an individual without a college education may not make as much money as an individual with a college education (as discussed at the beginning of this chapter), there is nothing inherently "good" or "bad" about having a particular level of income. If a student goes through a values training exercise and discovers that a college education is not in the service of his values, the student would likely not be happy continuing in that particular life direction and was likely doing so out of pliance (e.g., pressure from parents or peers) and not because he truly valued doing so.

In conclusion, the issue of student retention in our nation's universities is real and university administrators seem to be lacking the resources needed to address it. The preceding paragraphs outlined one possible solution. The online values training and choice module, added to a goal-setting training package, discussed herein has been shown to increase cumulative GPA and student retention during that term among psychology students at a public university. The online and automated nature of the package is a format that is amenable to dissemination across a wide number of colleges and universities across the world. Although the effects produced by the training package were shown to be medium-term and not permanent, this is not surprising. Values are continuously evolving and need to be revisited throughout life. There is no reason institutions of higher education could not structure regular exploration of values choices in students. The effects are encouraging and warrant the continued development and evolution of the technology for future implementation.

References

American College Testing (2008). *What works in student retention.* Retrieved October 10, 2008 from http://www.act.org/path/postsec/droptables/pdf/All Colleges.pdf

Amigo, S., Smith, A., & Ludwig, T. (2008). Using task clarification, goal setting, and feedback to decrease table busing times in a franchise pizza restaurant. *Journal of Organizational Behavior Management, 28,* 176-187.

Astin, A. W., Tsui, L., & Avalos, J. (1996). *Degree attainment rates at American colleges and universities: Effects of race, gender, and institutional type.* Los Angeles: Higher Education Research Institute, University of California.

Bandura, A. (1997). *Self-efficacy: The exercise of control.* Stanford: W.H. Freeman.

Berger, J. B., & Braxton, J. M. (1998). Revising Tinto's interactionalist theory of student departure through theory elaboration: Examining the role of organizational attributes in the persistence process. *Research in Higher Education, 39(2),* 103-119.

Bowen, E., Price, T., Lloyd, S., & Thomas, S. (2005). Improving the quantity and quality of attendance data to enhance student retention. *Journal of Further & Higher Education, 29(4),* 375-385.

Branstetter-Rost, A.D., Cushing, C., & Douleh, T. (2009). Personal values and pain tolerance: Does a values intervention add to acceptance? *Journal of Pain, 10,* 887-892.

Chase, J. A. (2010). The additive effects of values clarification training to an online goal-setting procedure on measures of student retention and performance. *Dissertation Abstracts International: Section B: The Sciences and Engineering, 71(6-B),* 3921.

Cohen, G. L., Garcia, J., Apfel, N., & Master, A. (2006). Reducing the racial achievement gap: A social-psychological intervention. *Science, 313,* 1307-1310.

Creswell, J. D., Welch, W. T., Taylor, S. E., Sherman, D. K., Gruenewald, T. L., & Mann, T. (2005). Affirmation of personal values buffers neuroendocrine and psychological stress response. *Psychological Science, 16,* 846–851.

Dohm, A., & Wyatt, I. (2002). College at work: Outlook and earnings for college graduates, 2000-2010. *Occupational Outlook Quarterly, Fall 2002,* 3-15.

Easterbrooks, S. R., & Scheetz, N. A. (2004). Applying critical thinking skills to character education and values clarification with students who are deaf or hard of hearing. *American Annals of the Deaf, 149(3),* 255-263.

Frayne, C. (1991). *Reducing employee absenteeism through self-management training: A research based analysis and guide.* New York: Quorum Books.

Gerhardt, M. (2007). Teaching self-management: The design and implementation of self-management tutorials. *Journal of Education for Business, 83(1),* 11-17.

Gollwitzer, P. M., & Brandstatter, V. (1997). Implementation intentions and effective goal pursuit. *Journal of Personality and Social Psychology, 73,* 186-199.

Goomas, D. T., Smith, S. M., & Ludwig, T. D. (2011). Business activity monitoring: Real-time group goals and feedback using an overhead scoreboard in a distribution center. *Journal of Organizational Behavior Management, 31,* 196-209.

Hayes, S. C., Barnes-Holmes, D., & Roche, B. T. (2001). *Relational frame theory: A post-Skinnerian account of human language and cognition.* New York: Plenum Press.

Hayes, S. C., & Hayes, L. J. (1989). The verbal action of the listener as a basis for rule governance. In S. C. Hayes (Ed.), *Rule governed behavior: Cognition, contingencies, and instructional control* (pp. 153-190). New York: Plenum Press.

Hayes, S. C., Strosahl, K., & Wilson, K. G. (2011). *Acceptance and Commitment Therapy: The process and practice of mindful change.* New York: Guilford Press.

Herbst, S. A., & Houmanfar, R. (2009). Psychological approaches to values in organizations and organizational behavior management. *Journal of Organizational Behavior Management, 29,* 47-68.

Hood, R. (1999). Academic success class a tool in OSU's retention efforts. *OSU This Week, 38(35),* 1.

Karabenick, S. A., & Knapp, J. R. (1988). Help-seeking and the need for academic assistance. *Journal of Educational Psychology, 80,* 406-408.

Kerkvliet, J., & Nowell, C. (2005). Does one size fit all? University differences in the influence of wages, financial aid, and integration on student retention. *Economics of Education Review, 24(1),* 85-95.

Levin, M. E., Hildebrandt, M., Lillis, J., & Hayes, S. C. (2012). The impact of treatment components suggested by the psychological flexibility model: A meta-analysis of laboratory-based component studies. *Behavior Therapy, 43,* 741-756.

Locke, E. A., & Latham, G. P. (1990). *A theory of goal setting and task performance.* Englewood Cliffs, NJ: Prentice Hall.

Locke, E. A., & Latham, G. P. (2002). Building a practical useful theory of goal setting and task motivation. *American Psychologist, 57,* 705-717.

Locke, E. A., Shaw, K. N., Saari, L. M., & Latham, G. P. (1981). Goal setting and task performance: 1969-1980. *Psychological Bulletin, 90(1),* 125-152.

Loewy, S., & Bailey, J. (2007). The effects of graphic feedback, goal setting, and manager praise on customer service behaviors. *Journal of Organizational Behavior Management, 27,* 15-26.

Luthans, F., & Davis, T. (1979). Behavioral self-management: The missing link in managerial effectiveness. *Organizational Dynamics, 8,* 42-60.

McEwen, B. S. (1998). Protective and damaging effects of stress mediators. *New England Journal of Medicine, 338,* 171–179.

McLaughlin, G., Brozovsky, P., & McLaughlin, J. (1998). Changing perspectives on student retention. *Research in Higher Education, 39(1),* 1-15.

Mosconi, J., & Emmett, J. (2003). Effects of a values clarification curriculum on high school students' definitions of success. *Professional School Counseling, 7(2),* 68-78.

Nelson, D. L., & Quick, J. C. (2006). *Organizational behavior: Foundations, realities & challenges* (5th ed.). Mason, OH: South-Western.

Ohlde, C. D., & Vinitsky, M. H. (1976). Effect of a values-clarification workshop on value awareness. *Journal of Counseling Psychology, 23(5),* 489-491.

O'Hora, D., & Maglieri, K. A. (2006). Goal statements and goal-directed behavior: A relational frame account of goal setting in organizations. *Journal of Organizational Behavior Management, 26(1/2),* 131-170.

Pascarella, E. T., & Terenzini, P. T. (2005). *How college affects students: A third decade of research.* San Francisco, CA: Jossey-Bass.

Richardson, M., Abraham, C., & Bond, R. (2012). Psychological correlates of university students' academic performance: A systematic review and meta-analysis. *Psychological Bulletin, 138(2),* 253-387. doi:10.1037/a0026838

Seidman, A. (2005). Minority student retention: Resources for practitioners. *New Directions for Institutional Research, 2005(125),* 7-24.

Sheldon, K. M., & Elliot, A. J. (1999). Goal striving, need satisfaction, and longitudinal well-being: The self-concordance model. *Journal of Personality and Social Psychology, 76(3),* 482-497.

Sheldon, K. M., & Houser-Marko, L. (2001). Self-concordance, goal attainment, and the pursuit of happiness: Can there be an upward spiral? *Journal of Personality and Social Psychology, 80,* 152-165.

Sheldon, K. M., Ryan, R., Deci, E. & Kasser, T. (2004). The independent effects of goal contents and motives on well-being: It's both what you pursue and why you pursue it. *Personality and Social Psychology Bulletin, 30,* 475-486.

Simon, S. B., Howe, L. W., & Kirschenbaum, H. (1972). *Values clarification: A handbook of practical strategies for teachers and students.* New York: Hart.

Stover, C. (2005). Measuring and understanding student retention. *Distance Education Report, 9(16),* 1-7.

Thomas, L. (2002). Student retention in higher education: The role of institutional habitus. *Journal of Education Policy, 17(4),* 423-442.

Tinto, V. (1993). *Leaving college: Rethinking the causes and cures of student attrition (2nd ed.).* Chicago: The University of Chicago Press.

U.S. Bureau of Labor Statistics News Release (2010). Usual weekly earnings of wage and salary workers fourth quarter 2009. Retrieved February 27, 2010 from http://www.bls.gov/news.release/pdf/wkyeng.pdf

U.S. Census Bureau (2002). The big payoff: Educational attainment and synthetic estimates of work-life earnings. *Current Population Reports.* Retrieved February 27, 2010 from http://www.census.gov/population/www/socdemo/educ-attn.html

U.S. Department of Education (2007). Persistence and attainment of 2003–04 beginning postsecondary students: after three years. Retrieved September 10, 2009 from http://nces.ed.gov/pubSearch/pubsinfo.asp?pubid=2007169

Wilson, K. G., & DuFrene, T. (2009). *Mindfulness for two: An Acceptance and Commitment Therapy approach to mindfulness in psychotherapy.* Oakland, CA: New Harbinger.

Zimmerman, B. J., & Risemberg, R. (1997). Self-regulatory dimensions of academic learning and motivation. In G. D. Phye (Ed.), *Handbook of academic learning: Construction of knowledge* (pp. 105-125). San Diego: Academic Press.

CHAPTER 10

Teaching Mindfulness and Acceptance within College Communities to Enhance Peer Support

Charles Morse

Worcester Polytechnic Institute (WPI)

It's 2 a.m. and Nathan is sitting at his desk, trying to memorize formulas for his Calculus test tomorrow morning. His phone vibrates with another text from Emily, his ex-girlfriend who lives across campus. He knows she's been having a hard time since they broke up and he's tried to be supportive, but she just doesn't seem to be able to move on with her life. This text is even more concerning than the one he received 20 minutes ago; she feels helpless, she's tired of the constant pain, and she just cut herself to make the pain stop. Nathan's feelings of frustration and helplessness mount. What should he say to her? What should he do? It's not the first time Emily has hurt herself. In fact, her self-harm was one of the main reasons Nathan had broken off the relationship. He couldn't understand why she'd hurt herself when she was upset and he struggled with keeping her self-harm a secret, as Emily had insisted. He'd tried to get her to agree to go to the college counseling center (CCC) but Emily angrily refused, saying that she wasn't crazy and could manage things on her own. Nathan's friends have told him he should stop talking to Emily, but he feels she needs him now more than ever. Nathan's afraid that if he doesn't respond to Emily, she might kill herself. He feels lost and overwhelmed in his relationship with Emily.

Emily was devastated when Nathan broke up with her two months ago. They had been dating for almost a year and she'd taken great risks to open up emotionally in her relationship with him. Nathan had become her lifeline in many ways, her family life being chaotic and abusive. She'd finally found someone she could trust, someone she could really talk to about her issues. He was the first person she'd ever told about her cutting, and though he seemed to handle it well, he insisted that she stop hurting herself. Emily tried to stop cutting and was successful for a few months until a visit home during break when, with her parents in the midst of a drunken argument, she cut her shoulder to ease the pain. A week later, when Nathan saw the cuts, he gave her an ultimatum: get help at the counseling center or the relationship is over.

This scenario and many others like it play out frequently on college campuses in the US and throughout the world. Students turn to other students for help with significant mental health issues and friends experience helplessness and frustration in their attempts to provide them with support. Significant numbers of students on college campuses struggle with mental health issues in isolation, afraid to talk to family or friends about their problems, sometimes due to fear of being a burden or because they think it means they're crazy. Many other students share freely of their struggles, but refuse to seek professional help because they "don't have time" or "want to solve things on their own" (Eisenberg, Downs, Golberstein, & Zivin, 2009). Ultimately, the significant prevalence of student mental health issues on college campuses impacts entire campus communities, not just those who are directly suffering. Students, functioning in close living and learning environments, are quite aware of their peers' distress, but feel ill equipped and overwhelmed in the face of attempting to provide support for their friends (Drum, Brownson, Denmark, & Smith, 2009). Fortunately, campus communities can be enriched by enhancing mental health awareness and community members' willingness and ability to recognize and connect effectively with their peers when they're in distress.

This chapter will describe one such initiative, a peer support enrichment program, which utilizes a mindfulness- and acceptance-based approach to train college students to help other college students struggling with mental health issues. We will first review relevant literature regarding student mental health problems on campus and establish the relevance of peer-based programs. Additionally, we will describe a peer support enrichment program and highlight its infusion with mindfulness and acceptance processes. This peer support training program, Student Support Network (SSN), is available for download as Appendix 10A at www.newharbinger.com/22225.

Some studies have estimated that between 30 – 50% of college students have diagnosable psychiatric disorders (Eisenberg, Gollust, Golberstein, & Hefner 2007; Blanco et al., 2008), while in annual surveys over half of college students report feeling overwhelming anxiety and 31% feeling so depressed it's difficult to function. Of great concern are students who are so distressed they are contemplating suicide (6.1%) or have made a suicide attempt (1.1%; American College Health Association [ACHA], 2011). Drum, Brownson, Denmark, & Smith (2009) examined more closely the nature of college student suicidal ideation and found that 46% of students with thoughts of ending their life never told anyone else, and when they did share their distress, 67% of the time they first told a peer. In summary, mental health distress is widespread and college students tend to hide their struggles from others, particularly when their struggles are more significant and involve suicidal ideation. When students do share their struggles, most often this sharing happens first with friends.

Typically, easy-to-access professional mental health resources are available on college campuses; yet, students seem reticent to seek help. Eisenberg, Downs, Golberstein, & Zivin (2009) sought to detail student resistance to help seeking; major reasons included lack of time, lack of perceived need for help, unawareness of services or insurance coverage, and skepticism about treatment effectiveness. Additional evidence is emerging that biomedical descriptions of mental health distress can add to stigmatizing attitudes and ultimately decrease potential help-seeking behaviors (Rusch, Kanter, & Brondino, 2009). Diagnostic labeling and biomedical descriptions of mental health distress, both inherent in a medical model conceptualization, may reduce the likelihood that individuals will access help for mental health distress.

Acceptance and Commitment Therapy (ACT; Hayes, Strosahl, & Wilson, 2011), with its functional/contextual orientation to understanding mental health distress, may provide a compelling alternative to the medical model when designing and implementing psychoeducational programming intended to enrich support for students within campus communities.

College counseling, health, or wellness centers can show initiative and assume leadership and responsibility for the strategic design and implementation of population-level interventions intended to improve overall student support, safety, and well-being. Many CCCs see themselves as more traditional clinical settings, providing professional mental health assessment and treatment and occasional training and outreach programming within the campus community. Under the weight of ever-increasing student requests for services (Gallagher, 2011), a call for more clinical staff is often the first reaction. But with such widespread prevalence of mental health distress on college campuses, no CCC could ever be adequately staffed to meet the clinical needs of all students on campus. New paradigms of treatment and community intervention need to be investigated, developed, and evolved in order to address the overall mental health needs of the campus community.

Fortunately, much has been learned over the past decade about college campuses adopting public health models for suicide prevention and mental health promotion. This work has been largely supported by the Garrett Lee Smith Act of Congress in 2004, which under the guidance of the federal Substance Abuse and Mental Health Services Administration (SAMHSA) has authorized grants to, as of 2012, 98 different colleges to study and evolve best practices as they relate to suicide prevention and mental health promotion on college campuses (Suicide Prevention Resource Center, 2012). The Act has also funded the creation of the Suicide Prevention Resource Center (SPRC), a clearinghouse for information and research, and a major provider of technical support for college campuses invested in designing and implementing strategic initiatives to promote mental health and prevent suicide on college campuses.

In light of the widespread prevalence of mental health distress on college campuses and the impossibility of providing individual or even group support to all these students, CCCs continue to evolve toward engaging in local, strategic, population-based mental health education and promotion activities as a central component of their mission on campus. While providing leadership for these efforts, CCCs must involve the entire campus community in development and implementation of such activities. Such efforts will help build trusting connections between helping resources within campus communities and open up conversations about mental health issues that can result in less overall mental health stigma. This chapter describes one such mindfulness and acceptance-informed approach to building community support for students with mental health distress.

Let's return to Nathan and Emily, the students introduced at the beginning of this chapter. Nathan has tried talking to family and friends about the situation with Emily and how he feels responsible for her well-being. Typically, they've tried to be supportive by giving him advice: break off the relationship, stop getting sucked into her drama, turn off your cell phone, forget about her. All this is meant to make Nathan feel better, but in the end he feels guilty about pulling away from Emily and to some degree he feels responsible for her pain. He still cares about Emily deeply. No one seems to understand this part of his experience.

Emily has lost her best friend in Nathan. They used to spend much of their time together and she met most of her friends through Nathan's involvement in the fraternity house. Now that they're not dating, she doesn't feel comfortable going to the fraternity house and hanging out. She's lost her boyfriend and her social life, all because of cutting. She feels that nobody understands her perspective: that the cutting is not that big a deal, it's not like she's going to kill herself. Emily is lost, alone, and afraid to ask for help. Every day she thinks of calling the counseling center to make an appointment as Nathan had suggested, but then she talks herself out of it. She's never been to see a counselor before and has no idea what it would be like or whether it could be helpful.

This chapter will follow these two students and show how a peer support enrichment program might be helpful in such a context. We will start by describing our program.

Student Support Network (SSN)

On the campus of Worcester Polytechnic Institute (WPI) and with the support of Garrett Lee Smith funding, the Student Development & Counseling Center (SDCC) has developed, evolved, and implemented a training program intended to enhance peer support for mental health issues on campus. The six-week training program, called Student Support Network (SSN), is a major component of WPI's comprehensive suicide prevention strategy. The program was designed to identify and train a wide range of connected and concerned students in how to recognize and best support other students in distress. Additionally, these students learn when and how to connect their peers with professional help for mental health concerns. Once trained, these students become part of WPI's SSN, a group of students dedicated to, and supported in, reaching out and helping other students in distress.

The program is designed with the understanding that there are naturally existing and evolving networks of student support, formal and informal, on any given college campus. Effectively identifying, recruiting, training, and supporting students from these existing peer networks can enhance the overall supportive and responsive atmosphere within a campus community. Embedded within these networks of support are "key" students on campus such as captains of athletic teams, fraternity and sorority presidents, leaders in student government and student clubs and organizations. Less formally, supportive networks form around students who are perceived by their peers as "natural helpers" within existing social, living, and academic networks. While recruiting student leaders is an important element of the training program, any student who wishes to be part of SSN is welcome to apply. Ultimately, SSN is about forming and enhancing connections between professional helping resources and a wide range of students within the campus community.

Program Development and Implementation

SSN incorporates elements of several different evidence-based approaches to suicide prevention and mental health promotion. Foundationally, SSN is a gatekeeper training for students, drawing core elements from the Question, Persuade, Refer (QPR) program (Quinnett, 1995). Additionally, SSN was influenced by the Campus Connect Training Program, developed at Syracuse University, in that it emphasizes skill building in empathic responding (Syracuse University Counseling Center, 2011). Perhaps unique to the SSN training program are 1) its strategic focus on building and sustaining connections between campus support resources and a significant number of student helpers within the campus community, and 2) its heavy reliance on Acceptance and Commitment Therapy (ACT; Hayes et al., 2011) in its view of psychological flexibility as a core component of mental health. We will first describe SSN generically and later point out how mindfulness and acceptance, through ACT, have been brought to bear on the development and implementation of this program.

SSN recruits students into the program through nomination and open invitation. During recruitment phases, members of the campus community are asked to nominate students who are well connected on campus and who may be perceived by their peers as "natural helpers." The SSN program is also advertised throughout the year to promote program recognition and invite open application for training. All interested students are welcomed into the program. There is no attempt to screen out candidates as the program is a gatekeeper training, not a peer education or peer counseling program. As student trainees are already connected within variously effective networks of support, SSN training seeks to enhance their ability to recognize and respond effectively to their peers' distress within their current networks of influence and support.

Recruitment results in diverse groups of 15 students per training session. Generally, two to three groups are trained simultaneously over six-week training periods occurring several times during the year. The 50-minute daytime classes fit into students' weekly schedules. Students are told they must complete the entire six-week training to be part of SSN and that no further commitment will be asked of them after the training. The existence of parallel training groups allows for both success in initial scheduling and the availability of make-up sessions. This system, and the compelling nature of the training itself, has led to over 97% retention rate for students who begin the training series.

The SSN training program is co-led by two group leaders with separate and complementary functions. The Program Manager oversees all efforts at student recruitment and involvement, arrangements for all SSN training meetings as well as SSN related events on campus. This role may be carried out by someone in the CCC, but other individuals working within student activities and/or student life, or graduate students, may be qualified for this function. The second group leader is someone with a mental health background; preferably a licensed clinician working within the CCC. This individual's primary role is to provide leadership and expertise in each of the SSN training sessions as well as to provide consultative advice to SSN trainees who may be concerned about a friend. This role can be filled by multiple individuals from the CCC, allowing student trainees to be exposed to a number of different individual clinicians and their specialties.

Six-Week Training Program

The SSN training series encompasses areas of key knowledge, skill, and perspective development. Each of the 50-minute training meetings involves roughly equal amounts of information sharing, group discussion, and experiential exercises. Limiting the size of training groups to 15 students enhances the formation of enduring connections both between group members and between trainees and trainers. The formation of these supportive connections, essentially networking helpers in various roles on campus, is central to the SSN philosophy.

Key knowledge areas include information on recognizing others with symptoms of depression, anxiety, substance abuse, non-suicidal self injury (NSSI), and suicidal ideation and attempts, and an awareness of the campus/community supports available to students experiencing various kinds of distress. Students are oriented to the entire continuum of suicidal behavior and the importance of being willing to ask directly about suicidal thinking and/or behavior. It is most helpful to highlight that suicidal thoughts are quite common when people are experiencing mental health distress, yet acting on these thoughts is quite rare. Individuals in distress experience significant relief from being able to directly express suicidal thoughts to another person without being perceived as crazy. This helps to reinforce the importance of asking directly about thoughts of self-harm and suicide, the thought of which is particularly anxiety provoking for trainees.

All content-oriented discussions are highly interactive, attempting to draw accurate portrayals from students' experiences in the topic of concern. Training topics as well as additional mental health topics (e.g., problematic eating, thought disorders, relationship distress) are more thoroughly outlined in a training manual that each participant receives. Additionally, and largely due to SSN-trained student requests, more in depth "advanced SSN training" sessions have been organized around topics not included originally in the series. This has become one of many ways that already trained students sustain connection to the SSN program. Skill development in the area of empathic listening and compassionate responding is emphasized throughout the training series. Students are told that of all of the helping skills one can employ, empathy/compassion can be seen as the most important and effective way to provide support in the moment. Role play sessions during trainings revolve around the use of supportive responding skills and challenge students to better appreciate the importance and effectiveness of empathy. Additionally, students enhance their skill associated with meeting resistance around helping others connect with professional help. Trainees discuss the various reasons why people are reticent to seek professional help and are taught to understand and apply a "stages of change model" (Prochaska & DiClemente, 1984) when encouraging others to get help. This helps trainees recognize an internal process of decision making that happens for individuals contemplating making changes and/or seeking help, and reinforces trainees' understanding of the importance of sustaining connection and expressing ongoing concerns to friends in distress.

Throughout the training series students are encouraged to reach out to clinical staff and the program manager to let them know of concerns they might be having about a friend. Professional staff function in a consultative role in response to student concerns. Unless a situation involves significant risk, trainers/clinical staff do not move to take the situation out of the hands of the students. Concerned students are assisted in their efforts to support their peers and guided toward making referrals to professional resources where advisable. In this manner, students who are experiencing debilitating mental health distress are encouraged by friends to connect with professional counseling support far earlier than they may have without encouragement and support. Earlier identification of students in distress generally allows professional counselors far more latitude in effective intervention and short-term treatment.

Again, returning to Nathan and Emily and the distress they are both experiencing in the context of their recent breakup: A mutual friend of both Nathan and Emily, Sarah, has felt caught in the middle of their struggles and has been trying to support both of them. She is very worried about Emily, who has been avoiding going out with friends and over the past week has not been to classes. Sarah has been to Emily's room several times to try to talk with her, but Emily refuses to open up and won't leave her room. Nathan has also seemed much more stressed of late. Sarah knows he too is upset about the breakup and worried about Emily, but Nathan has shut her out as well, preferring to go out drinking with his fraternity brothers every night. Fortunately, Sarah has been involved in SSN training. She's often thought of Emily and Nathan during training sessions as she's learned about the different ways people struggle with mental health issues and how people often seek to escape their problems by avoiding them. Sarah has also learned how to be more supportive during the training by listening empathically. The concept of empathy seems so simple during the training, but the thought of listening and supporting Nathan and Emily without trying to "fix" their problems is terrifying to her. She's afraid listening empathically may even make things worse. Sarah decides to talk to one of the SSN instructors after class about the situation with her friends.

Elements of Mindfulness and Acceptance in SSN Training

Unique to our peer support enrichment program is the infusion of several ACT concepts and ideas, as well as a general stance of relating to students in our peer support enrichment program in an accepting fashion. We will outline these concepts below.

Universality of Human Suffering

Many core elements of the SSN training derive from ACT (Hayes et al., 2011). In fact, the main topic of the first week of training involves discussion and exercises oriented toward understanding what constitutes "good mental health." Central to this discussion is the ACT core observation about the ubiquity of human suffering. A starting point for this discussion is sharing the observation that we all seem to struggle at various times in our lives, some more than others. Many of us invest great effort in judging our thoughts and feelings, and generally keep our struggles to ourselves and often from ourselves. Young adults in particular, while attempting to establish themselves as autonomous and self-sufficient, feel the pressure to maintain the façade that they "have it all together." This potentially leads to a sense of isolation and loneliness in our struggles, as we are acutely aware of our own suffering while observing that "everyone else" seems to have their life together. Emphasis is placed on how we are all faced with challenges and emotional upheaval, and mental health should not be defined as an absence of distress.

Such de-stigmatizing perspectives are embedded throughout the training. Consistent with the ACT model (Hayes et al., 2011), in an attempt to further de-stigmatize the conversation about mental health issues, all use of diagnostic language and medical model conceptualizations are avoided. For instance, throughout the series there is no use of the phrase "mental illness" in describing the manner in which people struggle with mental health issues. Additionally, clinical labeling and diagnostic language is avoided in order to promote a better understanding of the universality of human suffering. Clinical labels can be stigmatizing in and of themselves, reinforcing an "us vs. them" mentality and driving individual and societal acceptance of mental health struggles into dark corners of embarrassment and shame. Trainers open up the discussion about mental health distress from a contextual perspective; relying more on descriptive language of how different people react to elevated levels of stress and various ways, effective and ineffective, people tend to attempt to cope.

Experiential Avoidance

A logical (but not so effective) strategy when struggling is to try to avoid or eliminate the things that cause us discomfort, such as uncomfortable feelings, scary thoughts, and disturbing memories. Through various means we may try to control our thoughts and avoid our feelings, but all too often these attempts to "cope" fall far short of success. In fact, attempts to avoid experience often cause additional problems. Students come to understand that many behavioral issues are related to individual attempts to escape emotional upheaval (Hayes et al., 2011): drinking or self-harm as a means of avoiding pain, social withdrawal and avoidance to manage anxiety, eating disorders as an attempt to control the internal experience of "helplessness," suicidal ideation as a means to escape acute stress. Students are oriented to the entire continuum of suicidal behavior and the importance of being willing to ask directly about suicidal thinking and/or behavior, even when feeling uncomfortable. They also discuss the significance of accepting one's own experience (e.g., discomfort or feeling helpless when asking a fellow student about suicide), which helps them appreciate the importance of both empathy and compassion as supportive responses.

Self as Context/History Is Only Additive

A unique, ACT-inspired metaphor is demonstrated to reinforce understanding of this conceptualization. The "Backpack" metaphor starts with the group leader borrowing a backpack from a student trainee and pointing out that the backpack, like all of the backpacks sitting in the room, is typically filled with a variety of "stuff." Some of it is helpful, some not so helpful, some old, some newer, some stuff we love to get rid of, and other stuff we want to carry forever. Ultimately though, the challenge in life is figuring out how to best carry the backpack with all its "stuff." History is only additive, so we can only add to the backpack but cannot use a delete button to undo some of its less desirable contents (e.g., sadness). The backpack is then held out to the side and out of view of the presenter. Participants are asked, "How is this for a solution?" Participants recognize that this (avoidance) is unworkable. Other suggestions are elicited from the group (give it to someone else, wear it on your back, leave it behind, sort through it and lighten the load), with the presenter playing out and commenting on the relative effectiveness or limitations of each approach. Several themes emerge in the discussion, most importantly that avoidance strategies, though effective in the short term, can cause problems when over-utilized over a longer period of time. Acceptance of all our "stuff" frees us up to move ahead most effectively toward the things most important in our lives. Students eventually see that wearing the backpack on their front, close to their heart, where they have easy access to all their stuff, may be the desired solution.

Mindfulness and Experiential Exercises

Experiential exercises are also employed to further re-enforce the importance and challenges involved in acceptance. At various points during the training series students engage in mindfulness and/or ACT defusion exercises that enhance and reinforce training goals. Depending on time, a brief centering exercise, a 3-minute breathing space (Segal, Williams, and Teasdale, 2002), or a longer "body scan" exercise (Kabat-Zinn, 1996) is used in the first training to help students experience elements of mindfulness and acceptance. Brief processing of these exercises further reinforces students' understanding of assuming a defused position relative to one's experience (see chapter 3 for a more detailed explanation of fusion/defusion). For instance, students will often express that they "can't do" or "don't like" these exercises or conversely that they "enjoy meditating." Instructors simply reflect that it's quite common that our minds will want to judge or criticize the exercises, and that we can gently and simply try to return to the exercise each time we're distracted.

Perspective Taking or Empathy Training

Empathy training is a central element of the SSN training series. In the second training session, empathy is presented to trainees as a most important element of overall supportive responding to others' distress. In ACT, the ability of the helpers, whether an experienced therapist or a college student peer, to put themselves in the place of the person they are attempting to help is essential. Therapists being trained in ACT are encouraged to work on their own experiences of pain and struggle in order to achieve this level of empathy and compassion (Hayes et al., 2011). In a similar vein, in our training, an empathy visualization exercise (Appendix 10A, p. 29, at newharbinger.com/22225) asks trainees to recall a recent personal experience involving emotional distress. Students are directed to ask themselves, "What do I want most in this moment?" as they visualize their distress. Invariably, the majority of students in the training group agree that they want to be understood, perhaps hugged, and most importantly listened to. This experiential exercise is referenced often during the training as students inevitably begin to question the efficacy of empathic responding.

Follow Your Experience, Not What Your Mind Says

While most students agree that empathic responding is important; actually responding empathically elicits a fair bit of resistance from students. This becomes evident in role playing sessions which are an integral part of each lesson in the training series. Early in the development of SSN training we found students resisted empathic responding during exercises, citing reasons such as "It's making it worse," "I'm only mimicking them," "We're going around in circles," and "It's just plain not helpful!" Trainers would often get mired in debates about the importance of empathic responding. As the training series evolved we learned to back off the debate and, as often done in ACT (Hayes et al., 2011), point student trainees more to their experience: "Don't believe a word we say, try out empathic responding and see what your experience tells you." Student trainees are given the assignment between training sessions to try to genuinely employ empathy when talking to friends and/or family members and observe how it affects the conversation. This practice experience has been transformative for many trainees who report, often with surprise, great success in supporting others with empathic responding.

Defusion

We found it helpful to trigger student trainee resistance early on in the training by constructing role plays with an "all empathy" condition. We then work at building awareness around trainees' resistance by employing cognitive defusion strategies (Hayes et al., 2011; see also chapter 3). For instance, we often respond, "Ah, so your mind is telling you responding this way is making them feel worse. Let's see what happens when we continue empathic responding even while our mind is criticizing it." Students discuss the various thoughts they experience during role plays, many of them negative or critical of the experience. Each time we just note the thought ("Thank you for sharing that thought") and ask that they continue with the exercise.

Integrating Various ACT Processes

Consistently, we encourage trainees to notice a strong urge to want to "fix the problem" when they are practicing empathic responding. It is our observation that attempts to fix the problem come from our own sense of wanting relief, as empathic responding can trigger significant personal discomfort. In order to maintain an empathic stance, we must anticipate and make room for some degree of discomfort: pain, anger, uncertainty, and helplessness to name a few. Repeated direct exposure of this discomfort and associated acceptance through defusion and mindfulness practices are essential to enhancing actual student empathy. It is only from this place of human vulnerability that we can truly provide another with empathy and compassion.

Going back to our situation in the beginning of the chapter, Sarah stayed after class after her final SSN training in order to talk with the instructor about her friends Emily and Nathan. She felt quite nervous about doing so, but was bolstered by the fact that she had gotten to know, respect, and trust the instructor, a counselor in the CCC. Instructors had also talked repeatedly in the series about "consulting" when one had concerns about friends; that one shouldn't feel that one had to be alone in this process of helping other students. As Sarah talked about her concerns regarding her friends, she noticed how the counselor was so empathic to her situation; he understood how she felt stuck in between her two friends and how worried she was. The counselor eventually suggested that she try to get her friend Emily to go to the CCC by offering to go with her for a consultation. Additionally he suggested that she find a time when Nathan was sober to gently express that she misses seeing him and feels worried about his drinking so often.

Sarah, feeling very nervous, did talk to Emily about going to the CCC with her. She was able to share what she had learned about counseling—that it was free and completely confidential (her parents wouldn't find out), and she was also able to share that she had met several of the staff at the CCC during her SSN training and they seemed very "nice." Emily, feeling very anxious and depressed after missing over a week of classes, agreed to go with her. Her cutting had recently become more severe, and over the past few days she had been experiencing suicidal thoughts. Emily did go to counseling and experienced great relief after her first session. She was very relieved that the counselor didn't "freak out" when she talked about her cutting or her suicidal thoughts, and she left the office with a plan to get back on track with her classes and follow up in counseling. Emily knows she has some work ahead, learning more effective coping skills and perhaps how to deal more effectively with her family, but she feels encouraged that she has professional support and a great friend in Sarah. Nathan was initially angry at Sarah when she said she thought he was drinking too much. Sarah felt disappointed that she was not able to get through to him, but she remembered the part of the SSN training where they had talked about the process of change, and not to be surprised if others react defensively to expressions of concern. A few days later Nathan contacted Sarah to see if she wanted to get together and play pool. When they met, Nathan said that Emily told him she was going to counseling and that he was greatly relieved in hearing this. He went on to talk about how stressed he'd been recently, at first about Emily's problems, then about his own concerns about drinking. Somehow he felt he could really open up to Sarah; she was such a great listener.

This scenario describes a situation where a student who underwent SSN training based on mindfulness and acceptance triggered a chain reaction that was helpful to at least two people, probably many more, and the campus community in general. Although not all cases will proceed so well, this example is not rare in our experience.

Empirical Considerations

Student trainee feedback about the training series has been excellent, with 98% of students saying they would recommend the training to other students on campus. SSN-trained students have successfully made numerous referrals of friends into the CCC, many of whom were experiencing suicidal ideation. While it is not possible to ascertain whether the training has actually saved student lives, clearly the training has resulted in more open discussion about mental health issues on campus and expressions of concern about members of the community. The number of student consults with CCC staff has tripled in the past three years; although this cannot be attributed to the SSN specifically with certainty, it is likely that the SSN contributed to it.

In five years of training at WPI, close to 400 students like Sarah, in groups of 15, have completed the series and are now part of the WPI SSN. The training has been very well received by students on campus; they genuinely enjoy the opportunity to speak openly about topics that are often considered taboo: self-harm, alcohol abuse, depression, and suicide. Students also comment about how interesting and challenging the role playing aspects of the training are. Consistently, many students who complete the training express an interest in staying involved and join mental health–oriented peer groups on campus such as Active Minds, peer education, and existing sexual assault prevention peer groups.

Pre-/post-training measures demonstrate consistent improvement in student trainee confidence, skills, and knowledge of how and when to intervene supportively with friends. Students' crisis-responding skills also show statistically significant improvement cumulatively and in all 15 cohorts of the training completed in the first three years of the program. Beginning in 2009, pre-/post- measures using the Acceptance & Action Questionnaire, AAQ-II (Bond et al., 2011) were implemented to measure the impact of the training on psychological flexibility. Early results indicate that students whose pre-training scores were in the lower half of the respondent pool (more experiential avoidance or lower psychological flexibility) demonstrated statistically significant improvement on the post-training measure. Students in the upper half of the AAQ-II pool remained about the same on pre-/post- AAQ-II measure, although this may have been due to a ceiling effect, as there was not much room to show increases in psychological flexibility. This provides some assurance that the embedded ACT-oriented discussions, metaphors, and exercises do lead to increased psychological flexibility among those students with relatively higher experiential avoidance before the training begins.

The SSN training series has also proved an excellent vehicle to establish contact with groups who are typically under-served in terms of reaching out for mental health support. Thus far the training series has been specifically delivered to groups of international students and under-represented student groups, both of which were quite successful and helped foster closer contact within these groups. SSN training has also been quite popular with "hard to reach" groups such as student athletes and students within the campus Greek system. SSN training would be very well suited to making contact with other high risk, help resistant groups such as returning veterans and graduate students. Our SSN Program described here was listed in the Suicide Prevention Resource Center's "Best Practices Registry" in 2010. As noted above, a program manual that includes detailed information on all aspects of the training series, including all lesson plans, is freely available as Appendix 10A at www.newharbinger.com/22225. Over 150 manuals have been requested and distributed to college campuses that have expressed an interest in learning more about the program. In the past few years, several other campuses are at various stages of implementing the SSN training program, which may help with further empirical testing of this model of enhancing peer support on campus.

Final Words

The prevalence of student mental health distress on college campuses is overwhelming, particularly for students who are often most acutely aware of their peers' struggles. Fortunately, college campuses offer connected and supportive communities with easily accessible mental health resources. Campuses can experience great benefit by adopting a preventive health approach to enhancing the level of understanding, compassion, support, and referral of those in the community who are experiencing significant distress, particularly students whose distress extends to suicidal ideation. This may require a somewhat challenging shift of perspective on college campuses, CCCs in particular, to allocate time and resources to strategic preventive models such as the SSN training program described here. Investing more time in preventive models also needs to be accompanied by adequately staffed counseling resources, to respond to critical referrals from the campus community. Upper level administrative support for initiatives such as this can be achieved by emphasizing that investing time and energy in community trainings oriented toward recognizing and responding to student distress enhances overall safety within the communities. Most students are uniquely situated and highly motivated to support their friends in distress, but often these young adults lack the confidence and skills to do so. Investing time and energy in connecting, training, and supporting students in their natural roles as helpers can make campus communities more supportive and responsive to the needs of those who may be struggling.

Conceptualizations and philosophical underpinnings inherent in ACT offer an excellent foundation from which to design and implement strategic preventive programming on college campuses to enhance the safety and well-being of students. Students enjoy and benefit from ACT's use of various and engaging modalities, such as metaphor and experiential exercises, in better understanding how to open up to and effectively support their peers' distress. Student trainees have eagerly embraced the concept that demonstrating openness and acceptance to friends in distress is foundational to their ability to provide support when their friends are struggling. More globally, widespread introduction and development of acceptance, mindfulness, and empathy on campus, particularly with students, can catalyze overall openness and support and make for healthier and safer communities.

References

American College Health Association. American College Health Association - National College Health Assessment (ACHA-NCHA) Web Summary. Updated 2011. Available at http://www.acha-ncha.org/data_highlights.html. 2011.

Blanco, C., Okuda, M., Wright, C., Hasin, D., Grant, B., Liu, S., & Olfson, M. (2008). Mental health of college students and their non-college-attending peers. *Archives of General Psychiatry. 65(12)*, 1429-1437.

Bond, F. W., Hayes, S. C., Baer, R. A., Carpenter, K. M., Guenole, N., Orcutt, H. K., Waltz, T., & Zettle, R. D. (2011). Preliminary psychometric properties of the Acceptance and Action Questionnaire - II: A revised measure of psychological flexibility and experiential avoidance. *Behavior Therapy.*

Drum, D. J., Brownson, C., Denmark, A. B., & Smith, S. E. (2009). New data on the nature of suicidal crises in college students: Shifting the paradigm. *Professional Psychology, 40(3)*, 213-222.

Eisenberg, D., Downs, M., Golberstein, E., & Zivin, K. (2009). Stigma and help-seeking for mental health among college students. *Medical Care Research & Review, 66(5)*, 522-541.

Eisenberg, D., Gollust, S. E., Golberstein, E., & Hefner, J. L. (2007). Prevalence and correlates of depression, anxiety and suicidality among university students. *American Journal of Orthopsychiatry, 77(4)*, 534-542.

Gallagher, R. P. (2011). *National survey of counseling center directors.* Alexandria, VA: International Association of Counseling Services.

Hayes, S. C., Strosahl, K., & Wilson, K. G. (2011). *Acceptance and Commitment Therapy: The process and practice of mindful change.* New York: Guilford Press.

Kabat-Zinn, J. (1996). *Full catastrophe living: How to cope with stress, pain and illness using mindfulness meditation.* London: Piatkus, 1996.

Prochaska, J. O., & DiClemente, C. C. (1984). *The transtheoretical approach: Crossing traditional boundaries of therapy.* Homewood, IL: Dow Jones-Irwin.

Quinnett, P. (1995). *QPR: Ask a Question, Save a Life.* The QPR Institute and Suicide Awareness/Voices of Education; 1995.

Rusch, L. C., Kanter, J. W., & Brondino, M. J. (2009). A comparison of the behavioral and biomedical models of stigma reduction for depression with a nonclinical undergraduate sample. *The Journal of Nervous and Mental Disease, 197,* 104-110.

Segal, Z., Williams, M., & Teasdale, J. (2002). *Mindfulness-based cognitive therapy for depression: A new approach to preventing relapse.* New York: Guilford Press, 2002.

Suicide Prevention and Resource Center (SPRC) (2012). *Garrett Lee Smith Grantees.* Retrieved March 26, 2012, from http://www.sprc.org/grantees/listing

Syracuse University Counseling Center (2011). *Campus Connect: A Suicide Prevention Training Program for Gatekeepers.* Retrieved March 26, 2012 from http://counselingcenter.syr.edu/campus_connect/connect_overview.html

CHAPTER 11

Acceptance and Commitment Therapy (ACT) in Classroom Settings

Jacqueline Pistorello

Steven C. Hayes

Jason Lillis

Douglas M. Long
University of Nevada, Reno

Vasiliki Christodoulou
City University, London, UK

Jenna LeJeune
Portland Psychotherapy

Jennifer Villatte
University of Nevada, Reno

John Seeley
Oregon Research Institute

Matthieu Villatte

Tami Jeffcoat

Jennifer Plumb-Vilardaga

Jamie Yadavaia
University of Nevada, Reno

"I have lived a sheltered life, with highly protective parents in a small town, where I was the big fish in a small pond. Since coming to the university, I've encountered people who are way smarter than I am, and I have had my small-town jokes fall flat over and over again. How can I learn to fit in without feeling like a big phony?"

"I miss my mama. I came here to play ball, but I miss being in my 'hood, hanging out with my pals. I have to sit out for one semester because of eligibility, and I think all the time about giving up and going home. I know it's weird to feel like that when most dudes my age would die to have a full-ride scholarship. I guess I'm homesick. I can't get out of bed. I skip classes and often just hang out eating pizza and watching movies. What can I do about being homesick?"

For several years, the first author was a guest speaker in classes to discuss "stress and coping" with college freshmen, usually around midterms. Over time, she developed an approach she called "Dear Jacque" (a la "Dear Abby" the advice columnist) to these presentations. All students would write an anonymous question on a piece of paper about a situation they were struggling with, from a stress and coping perspective. These two excerpts are paraphrases of some of these anonymous questions. "Dear Jacque" would then skim through these notes and pick 3-4 distinct questions to discuss with the rest of the class. Oftentimes, several different students would think that the question being read was "his" question. This experience alone illustrated a useful point to students—the ubiquity of suffering.

The first quote above is from a class with students coming from rural settings, and the second from a first year seminar for athletes. Both of these students, although struggling, are unlikely to walk into the college counseling center (CCC), perhaps because they don't feel like their concerns are severe enough, they are afraid of being stigmatized, or a range of other reasons (Eisenberg, Downs, Golberstein, & Zivin, 2009). The college athlete quoted above actually laughed when counseling was recommended, "I'm just homesick, dude." These two students are not alone. According to a recent survey of CCC directors, although CCCs see approximately 10% of the student body in individual or group therapy in a given year, only approximately 20% of college students who killed themselves in recent years had *ever* been seen at the local CCC (Gallagher, 2011).

Most young adults successfully negotiate developmental challenges in college—in a recent survey, 59% of college students showed no formal psychological distress and 20% were thriving while in college (Whitlock, in preparation). However, for others, the two vignettes above may mark the beginning of a downward trend that can result in dropping out of college or developing chronic mental health problems (Kadison & DiGeronimo, 2004). New approaches are needed to reach a large swath of the student population, some of whom would be unlikely to come into a CCC on their own.

College classrooms provide such an opportunity. Classes are not psychotherapy groups, however, and students vary widely in their degree of distress. Fortunately, the psychological flexibility models provide common core targets that can both ameliorate distress and promote learning (e.g., Varra, Hayes, Roget, & Fisher, 2008), reduce stigmatiza-tion of others (Masuda et al., 2007), and prevent the development of psychological problems (Muto, Hayes, & Jeffcoat, 2011).

This chapter will describe four instances of attempting to teach college students mindfulness and acceptance skills in classroom settings. The four projects described in this chapter relied on Acceptance and Commitment Therapy (ACT; Hayes, Strosahl, and Wilson, 2011) as their foundation. These projects either created ACT classes or infused ACT into existing types of psychology classes. In two instances, ACT classes were offered to students (one exclusively for freshmen and the other across all class standings) in order to prevent the development or exacerbation of mental health problems. In the two other instances, ACT was infused into existing course content for a psychology of racial differences or an abnormal psychology class, with the deliberate intent to reduce stigma about mental health problems among students. At the end of the chapter, issues having to do with bringing mindfulness and accep-tance into a classroom format in general will be discussed.

Project 1: Acceptance and Commitment Therapy (ACT) as a First Year Seminar (FYS)[4]

Jacqueline Pistorello, Steven C. Hayes, Jason Lillis, Douglas M. Long, Jennifer Villatte, John Seeley, Matthieu Villatte, Tami Jeffcoat, Jennifer Plumb-Vilardaga, and Jamie Yadavaia

Most universities offer some type of First Year Seminar (FYS) to fresh-men students (Padgett & Keup, 2011). The purpose of these classes is to teach various aspects of college life in order to help freshman college students adjust more effectively to college.

4   This project was supported by Award Number R01MH083740 (PIs: S. C. Hayes and J. Pistorello; Co-Is: J. Seeley and T. Biglan) from the National Institute of Mental Health (NIMH). The content is solely the responsibility of the authors and does not necessarily represent the official views of the National Institute of Mental Health or the National Institutes of Health.

There are many different types of FYSs, some of which date back to the early 1900s (Padgett & Keup, 2011), but a popular form of FYS is that of an "extended orientation" consisting of "an introduction to campus resources, time management, academic and career planning, learning strategies, and an introduction to student development issues" (Padgett & Keup, 2011, p. 2). Participation in FYS is associated with positive outcomes, such as persistence into the second year in college, improved academic performance, and positive changes in other related experiences associated with retention in college (Pascarella & Terenzini, 2005). FYSs seem well suited to deliver interventions designed to both prevent and ameliorate mental health problems among college students.

The purpose of this project was to design and test the acceptability and perceived usefulness of an FYS that taught skills to deal with psychological challenges through an ACT class composed of eight two-hour sessions. This 1-credit class covered all processes articulated in ACT (Hayes et al., 2011; see chapter 3), relying on a PowerPoint presentation in order to enhance fidelity to the research protocol by different instructors (class presentations and a manual for instructors and are available as Appendix 11A at www.newharbinger.com/22225). All instructors were trainees, either graduate students or postdoctoral fellows, trained in ACT previously. The credit for the class and the textbook, *Get Out of Your Mind and Into Your Life* (Hayes & Smith, 2005), were paid for by grant funds. The class was structured by covering 1-2 ACT processes each week, which roughly coincided with the workbook chapters (Hayes & Smith, 2005). Chapters 3 and 4 of this book contain a thorough description of ACT, thus our presentation here will be focused on our approach.

Principles in Adapting ACT to an FYS Format

The following are some of the principles used in the development and implementation of the ACT-based FYS. In ACT, principles take precedence over actual content (Hayes et al., 2011). Therefore, emphasis was placed on articulating key principles in adapting ACT to a non-clinical setting like a college classroom.

Speak to All Levels of Life Experience, Without Assuming Fragility

Class presentations had to resonate to a wide range of life experiences. For example, creative hopelessness as it is traditionally done (Hayes et al., 2011) might resonate with a freshman student struggling with anxiety or depression but might alienate students who are functioning well or dealing only with normal developmental issues, as in the first vignette above. We adjusted to this challenge by including examples across a wide range of life experiences. For example, when discussing the difference between pain and suffering, examples were drawn from common situations such as how avoidance of prompt payment of a parking ticket leads to a surcharge, as well as clinically serious ones such as how avoidance of trauma memories may lead to substance abuse (Follette & Pistorello, 2007). Some ACT techniques were bypassed in favor of those that were more generally applicable, but we did not treat students as if they were fragile, and material was included that had high emotional content.

The Process within the Class Is Just as Important as the Content

Consistency in content was important given the research nature of the project, but delivery itself occurred from an ACT stance (Hayes et al., 2011). For example, instructors participated in most exercises, and modeled vulnerability and taking responsible risks.

For example, in Class 8, the students and teacher reflected upon the "Label Parade" defusion exercise in which students and teacher wrote judgments about themselves they were ready to let go of on name badges they wore (see Appendix 11A for details), in a way that focused on fusion as a common human problem:

ACT Instructor:	You know, they're just words on paper. They won't hurt you. And, what about mine? It says, "I'm an imposter."
Student:	I'm curious as to why you put that.

ACT Instructor: Well, I think it's actually a thought that a lot of us teachers have. Every time they have me teach a class, I think, "Are they crazy? Why are they asking me to teach this?" "I'm an imposter" shows up every time. We could sit here and think of all the ways that is not true, but I know from experience that my mind will come up with just as many reasons as to why it could be true. Check and see in your own experience too... It could turn into a never ending discussion where my mind tries to render a verdict on whether I am or am not "an imposter." The more important question is this: can we accept having these sticky thoughts, which we can't get rid of anyhow, and move in the direction that matters to us? That's what I'm doing when I teach this class every week."

This is one of many opportunities for the instructor to illustrate the commonality of the human experience and model acceptance of, and defusion from, difficult thoughts and feelings.

Orienting and Re-orienting Students to the Interventions Is Necessary

The relevance of material was sustained by linking methods to their purpose. This included:

1. **Noting relevance to students' lives – now and in the future.** A challenge in prevention is to make content relevant not just to the current situation but to experiences not yet contacted. ACT instructors attempted to do so by linking methods to experiences they may be witnessing in others (e.g., a roommate who's depressed) or to experiences they may have in the future (e.g., relationships may end), or by highlighting possible examples from a range of current situations that show the core processes involved (e.g., "Have you guys ever had the experience of all of a sudden feeling hungry, in need of a nap, or a strong desire to check e-mail *right* when you were supposed to start studying?").

2. **Preparing students ahead of time for the different strategies used in ACT and why that matters** (e.g., language is the problem so we need to rely on metaphors instead). Within a classroom format, clear rationale needs to be used to ensure that ACT interventions make sense to students. For example, when introducing ACT, the instructor might say, "Sometimes our minds are so apt to come up with the same old way of doing things that we need to create a space where we wipe the slate clean, where confusion is allowed to occur and stay for a while, so that we can truly do something new. There is a Zen teaching device called a koan, a question that has no logical answer, that may allow one to look at things with 'beginner's eyes' (Kabat-Zinn, 2005). An example of a koan might be 'What is the sound of one hand clapping?' If you feel confused here on occasion, see if you can make room for that and still remain engaged."

3. **Providing purpose and choice for an unusual exercise.** With "Eyes On" (Hayes, Strosahl, & Wilson, 1999), where students sit across from each other and maintain eye contact in silence with their knees touching, we initially had some concern about the students' ability to tolerate this exercise. However, following our first principle of not treating students as fragile, we conducted this exercise as it is normally done. Nobody complained about the exercise later in evaluations, and several cited it as one of the exercises that had the most impact. To ensure a positive outcome we provided a strong rationale for the exercise: "This is about noticing and riding the waves of discomfort." We also emphasized that each student had a choice about whether or not he wanted to participate. Everyone did, but it seems important to maintain choice when entering into potentially uncomfortable and evocative experiences.

Accepting that Students Will Progress at Their Own Pace

Although in ACT as psychotherapy, control-based strategies are usually vigorously undermined, a more open approach is necessary in classes with students who may or may not be in distress. If a student appeared to be overly confused or in disagreement, teachers were instructed to fall back on "Let this percolate, see if it doesn't show up in some areas of your life this week."

Similarly, the ACT instructors were coached on how to respond in an ACT-consistent manner to overt efforts to avoid. Sample responses in these situations could be the following:

- Invite the student to bring the internal barrier along: "Would you be willing to try it anyhow and bring the thought 'This won't work' along?"

- Highlight the commonality of the experience: "How many people in this room have had a thought like that at least once in their life (or today)?"

- Encourage increased mindfulness, as opposed to changing behavior, by asking the student just to notice, in the coming week, how often her mind says this or that.

- Explore barriers: "What got in the way of your doing the homework?"

- Thank the student: "Thank you for bringing this up today."

- Move to process: "What was it like to share this with the whole class?"

Instructors Must Be Watchful of Their Own Anti-ACT Behaviors

There is a certain challenge maintaining an active and experiential approach while "teaching" a class on ACT to college students. Instructors were asked:

- If you find yourself talking too much or working hard to convince students, do something else (e.g., ask the class questions, have them read and reflect from a small section in the book, or split students into dyads to discuss an experience or idea).

- Try not to predict students' experience. When in doubt, ask them and use that in class.

- Focus on the current experience rather than "talking about" an experience.

- Look at everything as "grist for the mill." See if you can find a way to turn a "failed" experiment by a student into a teaching moment for the whole class: "That's a great example. How can we get back on track when we try really hard and it doesn't work?"

The More Relevant and Engaging to College Students, the Better

To increase engagement, instructors incorporated into the class animations, YouTube videos, movies, books, commercials, recent events, etc. For example, rather than using a generic question when President Obama was scheduled to be on campus, the instructor asked, "How would we set up a banquet for President Obama?" to demonstrate the power of our minds to problem solve.

"Emerging adulthood" (18-25 years of age) is a unique period marked by identity explorations, instability, renewed self-focus, and feeling "in between" (Arnett, 2000). The sensitivity of college students to the transition from childhood to adulthood was leveraged for a variety of purposes. For example, during a class targeting self-compassion, we showed a YouTube video that portrayed adults engaging in behaviors such as name calling or hitting someone, in front of children—who then imitated the same behavior. The instructor utilized this video to set up a discussion about compassion and self-compassion vis-à-vis our unique histories (see Appendix 11B for a detailed description of this exercise). Instructors were encouraged to be creative and try to reach these "emerging adults" in multiple ways.

Flexibility and Freedom for Instructors Is Essential

It is important for instructors to have some flexibility and freedom in the delivery of the content. To foster this, some of the material for the lecture was considered essential while other aspects were optional, leaving it up to the instructor to pick among several metaphors and exercises listed for that particular class. Instructors could bring in their own material, or improvise on an exercise. To elaborate on certain concepts, students themselves were encouraged to bring in their own materials (e.g., songs, poems) and initiate and shape discussions through their own experiences.

Empirical Considerations: Acceptability and Perceived Usefulness of an ACT FYS

This FYS class was compared to a well-crafted control condition consisting of a more didactic presentation of materials pertaining to adjustment to college: time management, making career choices, learning about resources on campus, and learning about depression, anxiety, substance abuse, and relationship problems among college students. Students in the more standard class had a book that consisted of handpicked chapters from an available FYS textbook. This book had a great deal of face validity for college freshmen. A total of 732 college freshmen, recruited across three academic years, were randomized. Approximately 38% of participants were male, 33% were ethnic or racial minorities, and 25% were diagnosable with a current mental health problem. The mean age was 18 ($SD=.4$). Data regarding the impact on mental health problems is not yet available, but below we provide a brief description of issues of acceptability and perceived usefulness of the class. Details of this study are reported elsewhere (Pistorello et al., 2012).

Satisfaction with Classes

Given its experiential nature, it is important to see if ACT, packaged as an FYS, is acceptable to college freshmen. At posttest, a standardized class evaluation instrument was used, with items such as "Course materials are well prepared and carefully explained," "You have learned and understood subject materials in this course," and "Instructor is enthusiastic about teaching the course." Ratings could range from 1-5, and classes from both conditions received high marks (almost all in the 4-5 range on average) indicating high satisfaction. There were no differences across conditions, suggesting that the ACT class showed an equally high degree of acceptability among college freshmen, as compared to a typical FYS specifically designed for college freshmen.

Perceived Usefulness of the Class

Students were asked to predict at posttest how useful the class will be for them in the next year. Ratings on the usefulness of the class immediately post-class were just below 4 (on a 1-5 scale, with higher scores indicating higher predicted usefulness) and did not differ by condition. However, when students from the first cohort (n = 235) came back one year later, those in the ACT class were significantly more likely to report the class as having been useful the year before than students in the control condition.

Project 2: One-Day ACT Well-Being Training for College Students

Vasiliki Christodoulou

The second project we will describe was conducted in the United Kingdom (UK) and was focused on the promotion of well-being. The need for such initiatives is emphasized by UK statistics showing an upward increase in student suicide rates from 2007 to 2011 (Office for National Statistics, 2012) as well as by surveys indicating a high prevalence of clinical distress in the UK student body (e.g., Bewick, Gill, Mulhern, Barkham & Hill, 2008). There is the hope that prevention initiatives could benefit students' psychological well-being, improve educational performance, and promote social inclusion and community relations (Universities UK/ Guild Higher Education Committee for the Promotion of Mental Well-Being, 2007).

The program delivered a five-hour (one-day) Acceptance and Commitment Therapy (ACT; Hayes et al., 2011) well-being training to volunteering university students. The training was delivered as a workshop at a university campus in groups of six to ten students. It was offered in the context of two randomized controlled trials evaluating the effectiveness of an ACT well-being training compared to a waitlist control.

Overview of ACT Well-Being Training

The protocol was adapted from an ACT well-being program previously delivered in the worksite (Flaxman & Bond, 2006). It was designed as a hands-on, generic ACT intervention providing elements of the model's central processes (see chapter 3). The primary aims of the intervention were to illustrate the unworkable nature of experiential avoidance and introduce mindfulness as an alternative, and to activate personal values as an effective guide to action. The trainer organized the day by making a tentative distinction between people's internal world (e.g., thoughts, feelings, and physical sensations) and people's external world (e.g., behavior). This distinction was illustrated on a flipchart by drawing a human figure and identifying examples of "internal world" (e.g., stress, relaxation) and "external world" experiences (e.g., procrastination, physical exercise). Mindfulness was presented as an effective way of handling internal experiences and values choice as a skill associated with greater life satisfaction and effective behavior. The trainer referred back to this diagram while introducing different exercises or metaphors (see also chapters 3 and 4). See Appendix 11C for an organizing diagram for the day-long training.

Students reflected on "what effectiveness means to them" and how it relates to personally meaningful actions. They identified barriers to effective living (e.g., fear, worry, anger) and strategies they previously used to get rid of these difficulties (e.g., avoidance, distraction, alcohol use). The effectiveness of these strategies in the short and long term was explored. After students experimented with a suppression exercise (trying not to think of an item), mindfulness was introduced as a way of noticing challenging internal experiences without having to change or remove them. Throughout the day participants tried a selection of mindfulness practices (e.g., physicalizing of thoughts and feelings; Hayes et al., 2011).

Students were encouraged to identify personally meaningful life directions and formulate associated goals and actions in written exercises (Bond, 2004, pp. 288-290). The trainer used the flipchart to draw a "Passengers on the Bus" metaphor highlighting how attempts to control internal experiences can side-track us from valued living (Hayes et al., 2011; see also chapter 7). To develop defusion skills, students partnered up to "take their minds for a walk" around the campus (Hayes et al., 2011, p. 259; 2011, p. 359; see Appendix 11D for questions to debrief this exercise effectively). Students often conclude that it is possible to move toward valued directions while having "busy" minds. The "observing self" was introduced through the "chessboard" metaphor using a real chessboard and pieces (Hayes et al., 2011). Finally, students were encouraged to practice mindfulness daily for a month using an audio CD containing a selection of short and long practices and behavioral homework where they could record value-consistent actions (see Appendix 11E for a form for students to record their values-based actions).

Empirical Considerations: Effectiveness of a One-Day ACT Well-Being Training

The training was evaluated in two randomized controlled trials comparing it to a waitlist control group, reported elsewhere in greater detail (Christodoulou & Flaxman, 2012). Questionnaire data were collected from both groups on various mental health outcomes and on hypothesized ACT process variables over a period of three months (at baseline, at one month, and at two months). After completing the final questionnaires, participants provided written feedback on the intervention.

In both studies participants were university students drawn from numerous courses. Approximately one third of students who originally expressed an interest in the training did not sign up for it later, for various reasons (e.g., schedule conflict). No participant dropped out during the training day although five students (across two studies) signed-up for the training and failed to attend.

In the first trial (n = 65, 70.5% female), at one month ACT showed improved stress, anxiety, and depression outcomes with medium effect sizes, but outcomes were not maintained at two-months. In the second trial (n = 71, 69% female), comparisons at two-months, but not at one-month, revealed significant differences benefiting the ACT group on stress, anxiety and psychological well-being with medium to large effect sizes. The two trials occurred during different parts of the academic year, which may help explain these differences. Across the two studies, ACT training showed significant differences when assessments were conducted during exam periods (at one-month in Study 1 and at two-months in Study 2), but not during holidays.

Results showed that ACT processes (see chapter 3) accounted for most improved outcomes in the ACT groups. Mediation analyses showed that reduced believability in "sticky" thoughts partially mediated the between-group differences at one-month for stress and anxiety in the first study. In the second study reductions in stress and improvements in psychological well-being at two-months were partially and fully (respectively) mediated by increases in mindfulness and psychological flexibility for the ACT group.

Qualitative feedback showed that about 38% of participants reported pursuing the skills in a systematic or sporadic way, whereas a similar percentage reported experimenting with the skills initially or not at all. About a quarter lost their enthusiasm a few weeks after the training. Informal mindfulness practices were used more frequently than formal mindfulness practices. Practicing had "low priority" when other concerns were dominant (i.e., coursework, tiredness, ill health, and spending time with family) and fluctuated with participants' emotional state.

Reflections on the Program

The program was advertised as "life effectiveness training" through flyers and e-mail announcements, and thus participants felt comfortable with enrolling and quoted their motivation as "self-development." The small group size seemed to facilitate participation, while helping the trainer keep an emphasis on students' experiential learning. Short, experiential practices were more successful. Students related well to metaphors that were either acted out physically or delivered in pictorial form. Mindfulness practices were also kept short (10 minutes maximum), as pilot sessions indicated that longer practices felt tiresome and students lost their interest.

Probably due to an informal, psychoeducational format, the program attracted students from a wide array of backgrounds, from different departments and academic years, and with different levels of psychological distress at entry. There was considerable interest in joining the program, although about 1/3 later decided not to participate, as attending for a full day was difficult given their busy schedules. The one-day format had the advantage of keeping the cost of the training low, and eliminating program drop out, but offering flexible formats may make similar interventions more accessible.

Project 3: Infusing ACT into Undergraduate Classes in Psychology of Racial Differences

Jason Lillis and Steven C. Hayes

Multicultural education has become a requirement for training in many mental health fields, such as psychology and counseling (cf. Smith, Constantine, Dunn, Dinehart, & Montoya, 2006). Originally emphasized in graduate training, racial differences or multicultural psychology courses are often now taught at the undergraduate level. Undergraduate courses provide a venue for changing prejudicial behaviors in a large swath of the emerging adult population. Delivery of information alone is not always effective in reducing prejudice (Corrigan & Penn, 1999), in part because it can apply social pressure to not appear prejudiced or have prejudiced thoughts, which can lead to thought suppression efforts. Such suppression efforts have consistently been shown to produce a subsequent *increase* in prejudiced thoughts as well as discriminatory behaviors toward the target group (e.g., Galinsky & Moskowitz, 2000; Kulik, Perry, & Bourhis, 2000).

However, given that research suggested that an acceptance-based approach might be effective in reducing stigma (Hayes et al., 2004), a study was conducted to infuse a 75-minute ACT lecture into two undergraduate courses on the psychology of racial and ethnic differences. The details are presented elsewhere (Lillis & Hayes, 2007); here we will describe some of the underlying theory and ACT interventions used to attempt to reduce prejudice.

ACT Content Infused into Racial Differences Class

From an ACT perspective, prejudice is the objectification and dehumanization of people as a result of their participation in evaluative verbal categories (Hayes, Niccolls, Masuda, & Rye, 2002). Trying to change or modify prejudiced verbal content is a difficult task. ACT provides an alternative approach using acceptance and mindfulness processes to reduce the impact of prejudicial thoughts, beliefs, and attitudes, and values and behavior change processes to promote behavior more consistent with chosen ideals (Hayes et al., 2011). The first key component of this approach is to undermine the literal impact of prejudicial thoughts, without directly trying to change them in form or frequency. From an ACT perspective, behaving in a prejudiced and discriminatory fashion is unacceptable, but ironically a powerful way to reduce the behavioral impact of prejudicial thoughts is to accept that we all have them.

Cognitive defusion techniques were used to illustrate the automatic nature of thoughts through experiential exercises. For example, the classic ACT exercise "What are the numbers?" asks participants to remember a series of innocuous and arbitrary numbers, such as 1, 2, 3, illustrating how easy it is to program thinking (Hayes et al, 2011). This was followed by simply asking participants to complete common sayings, such as "There's no place like….[home]" or "Only the good die… [young]." This set a non-shaming context for discussing the nature of programming, and the many influences we've been exposed to (parents, media, peers, internet).

The next step was to have participants observe these processes in relation to prejudicial stimuli. We asked participants to "notice their programming" by completing statements in writing, such as "Most black people tend to…" or, "People who live in this country and don't speak the language are…." It is important to create a safe space where students can simply be aware of and watch these verbal processes without having to suppress or censor what shows up, in order to promote awareness of the automatic nature of prejudicial thoughts. The ensuing discussion validated the normality of whatever thought content showed up but focused on our responsibility to address any overt behaviors traditionally evoked by being "fused" with these historical and automatic thoughts. Defusion exercises (e.g., word repetition) were used to provide examples of how to undermine their behavioral impact.

Another key component was teaching acceptance of unwanted emotions. We are commonly taught that our biased reactions, such as feeling anxious around a group of strangers of a different racial or ethnic background, are "wrong." From an ACT perspective, our emotional reactions are not directly controllable and are not themselves our enemy. Indeed, trying to eliminate or control emotional reactions can lead to avoidance behavior that violates our values. For example, despite pro-diversity values, a Caucasian teenager may come to avoid his African-American peers because he knows it is "wrong" to feel anxious around them. From an ACT perspective, the goal is to step out of the struggle with emotions and orient to behavior consistent with chosen values.

The intervention targeted mindful awareness of emotional experiences through guided imagery. We presented a series of scenarios and asked participants to notice any emotional reactions or changes in their body. For example, one scenario involved a person of a different race or ethnicity getting hired for a job instead of you. The class debriefing validated the normalcy of any emotional reactions that showed up while also pointing out the cost of emotion avoidance to values-based actions. Demanding the absence of difficult emotions can inhibit diversity seeking and pro-social behavior. The latter problem was illustrated using the "Polygraph" metaphor, a classic ACT metaphor that points out the impossibility of trying to force yourself to be calm while having a gun pointed to your head (Hayes et al., 2011).

We made an important distinction that acceptance is not about treating reactions as true or valid in a verbal sense. For example, if one feels anxious around Arabs, acceptance does *not* mean that it is "right" to act suspiciously around Arabs. Acceptance means being willing to experience that anxiety in the service of behaving consistently with chosen values, such as creating relationships.

Choosing values was another important component of the ACT intervention infused into these racial differences classes. We appealed broadly to relationship values by asking participants to imagine being at their 85th birthday party and having each important person in their life speak about them (Hayes et al., 2011). The goal is to imagine an ideal, if you were exactly the person you wanted to be in relation to the people you care about. Common themes included being a loving person, treating people with respect, being close and connected to others, being honest and open, learning from others, and being loyal and dependable. Once these core values were present, they were organized into values statements and broadened out to include a broader and broader range of people: coworkers; members of one's town, state, country, and world; all human beings, including those associated with stereotypes.

The final piece of the ACT intervention was making behavioral commitments. Any activity designed to get participants exposed to new experiences and people fit here, with specific attention to being mindful, defused, and accepting, while orienting to behavior consistent with chosen values. For example, students were prompted to attend a social club or party in which they would be the only person of their race or ethnicity.

Empirical Considerations: Outcome Findings of ACT Infusion in Racial Differences Classes

This 75-minute ACT intervention was studied using two undergraduate classes in psychology of racial differences (n=32), who were presented with the ACT intervention and a multicultural education-based intervention in counterbalanced order. Results indicated that the ACT intervention was more effective at increasing positive behavioral intentions to engage in pro-diversity activities at post- and 1-week follow-up. These changes were associated with other self-reported changes that fit the ACT model (for further review, see Lillis & Hayes, 2007).

Project 4: Using an Acceptance-Based Model to Reduce Mental Health Stigma within an Abnormal Psychology Course

Jenna LeJeune

The undergraduate abnormal psychology course is often the first, and frequently only, course where college students develop their basic ideas about psychological suffering and mental illness. Abnormal Psychology is highly encouraged or even required for a wide range of degree programs including nursing, pre-medicine, criminal justice, and occupational therapy. Previous research has shown that stigmatizing behaviors and beliefs toward those with psychological and behavioral disorders remain high even among therapists or others working with these populations (Maslach, Jackson, & Leiter, 1996). Therefore, those working "on the front lines," such as health professionals and law enforcement officers, would be key groups to target in stigma-reduction interventions.

While some have highlighted the unique opportunity of abnormal psychology courses as a place to target mental health stigma (Curtin, Martz, Bazzini, & Vicente, 2004), taking such a course may not necessarily help decrease students' stigma toward mental health problems. Indeed, at times traditional abnormal psychology courses may actually *increase* students' level of mental health stigma (Kendra, Cattaneo, & Mohr, 2012; Sadow, Ryder, & Webster, 2002). Previous attempts to target mental health stigma within the classroom have generally focused on one of three types of interventions: 1. educational/informational interventions, 2. contact-based education, and 3. verbal confrontation of negative attitudes (Corrigan & Penn, 1999). Although both educational and contact-based interventions may have some positive stigma-reduction results, these benefits appear to be short-lived. Verbal confrontation (e.g., instructing people why it's "bad" to stigmatize those with psychological problems) has generally been found to be ineffective (Corrigan et. al, 2001, 2002). Interventions based on acceptance-based models provide a new avenue toward stigma reduction (Hayes et al., 2004) that may be well suited for the classroom setting (Masuda et al., 2007).

ACT Content Infused into Abnormal Psychology Classes

For this project, we created a new curriculum informed by stigma- and prejudice-focused interventions previously tested in other settings (e.g. Hayes et al., 2004; Luoma, Kohlenberg, Hayes, Bunting, & Rye, 2008; Masuda et. al., 2007; Masuda, Hayes, Lillis, Bunting, Herbst, & Fletcher, 2009). The curriculum was organized around eight principles focused on core processes of ACT. These included helping students:

1. Notice the process of objectification of others and build awareness of biases and the automatic process of stereotyping.

2. Normalize the occurrence of prejudiced thinking, so that it need not be suppressed or avoided and can be accepted.

3. Differentiate between prejudiced thoughts and prejudiced behavior.

4. Accept and defuse from prejudiced thinking.

5. Facilitate a hierarchical frame of a "common humanity" in suffering that competes with the tendency toward "us vs. them" framing that is part of objectification and stigma.

6. Open up to difficult emotions rather than attempting to suppress difficult thoughts and emotions related to themselves and others.

7. Develop a positive sense of connection and empathy in relation to the target group (i.e., those identified as "mentally ill").

8. Articulate values and set intentions for how they would want to be toward people in the stigmatized group.

Based on these 8 principles, we developed five 30-45 minute modules. The link to the complete curriculum, including outcome measures used, can be found in Appendix 11F.

The curriculum was revised over the course of several semesters of pilot testing, based on student feedback. Our goal was to create a curriculum that could be imbedded into more traditional abnormal psychology curricula so as to maximize dissemination opportunities. The class in which this curriculum was implemented met once per week for four hours, and each module was conducted during the last 45 minutes of class for five consecutive weeks. For a class meeting multiple times per week, this curriculum could be implemented as a stand-alone section over five consecutive classes.

Each module was organized around a theme. Class one provided an introduction to the curriculum and focused on building awareness of social classification. Class two sought to normalize the occurrence of prejudice thinking and suggest acceptance as an alternative strategy. Class three focused on building a sense of common humanity and common suffering in relation to psychological suffering. Class four taught students to differentiate between prejudiced thoughts and prejudiced behavior. In addition, this module focused on helping students defuse from stereotype-based thinking while developing a positive sense of connection and empathy in relation to the stigmatized group. Finally, in class five, exercises focused on helping students set intentions for how they would want to behave toward people in the stigmatized group.

Each module incorporated several in-class exercises, each targeting one or more of the eight principles described above. The experiential exercises included were adapted from previously established acceptance- and mindfulness-based protocols used in other settings (e.g. training workshops in ACT, published ACT protocols, etc.) including commonly used ACT exercises such as "Milk, Milk, Milk," the "Cross-cutting Categories" exercise, and "Thoughts on Cards" (Hayes et al., 2011). After each of the first four modules, students were given an experiential task to complete outside of class that was connected to the lesson for that week and asked to write brief reflection papers on the experience. Participation in both in-class and out-of-class experiential exercises was voluntary and students were told that their decision to participate or not would in no way impact their grade. The written homework assignments were mandatory and students who declined the experiential activity were given the option of an alternative written assignment.

Empirical Considerations: Perceived Usefulness of the ACT Infusion into Abnormal Psychology Classes

Preliminary analyses of feedback from the first two pilot cohorts was highly positive. Anonymous written feedback included "These last 5 weeks have been extremely meaningful to me," "The assignments didn't stop when we turned in homework. The ideas lasted and stayed in my mind," "I felt this was a fantastic learning tool," and "It opened my heart a bit more and usually I feel I'm bad with empathy." The majority of students (n=36) "agreed" or "strongly agreed" with the statements "I felt what we did was meaningful" (81%) and "I learned something important that will impact my life outside of class" (83%). Feasibility was also demonstrated by more than a 95% completion rate for the optional experiential portions of homework assignments.

The curriculum is usable by teachers with a relatively small amount of training; formal research will be needed to see whether it is successful. These early findings suggest that the ACT model may provide a meaningful and effective way to target mental health stigma among those enrolled in an abnormal psychology course.

Final Words

This chapter illustrated four different ways of bringing mindfulness and acceptance into classroom settings, either as stand-alone interventions or as infused into psychology classes. The data suggest that these methods have high acceptability and perceived usefulness in classroom settings;

formal research on other outcomes is early but is tentatively supportive. These are merely examples, however; exploration and creative development is the order of the day.

Presenting ACT content outside of the academic curriculum (see Project 2) has both advantages and disadvantages. On the one hand, greater recruitment barriers may arise outside of the university curriculum, as students may have to miss other classes or change work schedules to participate. On the other hand, when ACT is outside of the curriculum, students volunteer on their own accord. This type of recruitment may select more for students already in some form of distress relative to students who are taking a class, which may allow more targeted programs. Conversely, presenting mindfulness and acceptance concepts as part of an existing class (see Projects 1, 3, and 4) offers the possibility of reaching students who would not seek help on their own accord, such as those described in the two opening vignettes to this chapter.

The issues of dosage (how long an ACT intervention is needed) and duration of effects (whether the ACT intervention will continue to have an effect in the long run) need to be investigated. For example, some participant feedback suggested that motivation to use the training skills may lessen over time (see Project 2). Therefore, additional forms of engagement to bolster these ACT classroom interventions could be added in the future. Recommendations include sending e-mail reminders to practice the training skills, setting up an online forum where participants discuss their experiences and pose questions, and developing highly engaging, multi-media, interactive web-based ACT programs (see Levin, Pistorello, Seeley, & Hayes, under review, for an example of an online ACT program designed specifically for college students).

We do know that among college students with some level of distress, ACT in a classroom/training setting does reduce psychological distress (see Project 2), but we do not yet know if students who are not currently distressed will be less likely to develop mental health problems later in life if exposed to ACT concepts early in their college career. Project 1 above will likely help elucidate this question, as freshman students, 75% of whom are not currently diagnosable with a mental health disorder, will be followed up to three years through structured interviews. Whether the data are negative or positive, it is clear that a good deal of additional development needs to occur.

Curriculum infusion (CI) has been utilized by many colleges and universities in substance abuse prevention efforts (e.g., Lederman, Stewart, & Russ, 2007). CI usually involves the recruitment of professors to incorporate information about alcohol and/or other drugs into the subject matter of their courses. Two of the projects described above (Projects 3 and 4) utilized a similar strategy, where they imparted skills in mindfulness and acceptance, delivered experientially, to decrease stigma/prejudice. These two projects showed that ACT content infused into psychology classes is not only acceptable (see Project 4) but also effective in increasing positive behavioral intentions towards members of different racial/ethnic origins (see Project 3). Colleges are increasingly more diverse both in terms of race/ethnicity and mental health disabilities; yet, contact with different groups alone may not be enough to change behavior (see Hewstone, Rubin, & Willis, 2002). Infusion of mindfulness, acceptance, and values may provide an effective way over time for higher education settings to change cultural norms.

All four projects described above relied on mental health providers highly trained in ACT, but mindfulness is becoming widely applicable across campuses (see chapters 1, 10, and 12 also). Therefore, individuals who are not mental health providers may become involved in the delivery or infusion of mindfulness and acceptance content into classroom settings. As this occurs, it will become important to learn how to deliver these interventions with fidelity across varying levels of expertise. Overall, although it is still early and much needs to be learned, there are clear indications that mindfulness- and acceptance-based approaches can make a positive difference in classroom settings.

References

Arnett, J. J. (2000). Emerging adulthood: A theory of development from the late teens through the twenties. *American Psychologist. 55*, 469-480.

Bewick, B., Gill, J., Mulhern, B., Barkham, M., & Hill, A. J. (2008). Using electronic surveying to assess psychological distress within the U.K. student population: a multi-site pilot investigation. *E-Journal of Applied Psychology, 4*(2), 1-5.

Bond, W. F. (2004). ACT for stress. In S. C. Hayes & K. D. Strosahl (Eds.) *A practical guide to Acceptance and Commitment Therapy* (pp. 275-292). New York: Springer-Verlag.

Christodoulou, V., & Flaxman, P. (2012). *Assessing the effectiveness of Acceptance and Commitment Therapy as a brief intervention for students in higher education.* Manuscript in preparation.

Corrigan, P. W., & Penn, D. L. (1999). Lessons from social psychology on discrediting psychiatric stigma. *American Psychologist, 54,* 765-776.

Corrigan, P. W., River, L. P., Lundin, R. K., Penn, D. L., Wasowski, K. U., Campion, J., ...Kubiak, M.A. (2001). Three strategies for changing attributions about severe mental illness. *Schizophrenia Bulletin, 27,* 187-196.

Corrigan, P. W., Rowan, D., Green, A., Lundin, R., River, P., Uphoff-Wasowski, K., White, K., & Kubiak, M. A. (2002). Challenging two mental illness stigmas: Personal responsibility and dangerousness. *Schizophrenia Bulletin, 28,* 293-310.

Curtin, L., Martz, D. M., Bazzini, D. G., & Vicente, B. B. (2004). They're not "abnormal" and we're not making them "abnormal": A longitudinal study. *Teaching of Psychology, 31(1),* 51-53.

Eisenberg, D., Downs, M., Golberstein, E., & Zivin, K. (2009). Stigma and help-seeking for mental health among college students. *Medical Care Research & Review, 66(5),* 522-541.

Flaxman, P. E., & Bond, F. W. (2006). Acceptance and Commitment Therapy in the workplace. In R. A. Baer (Ed.), *Mindfulness-based treatment approaches.* San Diego, CA: Elsevier.

Follette, V. M., & Pistorello, J. (2007). *Finding life beyond trauma.* Oakland, CA: New Harbinger.

Galinsky, A. D., & Moskowitz, G. B. (2000). Perspective-taking: Decreasing stereotype expression, stereotype accessibility, and ingroup favoritism. *Journal of Personality and Social Psychology, 78,* 708–724.

Gallagher, R. (2011). *National Survey of Counseling Center Directors.* Pittsburgh, PA: University of Pittsburgh.

Hayes, S. C., Bissett, R., Roget, N., Padilla, M., Kohlenberg, B. S., Fisher, G., Masuda, A., Pistorello, J., Rye, A. K., Berry, K., & Niccolls, R. (2004). The impact of acceptance and commitment training and multicultural training on the stigmatizing attitudes and professional burnout of substance abuse counselors. *Behavior Therapy, 35,* 821-835.

Hayes, S. C., Niccolls, R., Masuda, A., & Rye, A. K. (2002). Prejudice, terrorism, and behavior therapy. *Cognitive and Behavioral Practice, 9,* 296-301.

Hayes, S. C., & Smith, S. (2005). *Get out of your mind and into your life.* Oakland, CA: New Harbinger.

Hayes, S. C., Strosahl, K., & Wilson, K. G. (1999). *Acceptance and Commitment Therapy: The process and practice of mindful change.* New York: Guilford Press.

Hayes, S. C., Strosahl, K., & Wilson, K. G. (2011). *Acceptance and Commitment Therapy: The process and practice of mindful change* (2nd edition). New York: Guilford Press.

Hewstone, M., Rubin, M., & Willis, H. (2002). Intergroup bias. *Annual Review of Psychology, 53,* 575-604.

Kabat-Zinn, J. (2005). *Coming to our senses.* New, NY: Hyperion.

Kadison, R., & DiGeronimo, T. F. (2004). *College of the overwhelmed: The campus mental health crisis and what to do about it.* San Francisco, CA: Jossey-Bass.

Kendra, M. S., Cattaneo, L. B., & Mohr, J. J. (2012). Teaching abnormal psychology to improve attitudes toward mental illness and help-seeking. *Teaching of Psychology 39(1),* 57-61.

Kulik, C. T., Perry, E. L., & Bourhis, A. C. (2000). Ironic evaluation processes: Effects of thought suppression on evaluations of older job applicants. *Journal of Organizational Behavior, 21,* 689–711.

Lederman, L. C, Stewart, L. P., & Russ, T. L. (2007). Addressing college drinking through curriculum infusion: A study of the use of experience-based learning in the communication classroom. *Commun Educ, 56,* 476–494.

Levin, M. E., Pistorello, J., Seeley, J., & Hayes, S. C. (under review). Transdiagnostic web-based prevention for mental health problems among college students: Results from a pilot trial.

Lillis, J., & Hayes, S. C. (2007). Applying acceptance, mindfulness, and values to the reduction of prejudice: A pilot study. *Behavior Modification, 31,* 389-411.

Luoma, J. B., Kohlenberg, B., Hayes, S., Bunting, K., & Rye, A. (2008). Reducing self-stigma in substance abuse through acceptance and commitment therapy: Model, manual development, and pilot outcomes. *Addiction Research and Theory, 16(2),* 149-165.

Maslach, C., Jackson, S. E., & Leiter, P. (1996). *Maslach Burnout Inventory (3rd ed.).* Palo Alto, CA: Consulting Psychologists Press.

Masuda, A., Hayes, S. C., Fletcher, L. B., Seignourel, P. J., Bunting, K., Herbst, S. A., Twohig, M. P., & Lillis, J. (2007). The impact of Acceptance and Commitment Therapy versus education on stigma toward people with psychological disorders. *Behaviour Research and Therapy, 44,* 2764-2772.

Masuda, A., Hayes, S. C., Lillis, J., Bunting, K., Herbst, S. A., & Fletcher, L. B. (2009). The relation between psychological flexibility and mental health stigma in Acceptance and Commitment Therapy: A preliminary process investigation. *Behavior and Social Issues, 18,* 25-40.

Muto, T., Hayes, S. C., & Jeffcoat, T. (2011). The effectiveness of Acceptance and Commitment Therapy bibliotherapy for enhancing the psychological health of Japanese college students living abroad. *Behavior Therapy, 42,* 323–335.

Office for National Statistics. (2012). *Deaths by suicide for students aged 18 and above, 2007-2011.* Retrieved February 3, 2013, from http://www.ons.gov.uk/ons /about-ons/what-we-do/publication-scheme/published-ad-hoc-data/health -and-social-care/november-2012/deaths-by-suicide-for-students-aged-18-and -above--2007-2011.xls

Padgett, R. D., & Keup, J. R. (2011). 2009. *National Survey of First Year Seminars: Ongoing efforts to support students in transition* (Research Reports on College Transitions No. 2). Columbia, SC: University of South Carolina, National Resource Center for the First-Year Experience and Students in Transition.

Pascarella, E. T., & Terenzini (2005). *How college affects students, Vol. 2: A third decade of research.* San Francisco, CA: Jossey-Bass.

Pistorello, J., Hayes, S. C., Lillis, J., Villatte, J., Long, D., et al. (2012). Acceptance and Commitment Therapy (ACT) as a First Year Seminar (FYS): Preliminary findings on acceptability and perceived usefulness. Manuscript in preparation.

Sadow, D., Ryder, M., & Webster, D. (2002). Is education of health professionals encouraging stigma towards the mentally ill? *Journal of Mental Health, 11,* 657 -665.

Smith, T., Constantine, M., Dunn, T., Dinehart, J., & Montoya, J. (2006). Multicultural education in the mental health professions: A meta-analytic review. *Journal of Counseling Psychology, 53,* 132-145.

Universities UK/Guild Higher Education Committee for the Promotion of Mental Well-being in Higher Education. (2007). *Final guidelines for mental health pro-motion in higher education.* Retrieved February 3, 2013 from http://www.mhhe .heacademy.ac.uk/silo/files/uuk-student-mh-guidelines.doc

Varra, A. A., Hayes, S. C., Roget, N., & Fisher, G. (2008). A randomized control trial examining the effect of Acceptance and Commitment Training on clinician willingness to use evidence-based pharmacotherapy. *Journal of Consulting and Clinical Psychology, 76,* 449-458.

Whitlock, J. L. (in preparation). Mental health trajectories and psychological and social antecedents: The role of emotion regulation, social connection, and meaning.

CHAPTER 12

Mindfulness in Student Affairs Practice

Eileen Hulme

Christy Tanious

Azusa Pacific University

Yolanda, the dean of students at a large public university, sits across the table from Ryan, a student withdrawing from the institution. As she probes into the reasons behind his desire to leave, it becomes evident that although he states the lack of financial resources as the impetus for his departure, he is actually detached from any meaningful community, without a sense of purpose for his education, and genuinely bored with his classes. He claims that he is simply "going through the motions" of attending college and that he would prefer not to "waste his parents' money" by continuing in an endeavor that he views as pointless. Regardless of the options that Yolanda presents, Ryan is unable to consider a divergent perspective. This type of scenario is common across student affairs departments, yet traditional approaches to student disengagement have been unable to significantly impact student departure rates.

Introduction

Today's student services are situated within a context of rapid and profound change, including increasing globalization, significant growth in diversity and multiculturalism, low graduation rates, high levels of student disengagement, and ever-evolving technology. Student affairs practitioners are left with a choice: Do we keep doing what we've always done, attempting to avoid the challenges and inconveniences presented by change, or do we embrace these changes and explore the ways in which they offer the greatest opportunities for our institutions and students? Our response to this question will determine whether we are relegated to the sidelines of higher education, or become critical partners in the mission of promoting relevant learning and preparing our students for service to society.

Furthermore, the impact of our effectiveness will be influenced by the quality of our response. If we commit to embracing change, yet continue to view and present information as fixed, implying that it is true regardless of new or changing contexts, we will find ourselves engaged in frenzied attempts to respond to each wave of change. Likewise, our students may retain several versions of context-specific information, but this information is likely to become irrelevant within a context of continuous change. However, if we incorporate flexible ways of embracing change that emerge from attitudes and orientations of openness, not only will our experience as educators be more coherent, but our students may also develop more complex and fluid frameworks for understanding, making their learning more relevant. If Ryan had taken a more flexible approach to addressing his discontentment with the college environment, perhaps his experience would have been more satisfying and meaningful.

A growing number of educators and business leaders recognize that education within, and preparation for, a context of change requires a dynamic learning environment, wherein students are actively engaged in the learning process and actively involved with others (Association of American Colleges and Universities (AAC&U, 2002; Chickering & Reisser, 1993; Komives & Wagner, 2009). They emphasize the need for learning environments to incorporate characteristics such as openness, creativity, flexibility, and inquiry (AAC&U, 2007; Duderstadt, 2000; Tagg, 2004). Within such environments, learning transcends mere knowledge acquisition, and students have the opportunity to develop increasingly complex frameworks for understanding—and are thus better prepared to navigate unforeseen change. However, despite this widespread recognition, many institutions of higher education do not reflect these characteristics, a discrepancy that suggests the significant challenge of creating dynamic learning environments.

Psychologist and educator Ellen Langer is among those who highlight these shortcomings of formal education. In response, she advocates for an educational approach in which students "remain open to ways in which information may differ in various situations" (1997, p. 87). This approach, labeled mindful learning, is based upon the psychosocial concept of mindfulness and has implications for staff and students. The remainder of this chapter will describe the differences between mindlessness and mindfulness, will explore the possible implications of a mindful orientation for both student affairs administrators and student life programming, and will address several inherent areas of resistance within higher education structures to a mindful orientation.

Langer's Mindfulness

Mindfulness in this context has been defined as "the process of drawing novel distinctions" (Langer & Moldoveanu, 2000b, p. 220). It is characterized by openness to new information, the continuous creation of new categories, and an increased awareness of multiple perspectives (Langer, 1989, 1997). In contrast, mindlessness is characterized by automatic behavior that prevents attention to new signals, by entrapment in previously established categories, and by actions that are based upon a single perspective (Langer, 1997).

Mindlessness

Langer's definition of mindlessness pertains to a few areas.

AUTOMATIC PILOT

Most of us can, in retrospect, identify times that we have functioned on automatic pilot. We may have arrived at work one day and wondered how we got there, unable to remember any of the details of that day's commute. Or, on a Saturday when preoccupied with a lengthy to-do list, we may have intended to go to the store and instead found ourselves accidentally en route to work. These experiences demonstrate a tendency to rely on previously created categories without engaging active thought—a phenomenon described by Langer as mindlessness. The experience of being on automatic pilot is often related to repetition, which can lead to a tendency to rely on previous ways of learning, understanding, and acting (Langer, 2000). Mindlessness becomes problematic when these thoughtless ways of thinking become so ingrained that the ability to change or vary them in light of new information is lost (Langer & Moldoveanu, 2000a).

CONTEXT AND PERSPECTIVE

In addition to resulting from repetition, mindlessness can emerge in response to a single exposure to information. Such a situation can breed mindlessness if the information is presented as absolute and is received without consideration of alternate ways of understanding the information (Langer, 2000). This is also described as a premature cognitive commitment, wherein one forms a mindset upon an initial encounter with a person or idea, then clings to that initial mindset during similar encounters and fails to explore other understandings or applications of the information (Chanowitz & Langer, 1981; Langer, 1989). Thus, mindlessness is associated with a lack of sensitivity to context, as information is viewed as fixed regardless of changes in circumstance or environment. Mindlessness therefore tends to freeze meaning and, as a result, limits one to a single perspective on information, ideas, and even people (Langer, 1989).

Mindfulness

In contrast, "mindfulness is a flexible state of mind in which we are actively engaged in the present, noticing new things and sensitive to context" (Langer, 2000, p. 220). The key characteristics of mindfulness include a continual creation of new categories, openness to new information, and awareness of multiple perspectives.

CREATING NEW CATEGORIES

Continually creating new categories keeps one attuned to the present context instead of being trapped in previously created categories and thus oblivious to new distinctions (Langer, 2000; Tanious, 2012). Reliance on previous categories can promote a tendency to interpret events through an existing lens, therefore limiting the extent of one's engagement with, or efforts to accurately understand, new information. In contrast, the continuous creation of categories can expand one's mind and scope of understanding, thus helping individuals to engage in ongoing discovery and preparing them for functioning within contexts of rapid change. The difference between being trapped in categories and constantly creating new categories can be observed in a myriad of student experiences. For example, two students with similar previous high school math experiences may respond differently to having to take a college math course. One student may immediately express fear or anxiety about the course, while the other welcomes it. Mindfulness theory might suggest that one plausible explanation of the students' reactions is related to the extent to which they categorize information. It is possible that the first student holds a rigid view of "math" that was created by a previous negative experience, while the second student is open to the creation of new and evolving "math categories." The second student is therefore able to view this particular math course through a new lens and thus perceive it as a novel area for discovery and learning, rather than a guaranteed repeated bad experience.

OPENNESS TO NEW INFORMATION

Openness to new information refers to an active awareness of changed signals, resulting in an "increasingly differentiated information base" (Langer, 1989, p. 67). In addition to an awareness of changing information, openness refers to receptivity to new ways of thinking. Thus, openness has intrapersonal implications, as it is related to recognizing the limitations of one's existing way of knowing and the need for more complex ways of knowing (Wawrzynski & Pizzolato, 2006). In addition, it has interpersonal implications as the realization of one's own limitations can lead to an increased appreciation and valuing of the perspectives of others.

MULTIPLICITY OF PERSPECTIVES

The final characteristic of mindfulness, an awareness of multiple perspectives, directly opposes a single-minded perspective or label. As indicated above, this awareness may refer to internal consideration of various perspectives on information or ideas, or to openness to the points of view of others. Whereas mindlessness invites opportunities for misunderstanding or devaluing other people and perspectives (Galinsky & Moskowitz, 2000; Gehlbach, 2004), mindfulness encourages openness to and appreciation of other individuals and various points of view. This characteristic of mindfulness also incorporates an understanding that all ideas, people, and objects can be many things, depending on one's perspective or vantage point (Langer, 1989).

These key characteristics each have their own merit, but they also interact with and reinforce one another. For example, openness refers to a state of mind that is not only open to new information, but also open to different points of view (Langer, 1989). Openness is thus directly linked to an awareness of different points of view or multiple perspectives. The reciprocal is also true, given that "by viewing the same information through several perspectives, we actually become more open to that information" (Langer, 1997, p. 133). In combination, these three characteristics represent the broad concept of mindfulness, a flexible state of mind that tolerates and even welcomes uncertainty. This description highlights one of the concepts associated with mindfulness: curiosity (Langer, 2000).

Divergent Perspectives on Mindfulness

The multifaceted concept of mindfulness has been defined and explored through divergent perspectives across the ages. Embedded in a Western approach to scientific discovery, Langer's approach to mindfulness emerged from a study of the effect of mindless behavior. Whereas approaches such as Mindfulness-Based Stress Reduction (MBSR; Kabat-Zinn, 1984) have roots in ancient religious traditions such as Buddhism and Christian mysticism, these ancient approaches may place a high moral value on mindfulness as a means to right action and compassion. Additionally, some of these methods are designed to quiet one's thought processes. Conversely, Langer's approach encourages intentional thought through an emphasis on the creation of new categories and disrupting one's automatic thought processes (Langer, 1997, 2000). Both traditions, however, underscore the reduction in existing mental categories that leaves an individual reliant on stereotypes and trapped in binary conceptualizations (Langer, 1989; Langer, Bashner, & Chanowitz, 1985). Langer's conceptualization of mindfulness has been utilized throughout colleges and universities and was chosen as the focus of this chapter because of its clear conceptual alignment with curiosity and engagement in learning, two deeply held values of the higher education academy.

Mindfulness and Curiosity

Curiosity has been defined as:

The recognition, pursuit, and intense desire to explore novel, challenging, and uncertain events. When curious, we are fully aware and receptive to whatever exists and might happen in the present moment. Curiosity motivates people to act and think in new ways and investigate, be immersed, and learn about whatever is the immediate interesting target of their attention. (Kashdan & Silva, 2009, p. 368)

This description of curiosity captures many of the characteristics of mindfulness. Both promote a posture toward knowing that incorporates openness, a present awareness, and an ongoing pursuit of learning. As student affairs professionals, taking such a posture can help to ensure that the work we do is relevant within a context of change. Promoting such an orientation also has significant implication for students. Noticing and exploring novelty can increase interest, involvement, engagement, and motivation to learn (Kashdan & Silva, 2009; Langer, 1997). Thus, characteristics of openness to uncertainty and an interest in novelty, whether incorporated into the presentation of information or in the mind of the student, can enhance learning (Langer, 1997). Studies have found mindful learning to be associated with flexibility, creativity, enjoyment, and performance (Langer, 1997). Mindfulness, therefore, has implications for both the immediate learning experience as well as for future applications of learned material or applications in different contexts. In the midst of rapidly changing contexts, mindful learning can help prepare students for "the as-yet-to-be-known future" (Langer, 1997, p. 81).

Mindfulness and Engaged Learning

Engaged learning is considered to be one of the key factors for student learning and success (Kuh, Kinzie, Schuh, & Whitt, 2005; Newman, 1992), in part because of its association with a host of educational outcomes including student learning (Astin, 1993; Kuh et al., 2005), achievement (Greenway, 2005), and persistence (Milem & Berger, 1997). However, despite extensive research, disengagement is rampant in educational settings, where many students are not inclined toward active thinking. This problem was demonstrated in a recent survey of public university students, in which 15% of second-year students reported being so disengaged that they slept frequently during class (Hurtado, 2007). These findings suggest that active engagement or thinking cannot be assumed in educational settings (Bargh, 1997).

Schreiner and Louis (2006) define engaged learning as "a positive energy invested in one's own learning, evidenced by meaningful processing, attention to what is happening in the learning moment, and active participation in learning activities" (p. 6). This multidimensional conceptualization of engagement in learning theoretically aligns with the construct of mindfulness, particularly due to the emphases on meaningful processing and a focus on the present moment. Likewise, the rampant disengagement among students parallels mindlessness. The interactions between the concepts of engagement, curiosity, and mindfulness suggest that the promotion of mindfulness is critical for promoting effective learning contexts. The following section provides useful examples of institutional approaches to mindfulness education.

Use of Mindfulness in Student Life Programming

Promotion of mindfulness through student life programming requires both the development of a professional staff that regularly practices mindfulness and the provision of informative programs for students. Without the practical experience of living a nonjudgmental and aware life, we would have a difficult time imparting the benefits and challenges of mindfulness to students. Additionally, student services professionals must develop creative, novel ways to introduce the central tenets of mindfulness to student leaders, resident assistants, first-year students, peer leaders, athletes, and other students who are involved in student life programming.

Staff Development Initiatives

As student affairs professionals experience growing demands on our time and energy, staff development initiatives focused on introducing mindful practices are critical to maintaining a vibrant team of professionals. These efforts should focus on diminishing the negative effects of mindless behaviors resulting from a life lived on autopilot and encouraging the creation of new categories necessary to establish a fresh perspective on programs and individuals. The following programs exemplify ways to introduce these concepts to student development professionals.

In an effort to highlight the value of slowing the pace of life to experience the rewards of a more mindful life, Baylor University's Student Life Division executed a silent retreat. Participants were given periodic instructions that reflected the work of Brennan Manning, a Franciscan priest and author (2009), and asked to remain in silence throughout the morning. Silence was experienced in 10-minute intervals, with brief reflective thoughts spoken throughout a two-hour program. The experience of quieting the mind to allow for the creation of new mental categories was disconcerting for some and liberating for others.

Professional conferences provide another avenue for the introduction of mindful practice into student affairs work. During the 2010 National Association of Student Personnel Administrators (NASPA) conference, a presentation introduced mindfulness as an important element of developing curiosity in our students (Hulme, Shushok, & Klinger, 2010). The presentation covered such topics as the value of uncertainty, perspective-taking, and the deconstruction of mental categories and heightened attendees' perceived need to live a more mindful life. A practical exercise to illustrate mindlessness was enacted. Attendees were asked to retrace their path from the door to the building where they entered to their seat in the meeting room. Additionally, they were instructed to make a list of everything they missed as they walked through the building. Upon returning, a master list was created of items overlooked as the participants initially entered the room on autopilot. A lively discussion followed that revealed the amount of time each person spends in a state of mindlessness. Professional development activities such as these require a minimal investment of time and resources but help in the process of developing mindful awareness in student life administrators.

Additionally, programs that foster mindful practice in the Langer tradition challenge student development administrators to explore the multiplicity of perspectives. For example, the chief student affairs and academic affairs officers at George Fox University (GFU) spent 24 hours experiencing the life of a student. As a result of living in the residence halls and attending classes, the administrators viewed the university through new mental categories. Simple autopilot tasks like finding a parking space on campus became mindful activities that raised a new level of awareness of the GFU college experience.

Another similar program found on various campuses that allows the student body president and vice president for student services to shadow each other for a day encourages mindful exploration of divergent perspectives.

Student Programming Initiatives

Student affairs staff development programs create the foundation for the promulgation of mindfulness education across the entire co-curricular college experience; however, as illustrated in this book, programs directed at encouraging the development of mindfulness among college students primarily originate from counseling centers.

As described below, Virginia Tech and Azusa Pacific University (APU) serve as examples of universities attempting to encourage mindful behavior throughout their student affairs programs and services.

VIRGINIA TECH'S CURIOSITY ASPIRATION

Virginia Tech encourages mindful practice through a focus on developing curiosity. One of the Division of Student Life's five aspirations for student learning states: "Virginia Tech students will be inspired to lead lives of curiosity, embracing a lifelong commitment to intellectual development" (www.dsa.vt.edu/aspirations/curiosity.php). An initial staff retreat introduced the student affairs division to the concept of curiosity and mindfulness. As a result of this event, a cross-divisional team was formed to create meaningful curiosity-oriented programs. Additionally, in consultation with Todd Kashdan, author of *Curious?: Discover the Missing Ingredient to a Fulfilling Life* (2009), residence hall curriculum is being developed to encourage students to embrace uncertainty and divergent perspectives.

AZUSA PACIFIC UNIVERSITY'S STUDENT LEADERSHIP PROGRAM

The development of effective leaders is often stated within the mission of colleges and universities as well as appearing as a specific outcome related to student development and the out-of-class curriculum. APU's leadership development efforts combine a curricular and co-curricular approach through a leadership minor. In 2010, one of the five courses in the minor was chosen to integrate a four-week mindfulness curriculum and to measure its effectiveness in improving a student's level of mindful awareness and quality of socially responsible leadership. Below is a summary of the topic for each session.

Session 1: The Power of the Mind in Leadership. "The Power of the Mind in Leadership" served as the focus for the introductory session. The purpose of the first session was to demonstrate the relationship of one's thoughts to his or her ultimate effectiveness as a leader. The importance of a mindful perspective was introduced and examined in light of its practical application to each student's own life. Four aspects of Langer's mindlessness construct—including automatic behavior, category traps, acting from a single perspective, and contextual influences—were investigated through applied activities (1997).

One specific exercise used during the first session to bring attention to mindlessness was the APU picture hunt. Students were requested via e-mail before class to take pictures of objects on campus that they walk by every day and don't notice. They e-mailed five of their best pictures to the professor, and a slide show illustrating articles that were missed on campus was created for class. This particular exercise created significant discussion and was mentioned on end-of-semester evaluations as a note-worthy learning experience.

Another exercise was created to introduce mindfulness through embracing novelty. Each student was asked to perform two novel activities throughout the week and write a reflection paper on each. The array of novel activities performed provided great fodder for engaging and instructive conversations in class. One student who decided to wear his tuxedo to his classes remarked on the power of context and how this simple activity had created a newfound awareness of difference. (Power Point slides for Session One are available as Appendix 12A at www .newharbinger.com/22225.)

Session 2: The Leader's Strengths and the Impact of Context. "The Leader's Strengths and the Impact of Context" introduced students to the influence of individual personality traits on their attention to information in a particular context. Through the use of the Clifton StrengthsFinder (Gallup, 1999) students were introduced to the effect their strengths have on communication preferences, ability to deal with change, approach to time and structure, conflict management style, and study habits. Through interactive exercises utilizing their strengths, students began to understand that their personality characteristics actually create blindness to certain aspects of their environment and promote mindless evaluation of people, places, and activities.

Additionally, mindfulness based on Langer's conceptualization is sensitive to the impact of content on our systems of evaluation. To introduce the topic of context, students were asked to sit on the floor for the last fifteen minutes of class if they were physically able to accomplish this. A lively discussion occurred about the change in the dynamic of the class that resulted from sitting on the floor. Students who had not previously been vocally engaged in the class began to speak. The conversation was more animated and relaxed. This visible change in the class made students more aware of their surroundings and class dynamics.

The execution of this class raised issues related to the relationship of mindfulness to self-awareness and identity formation. Approximately 15% of the class appeared disengaged during the class discussions on individual strengths and subsequent exercises. Whether they were uncomfortable with the personal nature of the class or developmentally they were experiencing Marcia's (1993) moratorium or foreclosure stage of identity development, it is hard to ascertain from the visual evidence.

Session 3: The Social Mind of the Leader. The topic of perspective-taking was addressed in the third session, titled "The Social Mind of the Leader" (see Appendix 12B for associated Power Point slides). The objective for this session was to introduce students to Langer's emphasis on the mindful awareness of multiple perspectives. Perspective-taking was demonstrated through an exercise based on understanding life through another person's strengths. Utilizing the knowledge of the Clifton StrengthsFinder gained during the preceding class session, students were given randomly chosen strengths and asked to react to various scenarios as a person with those strengths might react. An example of a scenario would be:

> *You have been assigned a group project to create a leadership class for a local junior high school. Frank, a member of the group, is extremely competitive and drives the group to excellence in hopes of being the best group project in class. How do you respond to Frank?*

This was an extremely difficult task for some, as they were constantly reverting back to their own perspectives on Frank as opposed to the perspective of someone with their assigned strengths. The class discussion focused on the effect our strengths have on our tendency to see life through our own perspectives as opposed to a more mindful approach that encourages the seeking out of other viewpoints. An extensive list of barriers to considering other perspectives was also generated through class discussion, and an exercise based on active listening was assigned to further the students' development of a mindful awareness of divergent perceptions.

After completion of the third session, it was clear that although all students appeared to be readily engaged in the activity, their ability to hold opposing perspectives was idiosyncratic to the individual. Hobson (2002) posits that perspective-taking is an innate social and biological process that is sensitive to a gradual process of development over time. It was evident that the level of mindful awareness based on the ability to see life from varying perspectives is significantly influenced by one's developmental stage. A wide body of research on mindfulness-based interventions also shows that most of these processes can be learned and that such learning is crucial in effecting values-based changes in one's life (see Levin, Hildebrandt, Lillis, & Hayes, 2012, for a meta-analysis).

Session 4: Building a Hopeful Mind. The final session of the four-week intervention included the juxtaposition of living in a state of present awareness and developing a hopeful future, complete with goals and strategic pathways. The session, "Building a Hopeful Mind," introduced students to a process titled "strategic futuring," which allows for a careful consideration of present strengths and values as one sets future aims. Students were led through an exercise to quiet their mind and to allow their imagination to form pictures of their future. Additionally, students were asked to reflect on the past three weeks and write a two-page reflection paper on the impact of mindfulness on their daily activities. One student wrote: "I had no idea all that I was missing each day."

Upon further review of the last session, the impact of the overall intervention may have been strengthened if the last session had focused exclusively on present awareness and the creation of new categories. The complexity of balancing future and present awareness may have diminished the overall understanding of developing a mindful practice and perspective. It is possible that this might be an advanced skill that can best be presented after students have already developed solid mindfulness skills.

The following section will provide significant empirical support for the need for an increase in mindfulness education embedded in the curriculum, followed by a summary of findings from this Leadership Training program.

Empirical Considerations

Langer and colleagues conducted numerous short-term empirical research studies related to mindfulness and learning. These studies revealed prevalent learning myths that diminish creativity and curiosity and limit true learning, enjoyment in the learning process, and realization of learning potential (Langer, 1997). These myths are associated with mindlessness, whereas mindfulness, or the continual process of noticing new things or making novel distinctions, is associated with increased levels of involvement (Langer, 1997).

The internal or external presence of the mindful characteristics of an interest in novelty and openness to uncertainty can enhance involvement in learning (Langer, 1997). Internally, an individual can benefit from embracing these characteristics and utilizing them as a lens for understanding new experiences and information. Alternatively, these characteristics can be encouraged from an external perspective, such as when they are incorporated into the presentation of information. Studies have demonstrated associations between mindful learning and creativity (Langer, 1997; Langer & Piper, 1987), increased levels of enjoyment in learning (Langer, 1997), enhanced academic performance (Lieberman & Langer, 1995), improved memory (Bodner & Langer, 1995; Langer, 1997), and flexible application of information (Langer, 1997; Langer, Hatem, Joss, & Howell, 1989). Therefore, mindfulness has implications for the immediate learning environment, as well as for applications of learned material in future or different contexts.

Findings from our own project on Student Leadership training at APU showed some promising but not definitive results. This study used a quasi-experimental, pretest-posttest, non-randomized control group design. The participants were 45 undergraduate students who were enrolled in either mindfulness-based student leadership courses (treatment group) or traditional leadership courses (control group; Komives, Lucas, & McMahon, 2007). Ultimately, pretests and posttests of the four-week intervention revealed that the control group's mean mindfulness scores decreased slightly during four weeks of a traditional leadership course, supporting the notion that educational environments may inadvertently promote mindlessness, left to their own devices. Over the same time period, the treatment group's mindfulness scores increased slightly, suggesting the possibility that the intervention may have helped protect students against the tendency toward mindlessness. However, although these changes in mindfulness scores moved in the predicted direction, the differences were not statistically significant. Thus, the findings indicate that it may be possible to impact students' mindfulness levels, but they also indicate the necessity to increase the strength and duration of such interventions. Although this study had limited quantifiable results, class evaluations indicate a high level of satisfaction with the curriculum. However, upon reflection after completion of the intervention, the connection between leadership effectiveness and mindfulness may not have been compelling enough to create what Ritchhart and Perkins (2000) term as a mindful disposition. Traditional-aged college students might not possess the breadth of experience necessary to understand the relationship of mindful constructs and their personal approach to leading others; therefore, the intervention did not appear to create a strong inclination or desire for developing a mindful practice. Future studies, perhaps using a variety of methodologies, may be useful in understanding these obstacles.

Although there are numerous examples of efforts student affairs practitioners are making to promote mindfulness, creating an environment within a college or university that promotes mindful practice is challenging and often is not subjected to controlled program evaluation efforts. The final section will offer suggestions on how to develop a sustained program resulting in a deep and lasting impact.

Final Words

Programs encouraging the pursuit of mindful practice within higher education are frequently developed on the margins of an institution. However, to deeply impact the lives of college students, those programs must be intertwined through a variety of curricular and co-curricular offerings. The following section will offer three pieces of advice to student affairs practitioners striving to create a culture of mindfulness within their institutions.

Create a Compelling Case for Mindfulness

Despite being practiced for centuries in religious orders, mindfulness is a relatively new concept to higher education professionals. The term is laden with misconceptions and preconceived erroneous notions regarding the purpose of mindful practice. Therefore, a compelling case for why an individual or institution would endeavor to learn and practice mindfulness needs to be established.

The impact of a college student mindfulness intervention may be improved if three components of a mindful disposition are present: sensitivity, inclination, and ability (Ritchhart & Perkins, 2000; Tanious, 2012). Most college students will not have a natural sensitivity or inclination to the notion of drawing novel distinctions or examining the impact of preexisting mental categories. It appears that they are, however, drawn to information that promotes academic success, social integration, and life satisfaction. Successful promotion of mindfulness programming should establish a clear link to the outcomes that garner a student's attention. The possibility that most of a college student's life is spent in a mindless state, using Langer's definition, makes it difficult to arrest her natural disposition toward unreflective behavior; therefore, careful attention must be paid to establishing the connection to outcomes reflecting students' interests.

Student affairs professionals may be more inclined to understand the need for developing a greater level of mindfulness in their lives; however, our hectic schedules often inhibit our actual attention to novelty, perspective, and context. Harvard business school professor and change theorist John Kotter discusses the need to create a sense of urgency before change may occur (Kotter, 2008). Perhaps presenting the negative effect that mindlessness has on job performance, curiosity, and relationship satisfaction would produce the sense of urgency and requisite motivation to begin a mindful practice. Both students and professional staff must be provided with a compelling reason to change current habits to become more mindful in their daily lives.

Establish Ties to Behaviors that Are Valued in the Higher Education Domain

The term mindfulness is often associated with images of Buddhist monks and New Age bookstores. Because skepticism is a long-standing higher education value, proponents of embedding mindful practice in the co-curricular and curricular aspects of higher education may want to consider aligning the term with valued constructs such as curiosity and engagement. For some administrative leaders and faculty, developing mindfulness may seem like an inappropriate learning objective because of the personal nature of the practice. However, engagement in the educational process has gained significant attention over the last ten years. The relationship of mindfulness to engagement and curiosity demonstrated earlier in this chapter should be exploited to lessen the impact of preconceived notions and heighten the understanding of the role mindfulness plays in the learning process.

Create Division-Wide, Cross-Functional Ownership of Mindfulness Initiatives

If students such as Ryan, mentioned in the beginning of this chapter, are going to be impacted by mindfulness practice, the exposure to mindfulness constructs must not be relegated to one office or person. Ryan must learn about the value of making novel distinctions and searching for divergent perspectives in the residence halls as well as in the classroom. Creating alliances with individuals from a diversity of functions interested in the outcomes associated with mindful behaviors has a multiplying effect across a student services division and institution. Although those alliances may be small in number and difficult to find in the beginning, ultimately they have the power to transform Ryan's experience from disengagement to engagement.

In conclusion, Langer's work on mindfulness provides student services professionals and students a way to positively address the fast-paced environment that surrounds them. Through drawing novel distinctions, valuing divergent perspectives, and becoming receptive to new information, professionals can transform the student experience from one of mindless disengagement to curiosity-driven engagement.

References

Association of American Colleges and Universities. (2002). *Greater expectations: A new vision for learning as a nation goes to college.* Retrieved from www.greater expecatations.org/

Association of American Colleges and Universities. (2007). *College learning for the new global century.* Washington, DC: Author.

Astin, A. W. (1993). *What matters in college? Four critical years revisited.* San Francisco, CA: Jossey-Bass.

Bargh, J. A. (1997). The automaticity of everyday life. *Advances in Social Cognition*, *10*, 2-48.

Bodner, T. E., & Langer, E. (1995). *Mindfulness and attention*. Cambridge, MA: Harvard University Press.

Chanowitz, B., & Langer, E. J. (1981). Premature cognitive commitment. *Journal of Personality and Social Psychology*, *41*, 1051–1063.

Chickering, A. W., & Reisser, L. (1993). *Education and identity*. San Francisco, CA: Jossey-Bass.

Duderstadt, J. J. (2000). *A university for the 21st century*. Ann Arbor, MI: The University of Michigan Press.

Galinsky, A. D., & Moskowitz, G. B. (2000). Perspective-taking: Decreasing stereotype expression, stereotype accessibility, and in-group favoritism. *Journal of Personal and Social Psychology*, *78*, 708-724.

Gallup Organization. (1999). *Clifton StrengthsFinder*. Washington, DC: Author.

Gehlbach, H. (2004). A new perspective on perspective taking: A multidimensional approach to conceptualizing an attitude. *Educational Psychology Review*, *16(3)*, 207-234.

Greenway, K. A. (2005). *Purpose in life: A pathway to academic engagement and success* (Doctoral dissertation). Retrieved from *Dissertation Abstracts International*, *66(04A)*, 1292–1478. (UMI No. AAT3171374).

Hobson, P. (2002). *The cradle of thought: Exploring the origins of thinking*. London: Macmillan.

Hulme, E., Shushok, F., & Klinger, K. (2010). *Positive student development theory: A new lens for the field*. Presentation at the National Association of Student Personnel Administrators (NASPA) annual conference, Chicago, Illinois.

Hurtado, S. (2007). Linking diversity with the educational and civic missions of higher education. *The Review of Higher Education*, *30(2)*, 185-196.

Kabat-Zinn, J. (1984). An outpatient program in behavioral medicine for chronic pain patients based on the practice of mindfulness meditation: Theoretical considerations and preliminary results. *General Hospital Psychiatry*, *4*, 33-47.

Kashdan, T. (2009) *Curious? Discover the missing ingredient to a fulfilling life*. Harper Collins: New York, NY.

Kashdan, T. B., & Silva, P. J. (2009). Curiosity and interest: The benefits of thriving on novelty and challenge. In S. J. Lopez & C. R. Snyder (Eds.), *Oxford handbook of positive psychology* (pp. 367–374). New York, NY: Oxford University Press.

Komives, S. R., Lucas, N., & McMahon, T. R. (2007). *Exploring leadership: For college students who want to make a difference* (2nd Ed). San Francisco: Jossey-Bass.

Komives, S. R., & Wagner, W. (2009). *Leadership for a better world: Understanding the social change model of leadership development*. San Francisco, CA: Jossey-Bass.

Kotter, J. (2008). *A sense of urgency*. Harvard Business School Press: Boston, MA.

Kuh, G. D., Kinzie, J., Schuh, J. H., & Whitt, E. J. (2005). *Student success in college: Creating conditions that matter*. San Francisco, CA: Jossey-Bass.

Langer, E. J. (1989). *Mindfulness*. Reading, MA: Addison Wesley.

Langer, E. J. (1997). *The power of mindful learning*. Reading, MA: Addison Wesley.

Langer, E. J. (2000). Mindful learning. *Current Directions in Psychological Science, 9(6)*, 220–223.

Langer, E. J., Bashner, R., & Chanowitz, B. (1985). Decreasing prejudice by increasing discrimination. *Journal of Personality and Social Psychology, 49*, 113-120.

Langer, E. J., Hatem, J., Joss, J., & Howell, M. (1989). Conditional teaching and mindful learning: The role of uncertainty in education. *Creativity Research Journal, 2*, 139–159.

Langer, E. J., & Moldoveanu, M. (2000a). The construct of mindfulness. *Journal of Social Issues, 56(1)*, 1–9.

Langer, E. J., & Moldoveanu, M. (2000b). Mindfulness research and the future. *Journal of Social Issues, 56(1)*, 129–139.

Langer, E. J., & Piper, A. (1987). The prevention of mindlessness. *Journal of Personality and Social Psychology, 53*, 280–287.

Levin, M., Hildebrandt, M. J., Lillis, J., & Hayes, S. C. (2012). The impact of treatment components suggested by the psychological flexibility model: A meta-analysis of laboratory-based component studies. *Behavior Therapy, 43*, 741-756.

Lieberman, M., & Langer, E. (1995). *Mindfulness and the process of learning.* Unpublished manuscript, Harvard University, Cambridge, MA.

Manning, B. (2009). *Souvenirs of solitude: Finding rest in Abba's embrace.* NavPress: Colorado Spring, CO.

Marcia, J. (1993). *Ego identity: A handbook for psychosocial research.* Springer: New York: NY.

Milem, J., & Berger, J. (1997). A modified model of college student persistence: Exploring the relationship between Astin's theory of involvement and Tinto's theory of student departure. *Journal of College Student Development, 38*, 387–400.

Newman, F. M. (1992). Student engagement in academic work: Expanding the perspective on secondary school effectiveness. In J. R. Bliss, W. A. Firestone, & C. E. Richards (Eds.), *Rethinking effective schools: Research and practice* (pp. 58–75). Englewood Cliffs, NJ: Prentice Hall.

Ritchhart, R., & Perkins, D. N. (2000). Life in the mindful classroom: Nurturing the disposition of mindfulness. *Journal of Social Issues, 56(1)*, 27–47.

Schreiner, L. A., & Louis, M. C. (2006, November). *Measuring engaged learning in college students: Beyond the borders of NSSE.* Paper presented at the annual meeting of the Association for the Study of Higher Education, Anaheim, CA.

Tagg, J. (2004, March-April). Why learn? What we may really be teaching students. *About Campus*, 2-10.

Tanious, C. M. (2012). Mindful strengths development: Leveraging students' strengths for 21st century learning and leadership (Unpublished doctoral dissertation). Azusa Pacific University, Azusa, CA.

Wawrzynski, M., & Pizzolato, J. E. (2006). Predicting needs: A longitudinal investigation of relation between student characteristics, academic paths, and self-authorship. *Journal of College Student Development, 47*, 677–692.

Editor **Jacqueline Pistorello, PhD**, is a clinical and research faculty member at the University of Nevada, Reno Counseling Services, where she has worked with college students for fifteen years. She specializes in the application of two mindfulness and acceptancebased behavioral approaches with college students: acceptance and commitment therapy (ACT) and dialectical behavioral therapy (DBT). Pistorello has received grants from the National Institutes of Health to research the prevention and treatment of mental health problems among college students using ACT and DBT.

Index

A

abnormal psychology classes, 242–245; ACT content infused into, 243–245; results of using ACT in, 245

academic goal-setting module, 194–196

academic performance: ACT-based podcasts and, 180; self-management training and, 187; student retention and, 186

academic values module, 192–194

acceptance, 54, 56–58; emotional, 240–241; exercise introducing, 85; internal control vs., 150; interventions based on, 98; perfectionism treatment and, 154; scalability and flexibility of, 14–15; studies on college students and, 18, 22; willingness related to, 57–58

Acceptance and Action Questionnaire (AAQ-II), 219

Acceptance and Commitment Therapy (ACT), 48–49; abnormal psychology classes using, 242–245; beginning treatment with, 54–55; classroom settings for, 226–247;

core processes of, 56–66, 147; FYS class based on, 226–234; group format for, 73–92; integration of processes in, 66–70, 217–218; intervention strategies used in, 52; letting go of the struggle with, 55–56; MBCT compared to, 100–101; mental health distress and, 205–206; mindfulness in, 54, 101, 112–113; model of intervention in, 53–66; one-day well-being training, 234–238; overview of course protocols, 105–108; perfectionism and, 143–156; podcasts based on, 164–180; psychological flexibility in, 53–54; psychopathology model of, 49–51; racial differences classes using, 238–241; research on efficacy of, 70, 91, 108–113, 155–156; self-help programs in, 14; Student Support Network and, 209, 212–218, 221; study on MBCT and, 101–108; values work in, 112

ACT Conversation podcasts, 164–180; acceptability ratings, 176–177; development of, 165–172; dissemination strategy, 164–165;

empirical considerations, 175–179;
outcome findings, 177–179;
screenshot examples, 166, 167, 174,
175; translation process, 172–173
ACT groups, 73–92; benefits of, 76,
96; college counseling centers and,
77, 91–92; composition of, 77–78;
exercises used in, 75, 82–86,
88–90; facilitation of, 77–90;
format for, 80–90; homework
assignments in, 81–82;
mindfulness exercises in, 80–81;
norms observed in, 79–80;
orienting students to, 78–79;
sample flyer advertising, 79; study
on college students in, 91; working
in the here and now in, 86–88
ACT well-being training, 234–238;
empirical considerations, 236–238;
overview of, 235–236
action. *See* committed action
adaptive perfectionism, 141, 144
adulthood, emerging, 232
alcohol use disorders, 10
American College Health
Association (ACHA), 10, 205
American Psychological Association
(APA), 70
anxiety disorders, 13, 78
Appendix materials, 3
Armstrong, Andrew B., 139
attendance issues, 30–31
attention, inflexible, 51
audio podcasts. *See* podcasts
automatic pilot, 253–254, 260
avoidance and control, 55. *See also*
experiential avoidance
avoidant persistence, 51
Azusa Pacific University (APU),
261–264

B

Backpack metaphor, 214
Barriers and Counter-Strategies
worksheet, 171, 175
being vs. doing, 99, 127
Bjornsen, Abby, 23, 34
body scan meditation, 125–126
Boone, Matthew S., 47, 73
borderline personality disorder
(BPD), 25–26, 42
breath: awareness exercise, 170;
focusing on, 120, 124, 125
Butterfly exercise, 82–86

C

calendar of goals, 196
Campus Connect Training Program,
208
Canicci, James, 73
category creation, 255
CCCs. *See* college counseling centers
Center for Collegiate Mental Health
(CCMH), 25
Chase, Jared, 183
Chessboard metaphor, 236
Chocolate Cake exercise, 149
Christodoulou, Vasiliki, 223, 234
CIRP survey, 96–97
classroom settings for ACT, 225–247;
abnormal psychology course,
242–245; First Year Semester ACT
class, 226–233; one-day ACT
well-being training, 234–238;
racial differences class, 238–241;
summary consideration about,
245–247
clean pain, 54
Clifton StrengthsFinder, 262, 263
clipboard exercise, 82
Cognitive Behavior Therapy (CBT),
175–179
cognitive defusion. *See* defusion

cognitive fusion, 50–51, 145

cognitive therapy: mindfulness integrated with, 99. *See also* Mindfulness-Based Cognitive Therapy

college counseling centers (CCCs): ACT groups and, 77, 91–92; DBT at, 25–26; MBSR groups at, 120–136; need for services provided by, 206; new paradigms of treatment in, 206; podcast considerations for, 179–180; psychopathology treated by, 25; suicide prevention and, 206

college education: earnings advantage of, 184; student values related to, 198

college staff: acceptance and mindfulness for, 15–16; mindfulness development initiatives for, 259–260

college students: acceptance-based therapies and, 96, 114; accessibility of counseling for, 162; ACT studies with, 70, 91, 101–113; challenges in counseling, 12–13; CIRP survey of, 96–97; DBT applied to, 23–42; dropout rates among, 160–161; goal setting for, 187–188, 194–196; MBCT studies with, 101–113; MBSR groups for, 120–136; mental health problems of, 10–11, 25, 97, 204, 205; mindfulness practice for, 112–113, 260–264; opportunities for change in, 11–12; perfectionism in, 142–143; retention problem among, 160–161, 184–187; Student Support Network, 207–221; uses of this book for, 6; values training for, 189–194

committed action, 54, 65–66; perfectionism and, 154; podcast exercises on, 171; racial differences and, 241

compassion, 132, 211

conceptualized self, 51, 62

conflict: ACT for resolving, 71; created by language, 167–168

contact with the present moment, 54, 58; exercise introducing, 85; perfectionism and, 152–153

context: illustrating the impact of, 262; perspective related to, 254. *See also* self as context

control: acceptance as alternative to, 150; experiential avoidance and, 55, 146; perfectionism related to, 146, 148, 149–150

counselors: accessibility of, 162; meditation practice of, 135–136; self-disclosure used by, 90; uses of this book for, 4

creative hopelessness, 55, 149, 168

Crosby, Jesse M., 139

curiosity, 257–258, 261

Curious?: Discover the Missing Ingredient to a Fulfilling Life (Kashdan), 261

curriculum infusion (CI), 247

cutting behavior, 204, 207

D

DBT. *See* Dialectical Behavior Therapy

decision-making process, 211

defusion, 54, 58–62; dialog illustrating, 60–62; exercises encouraging, 85, 169, 228, 236, 239–240; perfectionism treated with, 150–151; podcast exercises on, 169; self as context related to, 62; SSN training in, 216

delayed graduation, 161–162

de-stigmatizing perspectives, 213

Dialectical Behavior Therapy (DBT), 23–42; attendance requirements, 30–31; consultation team meetings, 37; crisis counseling and, 37–38; empirical considerations, 38–40; group selection criteria, 35–36; involving parents/family in, 31–32; overview of, 26–28; pre-group meetings, 36; reasons for using, 25–26; recommendations for using, 41–42; running groups based on, 36–37; skills training, 27–28, 29–30, 34–40; study on college setting for, 28–33, 38–40; summary of treatment effects, 45; treatment targets, 27

dirty pain, 54

discovery learning, 98

distraction vs. mindfulness, 110, 112–113

distress tolerance skills, 28, 29–30, 37

doing vs. being, 99, 127

drawing out the system, 55

dropouts: DBT treatment and, 32–33; statistics on college, 160–161

E

Eating a Raisin exercise, 124, 170

eating disorders, 10, 214

educational workshops, 156

effective living, 235–236

emerging adulthood, 232

emotion dysregulation, 26–27

emotion regulation skills, 28, 37

emotional health ratings, 96–97

emotions: accepting, 240–241; managing, 28, 35, 36

empathy: listening with, 211, 212; responding with, 216, 217; SSN training in, 215, 216

engaged learning, 258

Erikson, Karen, 23, 28

evidence-based work, 18

Expansion exercise, 169

experiential avoidance: ACT theory of, 49–50, 77; control and, 55, 146; perfectionism and, 146–147; SSN training in, 213–214

experiential exercises, 52; body scan, 125–126; The Butterfly, 82–86; Chocolate Cake, 149; Eating a Raisin, 124, 170; Expansion, 169; Eyes On, 89–90, 230; Getting to Work, 66–70; Label Parade, 75, 89, 228; labeling private events, 64; Leaves in a Stream, 169; mindfulness meditation, 124–125; Noticing Thoughts that Hook You, 62; observing without judgment, 131; one act of generosity, 130; Pick a Metaphor, 58; play dough, 103–104; SSN training using, 215; standing-sitting, 169; strike a pose, 104; Thank Your Mind, 169; Thoughts on the Highway, 169; walking meditation, 129, 170; What are the numbers?, 239; Willingness with an Avatar, 82. *See also* metaphors

exposure therapy, 66

external experiences, 235

Eyes On exercise, 89–90, 230

F

family interventions, 31–32

First Year Semester (FYS) ACT class, 226–234; empirical considerations related to, 233–234; principles of adapting ACT to, 227–233

flexibility. *See* psychological flexibility

Foley, Elizabeth, 95

Fruzzetti, Alan, 23, 28

fusion, 50–51, 145

future-oriented ideal, 153

G

Garrett Lee Smith Act (2004), 206, 207
generosity exercise, 130
Get Out of Your Mind and Into Your Life (Hayes & Smith), 227
Getting to Work exercise, 66–70
goal setting, 187–188; calendar used for, 196; characteristics of effective, 188; long-term goals, 195; online module about, 194–196; for perfectionism treatment, 147–149; RFT perspective on, 190–191; SMART goals, 194–195; values training with, 191–192, 196–197
goal statements, 190
graduation, delayed, 161–162
groups: ACT used in, 73–92; benefits of therapy in, 76; college counseling centers and, 77; DBT skills training in, 34–40; MBSR group at a CCC, 120–136. *See also* ACT groups
Guthrie, Carrie, 23, 34

H

Harris, Russ, 169
Hayes, Steven C., 9, 223, 226, 238
Hexaflex in ACT, 56, 57
homework assignments, 81–82
hopeful mind, 264
hopelessness, creative, 55, 149, 168
Houmanfar, Ramona, 183
Hulme, Eileen, 251
human suffering, 54, 212–213

I

impulsivity, 51
inaction, 51
inflexibility, psychological, 144–146
inflexible attention, 51

inquiry, 99, 102–103
instructors: flexibility/freedom for ACT, 233; uses of this book for, 4–5
integrating ACT processes, 66–70, 217–218
internal experiences, 143–144, 235
interpersonal effectiveness skills, 28, 37
Italian Institute for Statistics (ISTAT), 161

J

Jeffcoat, Tami, 224, 226

K

Kabat-Zinn, Jon, 120, 121
Kashdan, Todd, 261
koans, 230
Kotter, John, 267

L

Label Parade exercise, 75, 89, 228
labeling private events, 64
Landsbaum, Holly, 23, 34
Langer, Ellen, 253–258, 264–265
language: conflict created by, 167–168; problem solving and, 17; RFT and, 145, 190
Latham, Gary, 187
leadership, 261–264, 266; hopeful mind and, 264; impact of context on, 262; personal strengths and, 262, 263; power of the mind in, 261–262; social mind and, 263–264
learning: discovery, 98; engaged, 258; mindful, 253, 264–266
Leaves in a Stream exercise, 169
LeJeune, Jenna, 223, 242
Levin, Michael E., 9
life effectiveness training, 238

Lillis, Jason, 223, 226, 238
Linehan, Marsha, 26, 36, 42
Locke, Edwin, 187
Long, Douglas M., 223, 226
long-term goals, 195

M

MacLane, Chelsea, 23, 28
maladaptive perfectionism, 141, 144
Man in the Hole metaphor, 149
mandated therapy, 33
Manning, Brennan, 259
MBCT. See Mindfulness-Based
   Cognitive Therapy
MBSR. See Mindfulness-Based Stress
   Reduction
McNally, Julian, 159
medical model, 205
meditation: body scan, 125–126;
   mindfulness, 120, 124–125; sitting,
   125; walking, 129. See also
   mindfulness
mental health problems: biomedical
   descriptions of, 205; college
   students and, 10–11, 25, 97, 204,
   205; counseling service
   accessibility for, 162, 205. See also
   psychopathology
mental health professionals:
   accessibility of, 162; meditation
   practice of, 135–136; self-
   disclosure used by, 90; uses of this
   book for, 4
metaphors, 52, 230; Backpack, 214;
   Chessboard, 236; Man in the Hole,
   149; Passengers on the Bus, 152,
   236; Pick a Metaphor exercise, 58;
   Polygraph, 149, 241; Sky metaphor,
   63; Tending the Garden, 193;
   Tug-of-War with a Monster, 55–56,
   150–151; Two Scales, 150. See also
   experiential exercises

mind: defusion exercises, 169, 236;
   leadership and the power of,
   261–262. See also thoughts
mindful learning, 253, 264–266
mindfulness: ACT processes and, 54,
   101; characteristics of, 254–256;
   college students and, 112–113, 135;
   contemporary need for, 16–17;
   creating a case for, 266–267;
   curiosity and, 257–258, 261; DBT
   skills training in, 28, 37;
   definitions of, 120, 253, 254;
   distraction vs., 110, 112–113;
   divergent perspectives on, 256–
   257; eating based on, 124, 125;
   engaged learning and, 258;
   evidence on benefits of, 131; group
   exercises based on, 80–81; Langer's
   approach to, 253–258; leadership
   and, 261–264, 266; learning
   related to, 253, 258, 264–266;
   MBCT program and, 101, 113;
   meditation exercise, 124–125;
   podcast exercises on, 170;
   scalability and flexibility of, 14–15;
   SSN training in, 215; student
   affairs promotion of, 258–264,
   266–268; studies on college
   students and, 18, 22; therapeutic
   effectiveness of, 120
Mindfulness-Based Cognitive
   Therapy (MBCT), 95–96, 99–114;
   ACT compared to, 100–101;
   description of, 99; empirical
   considerations, 108–113;
   facilitating inquiry in, 102–103;
   mindfulness presented in, 101, 113;
   modifications for college students,
   102–104; overview of course
   protocols, 105–108; study on
   college students and, 101–108
Mindfulness-Based Stress Reduction
   (MBSR), 15, 119–136; body scan
   meditation, 125–126; college

students and, 120–121, 134–136;
commitment required for, 124;
empirical considerations, 133–135;
group facilitators for, 123; home
practice assignments, 125, 126–
127, 128, 130, 131, 132;
introducing new concepts in, 127,
128, 130, 131, 132; post-group
continuation of, 132–133; pre-
group considerations for, 121–123;
research on efficacy of, 109,
133–135; screening interview for,
121–122; session content for,
123–133; walking meditation, 129;
workbook for, 124

mindlessness, 253–254, 267

Miselli, Giovanni, 159

mood disorders, 13, 78

Morse, Charles, 203

multicultural education, 238–239

multiplicity of perspectives, 256

Murphy, Michael C., 119

N

Nafziger, Mark A., 139

National Association of Student
Personnel Administrators
(NASPA), 259

natural helpers, 208, 209

negative thoughts: defusing from,
58–62; refraining from countering,
59

Nelson, Brendan, 160

nonjudgment, 120, 128–129

non-suicidal self-injury (NSSI), 10, 25

Noticing Thoughts that Hook You
assignment, 62

novelty, embracing, 262

O

observe without judgment exercise,
131

observing self, 236

one-day ACT well-being training,
234–238; empirical considerations,
236–238; overview of, 235–236

online modules, 192–196; academic
goal-setting module, 194–196;
academic values module, 192–194

openness to new information, 255,
256

Organization for Economic
Co-operation and Development
(OECD), 161

P

pain: ACT perspective on, 49, 54;
play dough depiction of, 103–104;
suffering distinguished from, 54,
228

parents: DBT strategies involving,
31–32; uses of this book for, 6

Passengers on the Bus metaphor, 152,
236

peer support. See Student Support
Network

perfectionism, 139–156; ACT
perspective on, 143–147; ACT
treatment for, 147–155;
characteristics of, 140–141; clinical
presentations of, 142–143;
cognitive defusion and, 150–151;
college students and, 142–143;
committed action and, 154;
contact with the present moment
and, 152–153; control related to,
146, 148, 149–150; creative
hopelessness and, 149; criteria for
defining, 140; educational
workshops on, 156; establishing
treatment goals for, 147–149;
evidence supporting ACT for,
155–156; experiential avoidance
and, 146–147; negative outcomes
linked to, 141; psychological

inflexibility and, 144–146; self as context and, 152; session outline for treating, 147–155; values work and, 153

perspective taking, 215, 256, 260, 263–264

Pick a Metaphor exercise, 58

Pistorello, Jacqueline, 1, 9, 23, 28, 223, 226

play dough exercise, 103–104

Plumb-Vilardaga, Jennifer, 224, 226

podcasts, 164–180; acceptability ratings for, 176–177; considerations for CCCs about, 179–180; development process for, 165–172; dissemination strategy for, 164–165; empirical considerations related to, 175–179; outcome findings for, 177–179; screenshot examples of, 166, 167, 174, 175; translation process for, 172–173

Polygraph metaphor, 149, 241

Pozzi, Francesco, 159

prejudicial thoughts, 238–241, 243

premature cognitive commitment, 254

present-moment interventions. See contact with the present moment

Prevedini, Anna B., 159

preventive models, 220

private events, 49

professional conferences, 259–260

professors, uses of this book for, 4–5

psychiatric disorders: biomedical descriptions of, 205; college students and, 10, 25, 205; counseling service accessibility for, 162, 205

psychological flexibility: increasing in students, 53–54; perfectionism and, 146–147; six core processes of, 56–66, 147; SSN training

measures of, 219; teaching through podcasts, 164–172

psychological inflexibility, 144–146

psychological pain: ACT perspective on, 49, 54; play dough depiction of, 103–104; suffering distinguished from, 54

psychopathology: ACT model of, 49–51; college counseling centers and, 25; generational increases in, 97; perfectionism related to, 143. See also mental health problems

Q

Question, Persuade, Refer (QPR) program, 208

R

racial differences classes, 238–241; ACT content infused into, 239–241; results of using ACT in, 241–242

Relational Frame Theory (RFT), 145, 190–191

relational validation, 29

relevance of content, 229

Renner, Philomena, 95

rescuing strategy, 79–80

responding, patterns of, 53

retention problem, 160–161, 184–187; factors related to, 185–186; self-management skills and, 187; university resources devoted to, 185

risk management, 92

RMIT University, 164n

role playing, 211, 216, 219

S

Seeley, John, 224, 226

self: conceptualized, 51, 62; observing, 236

self as context, 54, 62–64; exercises
to facilitate, 75, 85–86;
perfectionism and, 152; SSN
training in, 214
self-disclosure, 90
self-help ACT programs, 14
self-management training, 187
self-validation, 29
"shoulds," 148–149, 151, 152, 153
silent retreat, 259
Sit or Stand exercise, 169, 171
sitting meditation, 125, 170
Sky metaphor, 63
SMART goals, 194–195
social mind, 263–264
social support, 76
SSN. See Student Support Network
staff. See college staff
stages of change model, 211
standing-sitting exercise, 169, 171
stigma-reduction interventions,
242–245; acceptance-based models
for, 243–245; results of using ACT
in, 245
strategic futuring, 264
strengths, finding, 262
strike a pose exercise, 104
student affairs practitioners:
contemporary choice presented to,
252; promotion of mindfulness by,
258–264, 266–268; staff
development initiatives, 259–260;
student programming initiatives,
260–264; uses of this book for, 5–6
Student Development & Counseling
Center (SDCC), 207
student leadership program, 261–264
student life programming:
mindfulness used in, 258–264;
staff development initiatives,
259–260; student programming
initiatives, 260–264

Student Support Network (SSN),
205, 207–221; ACT concepts used
in, 212–218; descriptive overview
of, 207–208; empirical
considerations about, 218–220;
program development and
implementation, 208–210; six-week
training program, 210–212;
training program download, 205,
220
students. See college students
Substance Abuse and Mental Health
Services Administration
(SAMHSA), 206
substance use disorders: ACT for
treating, 70; curriculum infusion
for preventing, 247
suffering: pain distinguished from,
54, 228; universality of human,
212–213
suicidality: ACT model and, 92;
college students and, 10, 25, 205;
effectiveness of DBT for, 3; SSN
training program and, 210; suicide
prevention and, 206, 207–208
Suicide Prevention Resource Center
(SPRC), 206, 220
suppression exercise, 236

T

taking the mind for a walk, 236
Tanious, Christy, 251.
Tending the Garden metaphor, 193
Thank Your Mind exercise, 169
therapists. See mental health
professionals
thoughts: assignment on noticing, 62;
defusing from, 58–62, 169, 236,
239–240; leadership effectiveness
and, 261; mindfulness of, 170;
perfectionistic, 145; prejudicial,
238–241, 243

Thoughts on the Highway exercise, 169
time-oriented goals, 195, 196
Tinto, Vincent, 185
training a puppy concept, 130
transdiagnostic core process approach, 13–14
translating podcasts, 172–173
Tug-of-War with a Monster metaphor, 55–56, 150–151
Two Scales metaphor, 150
Twohig, Michael P., 139
tyranny of the should, 140

U

universality: felt in groups, 76; of human suffering, 212–213
university administrators, 6

V

validation skills, 29
values, 54, 65; ACT perspective on, 191; characteristics of, 193–194; college students and, 18, 22, 111–112, 189–194; committed action and, 65–66; disconnection from personal, 51; exploring and articulating, 65; goal setting based on, 191–192, 196–197; MBCT work related to, 111–112; online module about, 192–194; perfectionism related to, 153; podcast exercises on, 170–171, 174; racial differences and, 241; training students in, 189–192, 197–198
Values and Goals worksheet, 174
values training: challenge of, 197–198; designing an online module for, 192–194; empirical research on, 189–190, 196–197;

goal-setting training with, 191–192, 196–197
verbal rules, 151
Villatte, Jennifer, 223, 226
Villatte, Matthieu, 224, 226
Virginia Tech, 12, 261

W

walking meditation, 129, 170
Ward, Todd A., 183
Web of Science portal, 18
web-based modules, 192–196; academic goal-setting module, 194–196; academic values module, 192–194
well-being training, 234–238
What are the numbers? exercise, 239
willingness, 57–58, 169
Willingness with an Avatar exercise, 82
wisdom, cultivation of, 132
Worcester Polytechnic Institute (WPI), 207
working in the here and now, 86–88

XYZ

Yadavaia, Jamie, 224, 226
YouTube videos, 232
zone of proximal development, 111, 114

MORE BOOKS *from*
NEW HARBINGER PUBLICATIONS

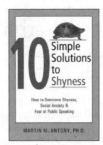

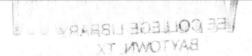

Register your **new harbinger** titles for additional benefits!

When you register your **new harbinger** title—purchased in any format, from any source—you get access to benefits like the following:

- Downloadable accessories like printable worksheets and extra content

- Instructional videos and audio files

- Information about updates, corrections, and new editions

Not every title has accessories, but we're adding new material all the time.

Access free accessories in 3 easy steps:

1. Sign in at NewHarbinger.com (or **register** to create an account).

2. Click on **register a book**. Search for your title and click the **register** button when it appears.

3. Click on the **book cover or title** to go to its details page. Click on **accessories** to view and access files.

That's all there is to it!

If you need help, visit:

NewHarbinger.com/accessories

new harbinger
CELEBRATING
40 YEARS